THE 11TH WAFFEN-SS

FREIWILLIGEN PANZERGRENADIER DIVISION "NORDLAND"

Massimiliano Afiero

SCHIFFER MILITARY

4880 Lower Valley Road   Atglen, PA 19310

Other Schiffer books by the author

The 27th Waffen-SS Volunteer Grenadier Division Langemarck: An Illustrated History, 978-0-7643-5072-6

The 7th Waffen- SS Volunteer Gebirgs (Mountain) Division "Prinz Eugen": An Illustrated History, 978-0-7643-5221-8

The 4th Waffen-SS Panzergrenadier Division "Polizei": An Illustrated History, 978-0-7643-6170-8

Type set in Minion Pro & Antique Olive Std

ISBN: 978-0-7643-6780-9

Printed in India

Published by Schiffer Publishing, Ltd.

4880 Lower Valley Road

Atglen, PA 19310

Phone: (610) 593-1777; Fax: (610) 593-2002

Email: Info@schifferbooks.com

Web: www.schifferbooks.com

For our complete selection of fine books on this and related subjects, please visit our website at www.schifferbooks.com. You may also write for a free catalog.

Schiffer Publishing's titles are available at special discounts for bulk purchases for sales promotions or premiums. Special editions, including personalized covers, corporate imprints, and excerpts, can be created in large quantities for special needs. For more information, contact the publisher.

We are always looking for people to write books on new and related subjects. If you have an idea for a book, please contact us at proposals@schifferbooks.com.

OTHER SCHIFFER BOOKS BY THE AUTHOR

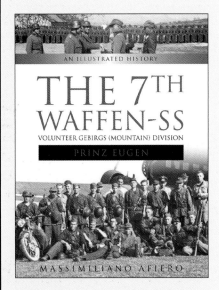

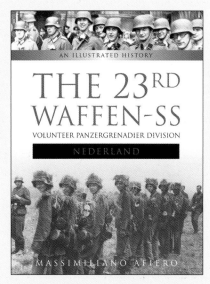

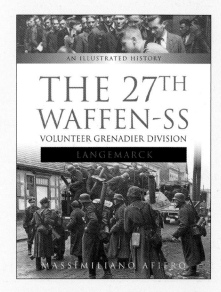

THE 7TH WAFFEN-SS VOLUNTEER GEBIRGS (MOUNTAIN) DIVISION "PRINZ EUGEN": *AN ILLUSTRATED HISTORY* (978-0-7643-5221-8)

THE 23RD WAFFEN-SS VOLUNTEER PANZERGRENADIER DIVISION NEDERLAND: *AN ILLUSTRATED HISTORY* (978-0-7643-5073-3)

THE 27TH WAFFEN-SS VOLUNTEER GRENADIER DIVISION LANGEMARCK: *AN ILLUSTRATED HISTORY* (978-0-7643-5072-6)

CONTENTS

SS-Brigadeführer Fritz von Scholz. *Berlin Document Center*

INTRODUCTION

In this volume, as for all the volumes in this series, in addition to archival documents, especially from German sources (the war diaries of the division and of its principal subordinate units, in addition to the personal records of decorated members of the unit), we have, as always, referred to numerous works already published on the division over the course of the years, especially those by Wilhelm Tieke, Jean Mabire, Erik Norling, Charles Trang, and Richard Landwehr. All of their books are fundamental works and crucial to the history of the "Nordland" Division and are full of unpublished documents and memoirs. Other publications regarding the war in general on the various fronts that the division fought, as well as other units that fought alongside it, are noted in the bibliography.

"Nordland" was the second SS division in which foreign volunteers who were not German but of German origin were included: Norwegians, Danes, Swedes, Dutch, Belgians, and French, as well as Volksdeutschen from Hungary, Romania, and Yugoslavia. Integrated into the SS Germanic III Corps and employed first in Croatia and then on the Eastern Front until the final battle in Berlin, the "Nordland" units fought strenuously and valorously until the end of the conflict. After being engaged for a brief period on the Croatian front, the Germanic volunteers of the Waffen-SS were able to deal with the Soviet advance in epic defensive battles, first on the Leningrad front, then at Narva, on the Blue Mountains, in Kurland, then continuing on to the front in Pomerania and East Prussia, until the final days of the war, continuing to fight in the ruins of the Berlin Chancellery alongside the French volunteers of the "Charlemagne" assault battalion. Overwhelmed by enemy superiority in men and equipment, the European volunteers of the "Nordland" fought valorously until the end and sacrificed themselves to defend European civilization from Soviet invasion, heedless of privation and suffering, faithful to their oath in the fight against Bolshevism.

As always, the subject matter is accompanied by many memoirs, period documents, extracts from official bulletins, the division's war diary, and hundreds of photographs and maps. We believe we have accomplished a significant amount of research, which lasted many years, but we do not pretend to have written the definitive work on the history of this division. We look forward to your comments, suggestions, and even criticisms to be able to improve our publications.

Massimiliano Afiero

ACKNOWLEDGMENTS

This volume has been made possible thanks to the collaboration of many friends and colleagues who have shared their research concerning the division with me, and in particular I would like to thank Lorenzo Barzaghi, Stefano Canavassi, Massimo Lucioli, Lorenzo Silvestri, Pierre Tiquet, Charles Trang, Cesare Veronesi, and all of the other Italian and foreign collaborators of our Cultural Association. Thanks also to all the friends and collectors for having provided previously unpublished images and documents from their collections and private archives and for having made valuable suggestions.

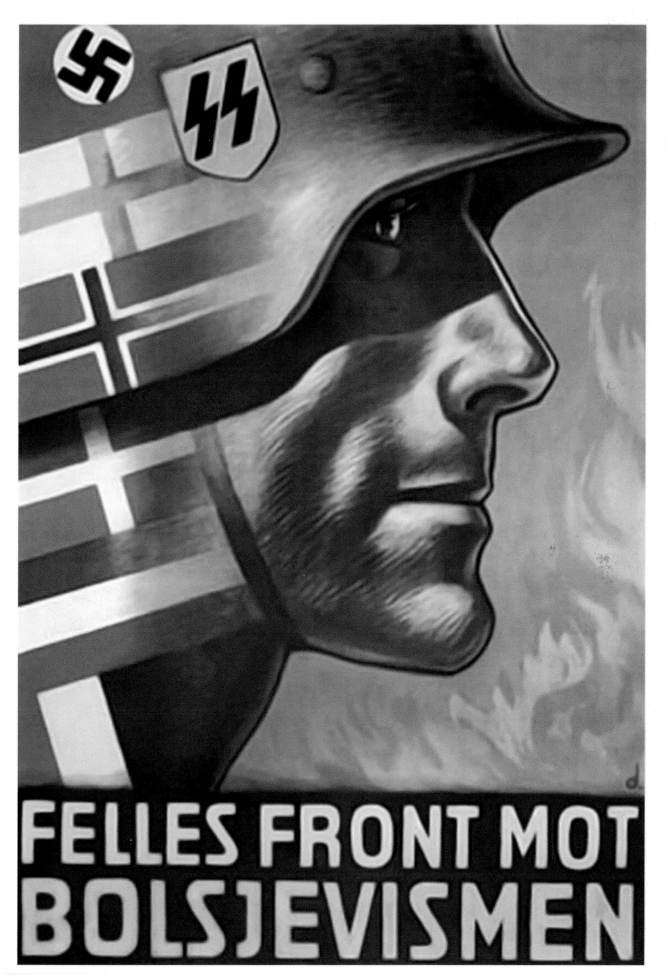

Norwegian poster by Harald Damsleth: "A united front against Bolshevism"

CHAPTER I
ORIGIN OF THE DIVISION

Reichsführer-SS Heinrich Himmler

SS-Ogruf. Gottlob Berger

SS-Gruf. Felix Steiner

SS-Hstuf. Franz Riedweg

The "Wiking," which was the first SS division to include foreigners of Germanic origin in its ranks, covered itself in glory beginning with its first actions on the Eastern Front in 1941 and was a success both militarily and politically. Thus, in late 1942, Hitler personally decided to authorize a second division with Germanic volunteers. Thus, on January 30, 1943, the anniversary of Hitler's rise to power, Reichsführer-SS Himmler issued the order for formation of this new division of Germanic volunteers, establishing that veterans of the European volunteer legions who had already fought on the Eastern Front and who had distinguished themselves should be assigned to the division. On February 8, 1943, a new circular by Himmler established that the new unit, initially designated as the Kampfverband Waräger,[1] should consist of Dutch, Flemish, Danish, Norwegian, and Estonian volunteers. As we shall see, Flemings and Estonians were later excluded so that they could form their own national units. Himmler hoped to gather together at least ten thousand Germanic volunteers with a minimum leavening of German officers and noncommissioned officers (NCOs) from the "Wiking," with the intent to integrate the formation into a new SS panzer corps, the III (germanische) SS-Panzer-Korps,[2] led by SS-Gruppenführer Felix Steiner.[3] The corps was to include the SS "Wiking" division as well.

Upon receiving Himmler's circular, SS-Ogruf. Gottlob Berger, head of the SS-Hauptamt, with the assistance of SS-Ostubaf. Franz Riedwig, immediately drafted a plan for formation of the new unit, which was sent to the Reichsführer-SS on February 10, 1943. Berger, as had happened in the past, amplified the orders that he had received from Himmler, and thus while

the original order spoke of integrating the Dutch, Flemish, and Danish legions, Berger considered integrating all the existing units of Germanic volunteers, such as the Norwegians and even Swiss volunteers. The reason for excluding the Norwegian legion from the original order is explained by the fact that it had been decided to disband it during that period. In addition, Berger soon began to talk about the formation of a corps and not only a division. In his plan, Berger specified at the outset that the

Den Norske Legion volunteers, summer 1942

Soldiers of the "Nordland" regiment of the "Wiking" division

Finnish volunteers of the "Wiking" during the ceremony disbanding their unit, 1943

corps should be commanded by Felix Steiner, which coincided with Himmler's ideas. In the second place, he accepted the idea of disbanding the so-called national legions but also all the other national units that existed, such as the Swiss company that was training at Sennheim, the Finnish battalion that was serving in the "Wiking" division, and the French volunteers who wished to serve in the Waffen-SS, such as Léon Degrelle's Wallonian legion. Berger also thought to integrate the Estonians in the Germanic units. If his plans had been realized, the "Nordland" undoubtedly would have become the most international of the Waffen-SS units. However, several reasons of a "political" nature prevented his ideas from coming to fruition. With respect to the Danish volunteer unit, the "Freikorps Danmark," Berger observed that relative to its particular political situation, not being a "politicized" formation like the others, but born with the authorization of the Danish monarch, it had to maintain its independence as a military unit, and for that reason a separate regiment had to be formed for the Danish volunteers

Formation of the Division

During that same month of February 1943, it was decided to use the "Nordland"[4] regiment as the nucleus of the new division, detaching it from the "Wiking" division, to which the Danish, Norwegian, and Dutch national legions would be attached, forming three infantry regiments designated "Danmark," "Norge," and "Nederland."[5] On March 3, 1943, Himmler issued a definitive memorandum that was later sent to the department heads of the Waffen-SS, who were to oversee the creation of the new SS corps. The Finnish volunteers were excluded from this project, since formation of a new regiment was planned, designated the "Kalevala," to be integrated into the "Wiking" division. However, political tensions in Finland made it impossible to form that regiment, and all the Finnish volunteers were repatriated in May 1943. For the Flemings as well, as mentioned before, it was decided to form a separate regiment, and it was Himmler himself who prohibited uniting the Flemings with the Dutch, for political reasons. The French were also to have formed a distinct unit, since the Walloons also were to have been integrated into the "Wiking," after having been grouped into another independent unit. With respect to the Estonians, they were to have replaced the Finns in the "Wiking."

On March 17, 1943, Hitler decided to call the new division the "Nordland" in order to carry on the military tradition of the regiment of the same name that had valorously distinguished itself during the recent campaign in the Caucasus. Himmler himself personally felt that the name of the famous regiment was most appropriate since it was planned that most of the volunteers would be Scandinavians, as the Reichsführer-SS himself expressed in a private letter to Steiner, sent on March 18, 1943. That same day, the SS-Regiment "Nordland" was detached from the "Wiking." The national legions would not be united with it until two months later, after May 20, 1943, when they were disbanded at the camp at Grafenwöhr and their men placed at the disposition of the new division. On March 22, 1943, the SS-Hauptamt assigned the first official designation to the unit: 14.(germ.) SS-Panzer-Grenadier-Division "Nordland."[6] Later the official identification number became 11. The camp at Mielau in Poland was chosen as the first assembly area, followed by the camp at Grafenwöhr in southern Germany. Between March and May 1943, the volunteers began to arrive at the Grafenwöhr camp.

SS-Brigadeführer Fritz von Scholz

July 28, 1943. SS-Ogruf. Felix Steiner meets Danish volunteers transferred to the new "Danmark" regiment. *Lars Larsen*

On May 12, 1943, Felix Steiner and SS-Brigadeführer Fritz von Scholz,[7] the latter designated as commander of the new division, inspected the units that were being formed. On May 20, by order dated May 17, the Germanic volunteer legions were officially disbanded, and their members transferred to the division. The Danish, Norwegian, and Dutch volunteers were joined by new recruits from those countries, and among them was a Norwegian Germanic SS company (Germanske SS "Norge") commanded by Hstuf. Olaf Lindvig, chief of staff of the same unit, about twenty Swedish volunteers,[8] and a large contingent of Danish volunteers.

At the last moment, the Dutch volunteers were excluded from the division; most of them considered it to be an affront to be integrated into a unit with a name that referred only to Scandinavian countries, which led them to request that they form their own independent unit. The Dutch nationalist leader, Anton Mussert, intervened in the matter, and in the end, Himmler authorized the formation of a new SS brigade for the Dutch volunteers, named "Nederland." However, about a hundred Dutch volunteers served in the new division, mainly in the reconnaissance battalion. With the exclusion of the Dutch volunteers, the division was left with only two grenadier regiments, formed on the basis of the remnants of the Danish legion and the Norwegian legion.

SS-Grenadier-Regiment 1 "Danmark"

On May 20, 1943, the "Freikorps Danmark"[9] arrived at Grafenwöhr, where it was officially disestablished. The members of the unit, around nine hundred men, were invited to voluntarily join the new SS-Grenadier-Regiment 1 "Danmark." These were joined by 250 new volunteers from the unit's depot company, under the orders of SS-Hstuf. Hansen. The presence of non-Danish personnel in the unit, however, raised protests by the volunteers who desired an exclusively Danish formation. The regimental commander himself, SS-Obersturmbannführer Graf von Westphalen,[10] was a German. Thus, many Danish volunteers resigned. To avoid this sudden and unexpected loss of the Danes, SS-Gruf. Felix Steiner personally intervened in order to try to calm the situation. The general office also moved to reach an agreement with the Danish government. Ambassador Mohr, the representative of the Danish government in Berlin, was ordered to go to Grafenwöhr to convince his compatriots not to abandon the Waffen-SS. The Danish government considered the presence of its volunteers alongside the Germans a way to avoid having the country have a harsher occupation regime and the ability to affirm, in case of a German victory, that it had actively participated in its success. Thanks to the intervention of Steiner and Mohr, most of the members of the Freikorps decided to be integrated into the new "Danmark" regiment. To fill out the unit's ranks, it was, however, necessary to also enlist Volksdeutschen from Romania. Of about 3,200 men present at that time, in the end only 40 percent were of Danish origin. Another 25 percent consisted of Germans, and the remaining 35 percent of Romanian Volksdeutschen.

SS-Grenadier-Regiment 2 "Norge"

The remnants of the Norwegian legion[11] arrived in late March, coming from Mitau in Latvia. The legionnaires were allowed to be repatriated and resign, but nevertheless several hundred decided to remain and to fight in the German armed forces. Himmler had estimated that there would be 150–200 defections out of the roughly six hundred volunteers present in the unit at that time, but as Berger noted later, there were about three hundred. Along with another two hundred new volunteers coming from Norway and slated for the now-disbanded legion, the Norwegians were concentrated at the Auerbach camp, near Grafenwöhr, where they met up with their fellow countrymen of the "Nordland."

Another photo of SS-Ogruf. Steiner with Danish volunteers at the Grafenwöhr camp. *Lars Larsen*

Danish ambassador Mohr with SS-Ostubaf. Graf von Westphalen, commander of the "Danmark." *Lars Larsen*

March 1943, Mitau. Himmler addresses Norwegian volunteers to convince them to join the new "Nordland" division.

The regiment's I Battalion, led by Norwegian SS-Sturmbannführer Finson,[12] was formed with the veterans of the Norwegian legion, about six hundred men. The II Battalion was formed from the cadre of the II Battalion of the "Nordland" regiment, while the III with the remainder of the I Battalion of the "Nordland." New volunteers arrived from Norway to refill the unit's ranks, members of the Germanic SS, but also many Volksdeutschen coming from Hungary. The regiment was placed under the command of SS-Obersturmbannführer Joerchel,[13] a German officer, originally from Upper Silesia.

Unit Formation

A special staff (Aufstellungsstab) was created for the formation of the division under SS-Stubaf. Vollmer. Officially as of May 1, 1943, SS-Brigdf. Scholz had assumed command of the division. SS-Stubaf. Helmut von Bockelberg was designated chief of staff. The "Nordland" was to be structured as an armored grenadier (Panzergrenadier) division, so that in addition to the two grenadier regiments "Danmark" and "Norge," it was also to include an armored element and an assault gun unit, in addition to an artillery regiment, a reconnaissance group, an engineer battalion, an antiaircraft artillery group, a signals detachment, and logistic support detachments.

The maintenance battalion and the signals battalion (SS-Stubaf. Rüdiger Weitzendörfer) were created near Munich, while the depot battalion (SS-Feldersatz-Bataillon "Nordland") was made up with recruits who trained at the camp at Sennheim in Alsace, under SS-Stubaf. Franz Lang.

SS-Artillerie-Regiment 11, under SS-Ostubaf. Friedrich Wilhelm Karl,[14] began to be formed in the spring of 1943. It was to have consisted of three groups (battalions), the first two equipped with 105 mm le.FH18 howitzers and the third with 150 mm s.FH18 howitzers and a battery of 105 mm s.FK guns.

SS-Pionier-Bataillon 11, led by SS-Stubaf. Fritz Bunse,[15] also began to be formed in spring of 1943, with personnel from the SS-Pionier-Ersatz-und-Ausbildungs-Bataillon "Dresden" and from the engineer school at Hradischko.

SS-Sturmgeschütz-Abteilung 11 was created in summer 1943 at Grafenwöhr and was placed under command of SS-Hstuf. Ernst Röntzsch,[16] structured with a command battery and three assault gun battalions. It later became SS-Pz.Jg.-Abt. 11.

The most highly motorized unit undoubtedly was the reconnaissance group, SS-Panzer-Aufklärungs-Abteilung 11, under SS-Hstuf. Saalbach,[17] with SS-Ostuf. Georg Erichsen as his adjutant. Formed in summer 1943, the group was organized as a reinforced battalion, to be employed with its armored vehicles not only in recon activity but also as a quick-reaction-and-support unit. It consisted of a staff company and five recon companies. The staff company consisted of

- repair platoon, equipped with vehicles to tow damaged vehicles
- signals platoon equipped with Kfz.15 vehicles with radios
- headquarters platoon with BMW motorcycles and Schwimmwagen amphibious vehicles
- medical platoon equipped with two Schwimmwagen and two Sd.Kfz.251 half-tracks

The first recon company was equipped with four- and eight-wheeled light armored cars armed with 20 mm guns and heavy machine guns. There were also armored cars equipped with radios.

The second recon company was equipped with light armored cars with turrets, with Sd.Kfz.250/9 half-tracks armed with 20 mm cannon and a heavy machine gun.

The third and fourth companies were equipped with Sd.Kfz.250/1 light armored cars used to tow the antitank guns and their crews. One platoon was equipped with Sd.Kfz. 250/7 half-tracks armed with 81 mm mortars.

The fifth company, designated as heavy, consisted of a platoon of Sd.Kfz.251 half-tracks armed with 75 mm guns, two platoons equipped with Sd.Kfz.251/1 half-tracks to tow the artillery and antitank guns, and an engineer platoon equipped with Sd.Kfz. 251/7 half-tracks for building bridges and roadways.

Swedish Volunteers in the "Nordland" Division

Since the beginning of the war, Swedish volunteers had joined the Waffen-SS, mostly assigned to the "Wiking" division. The Swedish volunteers enlisted in "Nordland" were mainly assigned to the 3rd Company of the division's reconnaissance group. The idea was to create a completely Swedish company, but the lack of a sufficient number of men finally resulted in standing up only one platoon that was completely Swedish. Nevertheless, the company was called the "Swedish company" (Schwedenkompanie), as Felix Steiner recalled in his memoirs, since there were many Swedish volunteers in it. The 3.Kompanie was initially commanded by SS-Ostuf. Walter Kaiser. Three of the company's platoons were primarily Volksdeutschen from Romania, while the fourth company, designated as heavy, consisted almost exclusively of Swedish and Swedish Estonian volunteers. Leading the company was SS-Oscha. Walther Nilsson, a veteran militant of the Swedish National Socialist Party. Then, when Hans-Gösta Pehrsson arrived at the unit, thanks to his higher rank he assumed command of the unit.

The Other Units

The air defense group, commanded by SS-Stubaf. Walter Plöw,[18] was formed in the Arys training area in East Prussia. It consisted of elements coming from SS-Flak.Ausb.-u.Ers.-Rgt. and from the "Wiking" division. SS-Flak-Abt.11 was structured with a headquarters battery (Stabs-Batterie), three batteries equipped with 88 mm flak guns, and a battery with 37 mm guns. One of the last units to be formed was an armored regiment. Initially it was to have two battalions, one equipped with tanks and one with assault guns, but due to a lack of vehicles, it was reduced to a single battalion with four companies in November 1943, becoming SS-Panzer-Abteilung 11 "Hermann von Salza,"[19] commanded by SS-Stubaf. Paul-Albert Kausch.[20]

SS-Ostubaf. Friedrich Wilhelm Karl

An Sd.Kfz. 250 of SS-Pz.Aufkl.-Abt.11. *NA*

From left: SS-Hstuf. Erichsen and SS-Hstuf. Saalbach, commander of SS-Pz.Aufkl.-Abt 11

Reichsführer-SS Himmler meets with Swedish volunteers of the "Nordland" during training. Present in the photo are Walther Nilsson, Karl-Olof Holm, and Karl-Mattin Agrahn.

Swedish volunteers of the "Nordland"

Hans-Gösta Phersson

SS-Hstuf. Walter Plöw

An 88 mm flak gun of the SS

SS-Stubaf. Paul-Albert Kausch

Commanding the "Nordland" medical unit, the SS-Sanitäts-Abteilung 11, was Swiss surgeon and SS-Ostubaf. Franz Riedweg,[21] one of the first foreign volunteers in the SS, used by Himmler and Berger to recruit other foreign volunteers; thanks to his propaganda work about seven hundred Swiss citizens clandestinely joined the Waffen-SS.

Training the Units

During the spring and summer of 1943, the division's units were assembled at Grafenwöhr for training. Many men were transferred to various army and Waffen-SS specialization schools. To recruit a greater number of volunteers for the corps, negotiations were held with the minister of armaments, Albert Speer, to mount a recruitment campaign among Germanic-origin foreign workers throughout the Reich. By order dated April 27, 1943, Speer authorized the recruitment of six thousand volunteers from among the workers. The results of this campaign were, however, somewhat disappointing, since of the 8,105 "Germanic" workers in the Reich, only 3,154 were considered suitable by the Waffen-SS recruiters. Between June and July, about eight thousand Volksdeutschen from Romania were transferred to the division and parceled out among the various units, thanks to an agreement signed on May 12, 1943, with Marshal Antonescu. In the end, only about 10 percent of the division's personnel were Scandinavian volunteers. The rest consisted of about 30 percent Germans, Romanian Volksdeutschen, and, in small measure, Hungarian, Croat, and Baltic Volksdeutschen. The last of these were not volunteers, and their arrival within the division led to more than a few problems for the German trainers, especially with respect to language. By an order dated June 28, 1943, sent to his officers, Steiner reminded

SS-Ustuf. Johan Peter Balstad, originally from Koppang in Norway, commander of 6./"Norge." Note the special tab with the Sonnenrad and the Norwegian national patch on the left sleeve. On the right sleeve are three badges for destroying tanks, earned on the Kurland front.

Cover of a propaganda booklet for the "Norge" regiment of "Nordland"

them that these men were volunteers and that they had all come to "fight against Bolshevism and for Germanic brotherhood" and that they were to be treated as equals because they were German, even though they had lived far from the Fatherland.

Insignia and Special Badges

Unit training was completed in part during August 1943, when the division was officially assigned to III.(germ.)SS-Pz.Korps. Its regiments were renamed as SS-Panzergrenadier-Regiment "Danmark" and SS-Panzergrenadier-Regiment "Norge." The "Nordland" was subsequently officially designated as an SS-Freiwillige-Division since it was formed exclusively of Germanic and Volksdeutschen volunteers. Divisions that consisted only of German personnel were instead called "SS-Divisionen," while those that consisted of volunteers of other nationalities, including the eastern territories, were called "Waffen Divisionen der SS." Chosen as the division insignia was the runic symbol of the *sonnenrad* (the solar wheel), the ancient Nordic representation of the sun, which had already been adopted by the German Thule society and by the "Wiking" division; to differentiate it from that of the "Wiking," the sonnenrad for the "Nordland" was enclosed in a circle. This symbol would be used on all the division's vehicles. A special badge was also made with the same symbol, to be used on the uniform collar in lieu of the double runes. Nonetheless, most of the volunteers, especially those coming from other SS units, preferred to continue to wear the classic SS collar tabs. In addition, the Norwegian and Danish volunteers continued to wear on the left sleeve of the uniform, under the National Socialist eagle, badges with their national colors, authorized by German headquarters.

The Norwegian SS company led by SS-Ostuf. Olaf Lindvig, parading through the streets of Oslo, spring 1943. This company became the 1.Kompanie of the "Norge" regiment. *Munin*

SS-Standartenführer Fritz von Scholz

SS-Hstuf. Hermenegild von Westphalen

SS-Ostubaf Wolfgang Joerchel

Chapter II

THE III.SS-PZ.KORPS IN CROATIA

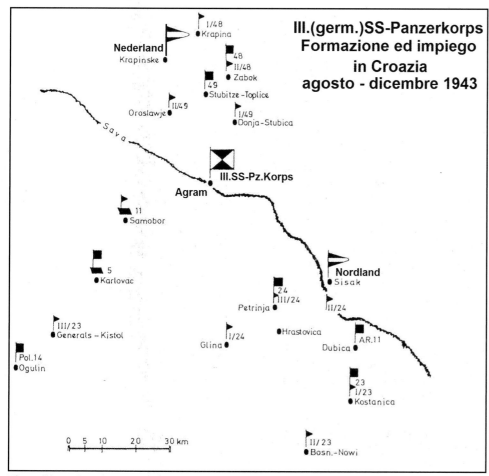

III.(germ.)SS-Panzerkorps
Formazione ed impiego
in Croazia
agosto - dicembre 1943

Disposition of III.SS-Pz.Korps in Croatia, August–December 1943

"Nordland" soldiers in Croatia

"Nordland" soldiers training in Croatia, 1943. *NA*

Between the end of August and the beginning of September, the units of III.(germ.)SS-Panzer-Korps and of the "Nordland" were transferred to Croatia to improve the training of the men and to accustom the new recruits to the hard fighting on the Eastern Front, according to the advice of Felix Steiner himself. The various units were billeted in the area of Agram (Zagreb) and south of it. At that time the division had 1,386 Danes (thirty-eight officers), 534 Norwegians (twenty officers), forty-five Swedes (one officer), forty-three Dutch (one officer), and twenty-five Flemings (one officer). Most of the units were equipped only with small arms; artillery, armored vehicles, and other heavy weapons had not yet been delivered. On September 8, 1943, at 2020 hours, headquarters of III.(germ.)SS-Panzer-Korps was informed of the Italian capitulation, and thus Steiner's units were to be involved in Operation Achse, the disarming of Italian units. All his units were placed on alert. For the occasion, the SS corps was attached to Armeegruppe von Weichs, directly subordinate to Lothar Rendulic's 2.Panzer-Armee. The first to be engaged in action were units of SS-Panzer-Regiment "Wiking"[1] and those of SS-Panzer-Abteilung 11, which shortly after having arrived in the Agram area were sent to Karlovac, where they disarmed the Italian troops of the Lombardia division, gathering up a large amount of equipment.

Many Italian soldiers, among them many officers, asked to join the SS division to continue to fight alongside the Germans. German headquarters authorized the recruitment of the Italians, according to dispositions made by Himmler himself, soon after July 25, 1943. In particular, SS-Stubaf. Kausch positively welcomed the presence of Italian soldiers in his unit[2] and thus had no problem using the many armored vehicles captured from the former ally, jokingly called by Germans as "Badoglio Panzers." The Italian tanks were quickly placed in service with SS-Pz.Abt.

A group of "Nordland" soldiers during a training session in Croatia, September 1943. *NA*

11, which at that time lacked its own armored vehicles. Meanwhile, the division completed its deployment in the area between Sisak, Glina, Bosnich, and Nowi, with its command post at Sisak in the Sava Valley, about 50 kilometers south of Zagreb. There, SS-Pz.Aufkl.Abt.11 was also billeted, while the SS-Nachrichten-Abteilung, the signals detachment, took up positions in the area south of Agram.

The SS-Panzer-Abteilung established itself in Samobor, where new assault guns and some PzKpfw.IV tanks arrived, joining the captured Italian tanks; 3./SS-Pz.Abt.11, still being fleshed out, was completely equipped with StuG.40 assault guns. The tank crews continued their training.

The Fight against the Partisans

Having completed Operation Achse, despite still not having completed their training, the III.SS-Pz.Korps units were engaged in antipartisan actions against Tito's Communist bands, especially in order to protect their own bases in the territory. By around late September, the first operation kicked off: in the village of Ogulin, southwest of Karlovac, men of Polizei Regiment 14, under Oberst Griese, had been surrounded by Tito's forces. Commandant Steiner landed with his Fieseler Storch in the besieged town to personally organize the relief operation. Meanwhile, III./"Norge," led by SS-Stubaf. Lohmann,[3] had been moved to the area by train. After having gotten off at the station at Dugaresa, the troops marched from north to south, reaching the village of Kistol, from where the attack against Tito's forces was to be launched. After having communicated by radio to Steiner that they had arrived at Kistol and were ready to attack, at the same time the troops in the village counterattacked, putting the partisan forces to flight. On October 23, a motorized patrol from the battalion was attacked in the Karlovac area while crossing a bridge; on that occasion, the first Scandinavian volunteer of the division, a nineteen-year-old Norwegian, Leif Otto Skuggen, was killed. On November 9, the first Norwegian officer was killed, SS-Ustuf. Oscar Lauritz Thunold, a platoon leader in 3.Kp./"Norge." He stepped on a mine while inspecting his platoon's forward positions.

On November 22, the III./"Norge" companies were attacked as they sought to keep their lines open between Dugaresa and Ogulin. The order was thus given to carry out sweeps throughout the area, during which another young Norwegian officer, twenty-two-year-old SS-Ustuf. Jens Bernhard Lund,[4] a platoon leader

A "Nordland" StuG.III in Croatia, September 1943

A Pak 40 used as an artillery piece to provide fire support to "Nordland" grenadiers during an attack against a position defended by Tito partisans, autumn 1943. *NA*

Jens Bernhard Lund

in 11./"Norge," was killed. According to a report by a member of the III./"Norge" staff, after having been surrounded by Communist partisans, a group from Lund's platoon managed to fall back to a position near a bridge while the rest of the company was engaged in a larger operation against a partisan band. When that operation had been concluded, Lund was ordered to protect the bridge and to cover the retreat of their comrades. The partisans attacked shortly thereafter with superior forces. Lund put himself at the head of his men, fighting until his last cartridge. After having been wounded, he was captured and executed by Communist partisans with a shot in the back of the neck. The next day, not having received any word from the group that had remained behind as a rearguard, Lohmann ordered the whole area to be swept. After various searches, five mutilated bodies of volunteers were found, among them that of SS-Ustuf. Lund. The "Norge" soldiers who had fallen in combat were buried with full military honors in the cemetery in Karlovac.

Employment of the "Danmark" Units

Units of the "Danmark" regiment as well were engaged in sweep operations to keep the partisan formations at bay. The regiment was completing its training in the area between Petrinja and Glina; the various companies protected each other reciprocally against numerous infiltrations by the partisans. The main inhabited areas were under control, but the forests and hills were in Tito's hands. The I./"Danmark," under command of SS-Stubaf. Alfred Fischer (who had replaced SS-Ostubaf. Martinsen), was garrisoned in Glina, a village with about 2,300 inhabitants, surrounded on three sides by hills that were firmly controlled by rebel formations. On November 20, the partisans attacked Glina with an entire brigade of the Yugoslav Liberation Army, more than five thousand battle-hardened Communist partisans, supported by several tanks. The battalion commander tried to contact other units of the division, but without success; the city was surrounded. Available to him were around three hundred men on the line, plus another 150 in reserve. The partisan attacks continued without letup, day and night, putting the resistance and combat capabilities of the Danish volunteers to the test.

Between November 21–22, the Danes repulsed all the enemy attacks, inflicting significant losses. From Petrinja, SS-Hstuf. Sörensen,[5] a Freikorps "Danmark" veteran, sent the 1st Platoon of his 1st Company to rescue the besieged forces, but a few kilometers from Glina, the Danish volunteers were ambushed and were wiped out; only SS-Ustuf. Bjärne Larsen and a couple of grenadiers made it back. On November 23, partisan forces again attacked Glina, this time with the support of several armored vehicles. The 4.(schwere). Kompanie under SS-Ostuf. Helmut Stenger,[6] with only one antitank gun available, managed to work miracles, destroying two enemy tanks and forcing others to turn back. During the next two days, the outposts around the city were overwhelmed by a new massive attack by the Communist partisans; several outlying areas of the city fell into enemy hands, but the Danish volunteers continued to defend themselves strenuously. The "Danmark" commander, SS-Ostubaf. Westphalen, not receiving any further reports from Glina, decided to intervene personally; he gave two companies to Danish Stubaf. Poul Neergaard-Jacobsen,[7] commander of III./"Danmark," and marched toward Glina with the rest of his regiment. The two companies that were left as a rearguard were soon attacked by large partisan forces. The 10.Kp./"Danmark," led by Ostuf. Hugo Jessen,[8] was able to hold its position at Petrinja, repelling reiterated enemy attacks, while 5.Kp./"Danmark," under SS-Ostuf. Poulsen, found itself again surrounded in the village of Hrvastovika. Meanwhile at Glina, just at the moment in which the Danish volunteers were at the point of being overwhelmed by an *n*th enemy attack, a providential intervention by the Luftwaffe managed to disperse the besieging forces. The Stuka dive-bombers hit the whole area around the town, scattering the partisan columns and enabling the other units of the division to link up with the besieged troops.

Having resolved the situation at Glina, Westphalen's attention turned to Hrastovika, where his grenadiers were on the verge of being overwhelmed. To liberate them, squadrons of Cossack cavalry, able horsemen and formidable fighters, that had been enlisted in the German army were thrown into the fight. However, the entire area around Hrastovika had been infested by partisan forces, and the efforts of the Cossacks to link up with the Danish grenadiers were fruitless. It thus became necessary for 7./"Danmark," under SS-Ostuf. Heinz Hämel,[9] to be committed to break the enemy ring around the village. But in reality, in the end the partisan forces withdrew only because they had completed their mission. Having in fact arrived at Hrastovika, Hämel's men found only ruins, flames, and corpses; all the grenadiers of 5.Kompanie of "Danmark" had fallen in combat, and the few remaining wounded had been massacred in cold blood by the Communist partisans. The men of SS-Pz.Abt.11 had also been engaged against the partisan forces, making many forays with their assault guns and Italian tanks, particularly in the Okitsch Mountain sector.

In the following weeks, "Nordland" units were engaged in other fighting against the Tito forces in the areas of Petrinja and Bosanski Novi, achieving new successes and suffering few losses.

A column of the "Danmark" regiment in Croatia

Men of the "Danmark" regiment engaged in antipartisan operations in Croatia, autumn 1943

SS-Ustuf. Robert L. Hansen, a platoon leader on 6./"Danmark," seated on a Schwimmwagen returning from an operation against Communist partisan bands in Croatia, autumn 1943

"Danmark" soldiers in a defensive position with an MG42. *NA*

On the left, a "Nordland" motorized column on the move in Croatia: a Kfz.15 is towing a Pak 40, followed by an RSO half-track. *Right*, "Nordland" assault guns moving on the Croatian front. *NA*

New Orders

On October 22, 1943, by order of the SS-Führungs-Hauptamt,[10] the division was officially renamed as 11.SS-Freiwilligen Panzer-Grenadier Division "Nordland." All the divisional units were assigned the number "11," while its two regiments were renumbered according to the new sequence of Waffen-SS regiments, becoming the SS-Panzergrenadier-Regiment 23 "Norge" and SS-Panzergrenadier-Regiment 24 "Danmark" on November 12, 1943.[11] Later, with a new order dated January 22, 1944, the two regiments received their final designations: SS-Panzergrenadier-Regiment 23 "Norge" (norwegishces Nr.1) and SS-Panzergrenadier-Regiment 24 "Danmark" (dänishces Nr. 1).

Divisional Order of Battle (Autumn 1943)

SS-Panzergrenadier-Regiment 23 "Norge"
SS-Panzergrenadier-Regiment 24 "Danmark"
Kradschützen-Regiment SS-Pz.Gren.-Division 11*
SS-Panzer-Regiment 11
SS-Panzerjäger-Abteilung 11**
SS-Artillerie-Regiment 11
SS-Sturmgeschütz-Abteilung***
SS-Flak-Abteilung 11
SS-Pionier-Bataillon 11
SS-Nachrichten-Abteilung 11
SS-Feldersatz-Bataillon 11

Kommandeur der SS-Divisions-Nachschubtruppen 11
SS-Instandsetzungs-Abteilung 11
SS-Sanitäts-Abteilung 11
SS-Wirtschafts-Bataillon 11

* Later transformed into SS-Panzer-Auflkärungs-Abteilung 11
** Not yet formed
*** Later transformed into SS-Panzerjäger-Abteilung 11

SS-Ostubaf. Graf von Westphalen awards the Iron Cross Second Class to two "Danmark" NCOs. *NA*

Another moment in the ceremony awarding Iron Crosses to two NCOs who had distinguished themselves during an antipartisan operation. *NA*

SS-Untersturmführer Erik Herløv Nielsen of the "Danmark" regiment on the Croatian front, a veteran of Freikorps "Danmark," autumn 1934. *NA*

Despite these new titles, the division's units continued not to receive the materials and equipment needed to continue their formation. Early to pay the price was the armored detachment, which as mentioned previously was reduced to a single battalion with four companies. On November 1, the II.Abteilung was therefore disbanded and part of its personnel transferred to schwere SS-Panzer-Abteilung 103.[12] That same day, the I.Abteilung assumed the designation of SS-Panzer-Abteilung 11. The title "Herman von Salza" was assigned to it later, in honor of the Grand Master of the Teutonic Knights.

Transfer to the Eastern Front

At the end of November, the order to transfer to the Leningrad sector of the Eastern Front finally came. Beginning on November 25, the movement of units that were to embark at Zagreb began, terminating completely only on December 2. The various companies were relieved in turn by other German units, while actions by partisan bands continued despite everything else. The division's motorized units were engaged in convoy escort duties.

Some units, such as SS-Pionier-Bataillon 11, 16./"Norge," and 16./"Danmark," never reached Croatia, remaining in the Beneschau training area, from where they were transferred directly to the Leningrad front. SS-Flak-Abteilung 11, still in training at Arys, also joined the division directly on the Russian front. The Panzer-Abteilung was the last "Nordland" unit to leave Croatia toward the end of December.

Up to the last minute, the units were engaged against the partisans. The men of the battalion passed Christmas on a train as they traveled to the Eastern Front. The arrival of the Panther tanks assigned to the battalion was, however, once again postponed. The units of the SS "Nederland" brigade, also attached to III.(germ.)SS-Panzer-Korps, remained in Croatia to complete their training and began to be transferred to the Eastern Front around the end of December.

SS-Ostubaf. Graf von Westphalen inspects a group of new recruits for the division. *NARA*

A group of new recruits for the "Nordland" division. *NARA*

Middle: a 15 cm infantry gun (s.IG-33) of the "Nordland" during operations in Croatia, autumn 1943. *NA*

CHAPTER III
THE ORANIENBAUM FRONT

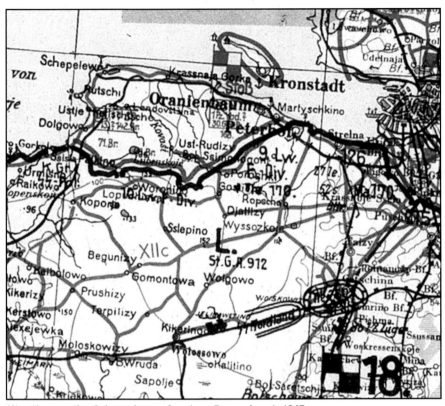

Situation on the Orianenbaum front on December 1, 1943

General Lindemann and Fritz von Scholz

The units of III./SS-Panzer-Korps began to be moved to the Leningrad front in early December 1943, where they were subordinated to Generaloberst Lindemann's 18.Armee. The army's operational front ran from Lake Ilmen in the south to the Gulf of Finland in the north. For many veterans of the volunteer legions, that area of the front was very familiar, having already fought there in the terrible winter between 1941 and 1942. The units of the SS "Nordland" division were deployed west of Leningrad, in a forward position along the Soviet Oranienbaum salient, which from the north dominated the German 18.Armee positions. In their advance to Leningrad in 1941, the Germans had left this large pocket to the west, butted up against the Baltic Sea, without bothering to eliminate it. After almost three years of siege, after having managed to break the encirclement around the city of Leningrad, Soviet forces now readied themselves to launch a great offensive to throw the German forces out of northern Russia and from the Baltic provinces.

A German artillery position on the Oranienbaum front

Disposition of German forces on the Oranienbaum and Leningrad fronts, 1944

Waffen-SS soldiers

German headquarters had for some time been expecting an imminent Soviet offensive coming from the Oranienbaum salient, and Steiner's SS corps was to have contained the attack and protected the retreat of German forces toward Estonia. The III.(germ.)SS-Pz-Korps units faced the Kessel, from the course of the Luga River until the city of Peterhof.

Situation of the Units along the Front Line

In the sector allotted to III.(germ.)SS-Pz-Korps were deployed the III.Luftwaffen-Feld-Korps under General der Flakartillerie Job Odebrecht, consisting of two Luftwaffe field divisions, the 9.Luft-Felddivision (Oberst Ernst Michael), and the 10. (Generalmajor Hermann von Wedel), and farther to the west was the Kampfgruppe-Polizei (SS-Staf. Bock), recently transferred from the Volchov front. These three units were attached to Steiner's corps as of December 13, 1943. At that time, Kampfgruppe SS-Polizei stood in for units of the "Nederland," which had not yet reached the Leningrad front. On December 4, 1943, the corps staff reached Wolossovo by train; that same night, the officers and service personnel took up positions in the suburbs of Klopitzy, where Steiner also set up his command post.

The first elements of the "Nordland" to reach the Oranienbaum front were the engineers of SS-Pionier-Bataillon 11, along with the engineers of the "Norge" and "Danmark" regiments: 16.(Pi.) Kp./23 and 24. These units had never been transferred to Croatia and had continued their training in Bohemia and Moravia, in the Beneschau area. Having also detrained at Wolossovo, they reached Klopitzy on foot. With the help of engineers from 10.Lw. Felddivision, they were soon engaged in preparing positions for units of III.(germ.)SS-Pz-Korps.

Beginning on December 10, men of the grenadier regiments also began to arrive; those of the "Danmark" took up positions in the Kotly area, while those of the "Norge" established themselves in the Ragovizy area, then to be shifted to the Dolgaja Niva-Voronino area. SS-Brigadeführer Scholz established his command post in Kirova. Several companies were immediately moved to the front line, in the sector between Voronino and Dolgaja-Niva,

Soldiers of a Luftwaffe field division, January 1944

An SS grenadier in a trench on the Oranienbaum front. *NA*

A German patrol on reconnaissance

SS-Ostubaf. Christian Peder Kryssing

in the central part of the Oranienbaum front, relieving Luftwaffe field units. The "Nordland" division was assigned a stretch of the front about 25 kilometers long, from Gorbowizy to the west as far as Nowaja-Burya to the east, with "Danmark" units deployed on the left flank (to the west) and those of "Norge" on the right (to the east). On the left, up to the coast, were men of the Kampfgruppe of the SS-Polizei-Division, while to the right were the two Luftwaffe field divisions previously mentioned (9. and 10.LFD) and the 126 Inf.Div. (L.Armee Korps). Beginning on December 12, recon patrols began to be sent out to gather information on enemy intentions and his positions and size of his forces.

The Soviets fielded two army corps, nine guards divisions, three tank brigades, and a coastal brigade in the Oranienbaum salient. On December 14, 1943, fearing enemy landings along the coast west of Leningrad, Steiner decided to constitute a separate command for the coastal sector, assigning command to SS-Ostubaf. Kryssing,[1] commander of the SS corps artillery. He was tasked with forming a combat group to employ in the assigned area, which was designated Kampfgruppe Küste (coastal combat group). Assigned as chief of staff of the coastal group (Chef des Stabes des SS-KG Küste) was SS-Stubaf. Ranzow-Engelhardt, and under his guidance, organization of the units was quickly ended. Available to Kryssing were eleven coastal batteries under Major Blum, well entrenched and hidden from the view of the enemy, a battalion of Estonian police, a naval infantry regiment, and an artillery battalion.

Completion of the Defensive Line

Toward the end of the year, thanks to the arrival of units of the "Nederland" brigade, it was possible to complete the defensive deployment of the SS corps; the two Dutch regiments of the "Nederland" brigade, commanded by SS-Brigdf. Jürgen Wagner, consisted of some six thousand combatants. The Dutch brigade's headquarters installed itself at Lutschki. Steiner decided to have the Dutch units relieve the SS-Polizei Kampfgruppe, which was being reorganized, on the left flank of the line. The first unit of the brigade to be put on the front line was SS-Ostuf. Kuhne's recon company, which relieved the 2. Kompanie of the Polizei engineers, southwest of Mustovo. Soon after, it was the turn of I. / "General Seyffardt." At the beginning of the new year, the Dutch units went to occupy the entire sector held by the SS-Polizei Kampfgruppe. Only III./SS-Pol.Art.Rgt. under SS-Hstuf. Wilhelm Schlüter remained on the line, since the Dutch brigade was still awaiting its own artillery regiment. The men of SS-Frw-Pz.Gr.Rgt. 49 took up positions east of those of SS-Frw-Pz.Gr.Rgt. 48, whose command had been assumed by SS-Ostubaf. Wolfgang Joerchel, to the west. After finally receiving its assault guns and its antitank guns, SS-Panzer-Jäger-Abteilung 54, under SS-Stubaf. Knud Schock, was deployed to the area south of Kotly, where it was quickly engaged against Soviet partisan forces that were very active in that sector. The "Nederland" engineer battalion, which in the meantime had come under command of SS-Stubaf. Günther Wanhöfer, became busy in constructing defensive works.

"Nordland" Deployment Posture

The "Danmark" regiment took up positions in the western part of the "Nordland" operational sector; SS-Ostubaf. Westphalen had set up his headquarters in several revetted bunkers about 4 kilometers north of the village of Saoserje, while the SS-Artillerie-Regiment 11 command post was farther south. In reserve was II./"Danmark" under SS-Stubaf. Kurt Walther,[2] an artillery group, and an engineer company. The I./"Danmark," led by SS-Hstuf. Karl Wichmann,[3] situated on the left flank, maintained contact with the Dutch units, and the III./"Danmark," under SS-Stubaf. Poul Neergaard-Jacobsen, maintained contact with units of the "Norge" regiment on the right. II./SS-Art.-Rgt.11 and 1./SS-Pi.Btl.11 were placed in support of the "Danmark" regiment.

The "Norge" units were deployed in the area between Voronino and Nowaja-Burje. Following the transfer of SS-Ostubaf. Joerchel to the "Nederland," command of the "Norge" regiment had been assumed by SS-Ostubaf. Arnold Stoffers,[4] who had in reserve the I./"Norge" under SS-Stubaf. Vogt[5] at Lopuschinka, while on the line were the II./"Norge" under SS-Stubaf. Albrecht Krügel,[6] located to the west, and the III./"Norge" under SS-Stubaf. Lohmann to the east. SS-Stubaf. Stoffers had placed his command post in a bunker complex at Dolgaja-Niwa. I./SS-Art.-Rgt.11 and 1./SS-Pi.Btl.11 were placed in support of the "Norge" regiment.

Toward the end of the year, on December 29, 1943, to be exact, the men of SS-Pz.Aufkl.-Abt.11, under SS-Hstuf. Rudolf Saalbach, arrived and took up positions in the rear area, between the villages of Begunizy and Greblovo, to continue their training. The "Nordland" reconnaissance battalion was structured with five companies: the first, led by SS-Ostuf. Lorenz,[7] was equipped with eight-wheeled vehicles (SdKfz 234) armed with 20 mm cannons and machine guns. The second, under SS-Ostuf. Heckmüller,[8] was equipped with half-tracks (SdKfz 250 and 252). The third and fourth companies consisted of grenadiers mounted on SPW (Schwerer Panzerspähwagen), which were armored troop transport vehicles. The 3.Kompanie was led by SS-Ostuf. Walter Kaiser and the 4. by SS-Ostuf. Heinz Viehmann. The fifth company, designated as "heavy," commanded by SS-Ostuf. Schmidt,[9] consisted of an antitank platoon, an infantry gun platoon, an engineer platoon, and a half-track platoon, with SdKfz 251/9 armed with 7.5 cm KwK 37 L/24 guns.

SS-Pz.Jg.-Abt.11 (SS-StuG-Abteilung 11), led by SS-Hstuf. Ernst Röntzsch, assembled at Jamburg, on the river Luga. Röntzsch had as his adjutant a German army officer, Hauptmann Schulz-Streek.[10] As soon as it arrived at the front, the unit received its assault guns: the Stabsbatterie was headed by SS-Ostuf. Krohmer,[11] the 1.Batterie under SS-Ostuf. Rennert,[12] the 2.Batterie led by SS-Hstuf. Knobelspeiss,[13] and the 3.Batterie under SS-Hstuf. Ellersiek.[14] SS-Pz.Abt.11 also arrived, whose crews, while awaiting issue of their Panthers, were billeted for logistics reasons in Hungerburg, along the Panther-Stellung, the defensive line set up in anticipation of a withdrawal of 16. and 18.Armee. Thirteen Panther Ausf. Ds with mechanical problems, abandoned by I./Pz.Rgt.24, had been salvaged by the battalion and integrated into its 1.Kompanie. Most of these tanks, which could not move under their own power, were dug in and transformed into static artillery positions so that at least their guns could be used. On December 31, 1943, the "Nordland" division numbered 11,393 men, of which 304 were officers, 1,734 were NCOs, and 9,355 were other ranks. The SS division still was short by many men to reach its theoretical manning level.

SS-Hstuf. Poul Neergaard-Jacobsen

SS-Ostubaf. Arnold Stoffers

An SdKfz 250 of 2./SS-Pz.-Aufkl.-Abt.11

German defensive position on the Oranienbaum front

German patrol on reconnaissance, January 1944

"Danmark" defensive position on the Oranienbaum front

Final Warnings

Since the early days of 1944, the Soviets began to bombard the German positions with artillery and air strikes, a clear presage of an imminent offensive. At the same time, they sent fresh forces into the Oranienbaum sector and intensified their aerial reconnaissance. In the Leningrad sector, a new army arrived, the 42nd, equipped specifically to attack. But despite all these advance signs, 18.Armee received no reinforcements and had in reserve only one division, the 61.Infanterie-Division, located between Krasnogwardiesk and Oranienbaum. In this situation, it had to face the offensive by the Leningrad front, with three armies, and by the Volchov front, with four armies.

On January 9, 1944, the "Danmark" commander, SS-Ostubaf. Westphalen, sent out a recon patrol under Danish SS-Oberscharführer Hvenekilde into enemy territory in an attempt to capture prisoners and obtain intelligence. The patrol ran into a Soviet ambush and all its members were killed or captured. Yet another sign that the Soviets were getting ready to attack.

On January 10, 2./SS-Pi.Btl.11 was shifted to the 9.Luft.Feld.-Div. sector in order to strengthen defensive works and to act as an operational reserve at the juncture point between 9. and 10.Luft.Feld.-Div. SS-Ostuf. Knepel[15] led his engineers of 2./SS-Pi.Btl.11 on a night march in the cold and snow to reach the new positions. The company dug in near the artillery batteries. After having carried out a detailed reconnaissance of the terrain, the SS engineers began to build fortifications immediately behind the main line of resistance. For their part, the Soviets intensified their artillery and air bombardment along the entire front line.

The Soviet Offensive Kicks Off

On January 4, 1944, Soviet forces of the Second Baltic Front launched an offensive from the east and from the Oranienbaum salient, overwhelming the German defenses: the 2nd Shock Army from the Oranienbaum salient, the 42nd Army from the Leningrad area, and the 67th Army from the front north of Mga. Naturally the offensive was preceded by massive preparatory fires, unleashed by the Kronstadt naval fortress, by the guns of several Soviet ships, and by the batteries of the 2nd Shock Army. East of the Oranienbaum front, the Soviets assaulted the German positions that were defended by Luftwaffe field divisions. That choice was not a casual one but was dictated by the conviction that those units were inferior in quality compared to those of the army and of the Waffen-SS. The poor Luftwaffe infantrymen, badly armed and even worse equipped, could in fact do little against the avalanche of fire and steel that fell upon them, and ended up being literally shattered. With the beginning of the attack by Soviet infantry and tanks, the situation became even more critical.

The engineers of 2./SS-Pi.Btl.11 soon found themselves in the center of the enemy attack. SS-Ostuf. Heinz Knepel was rudely awakened by the explosions. In an attempt to return to his command post, he ran across a group of soldiers who were running in all directions in an attempt to find shelter, completely seized by panic. SS-Hstuf. Hermann Voss,16 commander of 3./SS-Pi.Btl.11, managed to join Knepel's men: "What shall we do?" asked Voss. "We'll counterattack," responded Knepel decisively. "But there are too many of them," retorted Voss. Knepel again replied, "Maybe, but they will be surprised by our reaction." The two "Nordland" engineer companies thus threw themselves against the advancing Soviet columns. Spurred by that bold action, some of the survivors of the two Luftwaffe field divisions who had made it through the inferno also dived in behind them. But their courage lasted only briefly.

In fact, after having gone a couple of kilometers, the "Nordland" engineers realized that they had been alone to attack. The two SS officers, Knepel and Voss, found themselves and their engineers having to face thousands of enemy infantry supported by many tanks. Assessing that it was impossible to continue any further offensive action, the two SS officers agreed that they would pull their men back. Covering each other, the two companies began to fall back under constant enemy fire and continuing to be engaged in rearguard actions. It was not until they were under shelter of a small patch of woods that the men could catch their breath and tend to the many wounded. Among them was SS-Ostuf. Knepel himself, who had been seriously wounded. SS-Stubaf. Fritz Bunse, commander of the engineer battalion, personally went up to the front line to take command of the small combat group. After having managed to scrape together all the survivors on a farm, he had the men dig in in anticipation of new enemy attacks. After having been subjected to massive Soviet artillery fire, their position was soon attacked by Siberian infantry units. Fire from the engineers' heavy machine guns and all other automatic weapons was able to stem the attack in some fashion. Losses, however, were heavy. The next day, beginning in the morning, Soviet artillery again began to shell the SS engineer positions, prior to a fresh infantry attack, this time supported by three T-34 tanks. Two of them approached the SS engineer positions. Two courageous engineers left their foxholes in the snow, attaching hollow-charge magnetic mines onto the enemy's steel monsters, knocking them out of action. The third T-34 was destroyed by an antitank gun. Despite the destruction of the three tanks, the Soviet infantry carried on with its attack against the German positions, heedless of the large number of corpses that littered the battlefield. When the situation appeared to be lost, a sort of miracle occurred: a German soldier, possibly in a fit of madness, left his trench and, with a machine pistol, threw himself like a fury against the Soviet infantrymen. Others, less insane but encouraged by that gesture, followed him in the attack. Caught completely by surprise, the Soviet soldiers fell back.

German artillery position on the Oranienbaum front

Luftwaffe soldiers in combat, January 1944

SS defensive position on the Oranienbaum front

Soviet T-34 tanks attacking on the Oranienbaum front

German soldiers facing Soviet tanks at close range in a Russian village, January 1944

A soldier wounded in the face, after quick treatment, is carried by his comrades to the rear for further treatment.

50 mm antitank gun engaged against Soviet tanks. *Cremin*

The Knight's Cross for Fritz Bunse

For that decisive action, SS-Stubaf. Bunse was proposed for the award of the Knight's Cross, which was officially presented to him on January 30, 1944. Following is the text of the proposal, written by SS-Brigdf. Fritz von Scholz and approved by SS-Ogruf. Steiner himself: "On January 12, 1944, SS-Sturmbannführer Bunse and 2.Kompanie of his engineer battalion were engaged in building obstacles in the forest southeast of Poroshki. After having completed these works according to orders dated January 14, 1944, they pulled back to the 'Finnish position.' He and his men had barely established themselves at that position when they received a verbal order from the commander of 9.Lw.Feld.Div to launch a counterattack against enemy troops that had penetrated near Poroshki. He thus pushed against superior enemy forces without concentrating on either the right of the left, but as he was doing this he fell under enemy attack on his right flank while he was in the forest. On his own initiative he attacked the enemy that had shown up on the right behind his company, and from that moment on he fought to return to the 'Finnish position.' From there, he repelled eight enemy attacks made by superior enemy forces, with heavy losses both to attackers and defenders. His men were already exhausted by the attack over the deep snow, and their unfavorable positions were often only holes dug into the snow.

"The enemy preceded its attacks by heavy artillery fire and attacked for the most part with the support of tanks and aircraft. Both of the nearby units had already pulled back during the last two attacks. The fact that his young unit (which was newly constituted and consisted 605 youths) had been able to hold its positions for all that time was thanks only to his own determined and incessant personal efforts on the front line, as well as to his exemplary courage. As a result, his battalion was the only unit in the sector to hold its positions for two days.

"After the enemy had managed to break into the position on the night of 01.15.1944, he was again engaged in hand-to-hand fighting. He was the last man to leave the position after the wounded had been evacuated. Covering his men with his machine pistol, SS-Sturmbannführer Bunse and his men fell back to a new position on the southeast bank of the river between the farm and the village of Lewolowo. From there, covered on both flanks by two companies of Infanterie-Regiment 176, he repulsed two more Soviet night attacks with only one officer, one NCO, and eleven men (the rest of the members of his Kampfgruppe were by now dead or wounded). The enemy was forced to modify their plans because of the resistance by SS-Pz.Pi.Btl.11, as was learned from an analysis of radio messages to and from Bunse's unit. The battalion's exceptional sacrifice, inspired by the example of its commander, allowed his unit to be able to escape destruction by enemy forces."

SS-Ostubaf. Fritz Bunse with the Ritterkreuz

German defensive position with a medium mortar

An "old" MG34 defending a position, January 1944

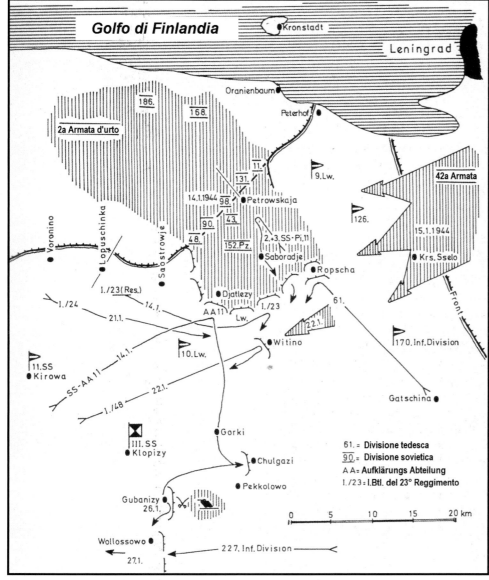

Movement of German units after the January 14 Soviet offensive

Defensive Battles

While the "Nordland" engineers were engaged in bitter fighting, the men of 9.Luft.Feld.Div., 126.Inf.Div., and 170. Inf.Div. were almost surrounded after the rapid Soviet advance. Only a few units were able to withdraw to the west in good order. At the same time, all the available German forces were sent to the area of the breakthrough, among them 61. and 227.Infanterie-Division. The 2nd Shock Army's objective was now clear: enemy forces aimed at seizing Ropscha and Gatschina, the key node in the German supply line and the main railway node. The 61.Infanterie-Division was hard pressed in the Ropscha area throwing back Soviet attacks. The III. (germ.)SS-Panzer-Korps sent all its available forces to the area of the Soviet penetration. Between January 17 and 18, Kampfgruppe "Küste" sent its three reserve battalions and its motorized artillery group to the combat zone.

On January 19, the two arms of the Soviet offensive that had left from the Oranienbaum front and from Leningrad linked up at Ropscha, not far from Krasnoje Selo, trapping the German forces south of Leningrad in a mortal grip. In that way, the first objective of the Soviet offensive had been achieved, with the elimination the northern wing of General Lindemann's 18.Armee. From the Ropscha area, enemy forces, which had now joined up, attacked to the west, toward Jamburg on the river Luga. With this new offensive, all the German forces engaged on the Oranienbaum front risked being taken from behind. To avoid annihilation of his forces, the commander of Heeresgruppe Nord, Field Marshal Küchler, asked Berlin for authorization to withdraw to a new defensive line along the course of the Luga. The führer, opposed to any withdrawal, not only prohibited any possible retreat but also decided to replace Küchler by Field Marshal Walter Model. In light of the seriousness of the situation, the new commander could do nothing other than to send all available forces to the front line, especially the units of III./SS-Panzer-Korps.

SS Reconnaissance Troops in Action

As soon as the axis of attack of Soviet forces became clear, on January 14, SS-Pz.Aufkl.Abt.11 was sent to the Djatlezy area. In the afternoon, it was engaged, along with units from 10. Lw.Feld.Div. The 2./SS-Pz.Aufkl.Abt.11, led by SS-Ostuf. Heckmüller, with his 20 mm armed half-tracks, arrived on the outskirts of the villages of Kapyloschka and Djatlezy. In those two villages, situated in the rear area, the Luftwaffe infantrymen had been overwhelmed by the Soviets and had thus fallen into their hands. The village of Djatlezy was quickly attacked by the SS recon troops and retaken. Soon thereafter, SS-Ostuf. Heckmüller gathered his platoon leaders together in an isba to discuss how to continue the counterattack. After having laid down a plan, the four of them left the isba to return to their vehicles. But just at that moment they came under fire from Soviet mortars. SS-Ostuf. Heckmüller came out of it unharmed, but two platoon leaders were badly wounded and a third, SS-Oberscharführer Gramlisch, died shortly after from his serious wounds. Heckmüller quickly assembled his vehicles and withdrew with them to a small woods. From there, with his 20 mm guns and his machine guns, he managed to halt the advance of the Soviet infantry. There were no radio communications, and it was an NCO, SS-Unterscharführer Poller, who had to run from vehicle to vehicle to relay his commander's orders. The road to Djatlezy was blocked, and thus the Soviets sought another passage farther north, through the village of Kapyloschka. SS-Ostuf. Heckmüller found himself forced to divide his forces: he sent half of his available vehicles to the threatened sector, under SS-Uscha. Poller. The SS scouts, however, needed infantry support to repel the enemy attacks, but the German headquarters could send only a labor battalion, consisting of old men armed with small arms, as reinforcements. Until January 21, the SS recon troopers and veterans of the Great War managed, however, to block all Soviet penetrations toward Bor and Kosserizy (Kosheritzy).

Sd.Kfz. 250 half-track on the Oranienbaum front, January 1944

Sd.Kfz. 250/9 half-track armed with a 20 mm gun. *NA*

German grenadiers in a woods, armed with automatic weapons and Panzerfaust, facing a Soviet tank attack, January 1944

SS-Hstuf. Fritz Vogt, *on the left*, with another SS officer. *Charles Trang*

A formation of assault guns on the Oranienbaum front. *Cremin*

An sIG.33 infantry gun providing fire support

On the Positions of I./"Norge"

During the night, Vogt led his battalion to the area where the Soviets had managed to break through. The German grenadiers marched over snowy paths, through bitter cold. On January 15, when dawn began to break, the SS grenadiers saw in front of the positions that they had occupied in Kosserizy in the darkness six Soviet tanks that were advancing, making a great noise with their motors and tracks. All hell broke loose along the front line. SS-Ostuf. Rendemann,[17] commander of 2./"Norge," was among the first to fall to enemy fire. The 3./"Norge," led by SS-Hstuf. Otto von Bargen,[18] was spared from enemy attacks until noon. At the stroke of noon, four assault guns from 3./SS-StuG. Abt.11, led by SS-Hstuf. Kurt Ellersiek, arrived as reinforcements and threw themselves into the counterattack along with the grenadiers. The well-camouflaged Soviet tanks responded to their fire. Ellersiek's assault gun took a direct hit from a Soviet shell, and in the explosion everyone in the crew was killed except for the commander, who sustained serious injuries. The 3./"Norge" was forced to withdraw, taking up new defensive positions farther west. The Soviet T-34s dogged the withdrawal of the SS grenadiers, but for the rest of the day they settled for shelling the positions of the volunteers with their guns. SS-Hstuf. Bargen and one of his platoon leaders were wounded, and command of 3./"Norge" was assumed by an NCO, SS-Hscha. Twesmann.[19] To support Vogt's battalion, division headquarters sent the guns of 5./SS-Art.Rgt.11, under Danish Ostuf. Björn Binnerup.[20] These began to hit the Soviet positions but were not able to silence the enemy rocket launcher batteries, whose intense fire inflicted heavy casualties on the men of I./"Norge." In the end, SS-Hstuf. Vogt was forced to shift his positions to a kilometer southwest. For two days, enemy pressure was intense, and in the end the grenadiers found themselves north of the road that ran from Vitino to Djatlezy. Vogt's battalion held out for an entire week, continuing to suffer heavy losses. SS-Hscha. Twesmann was badly wounded and 3./"Norge" was once again left without a commander. SS-Hstuf. Vogt entrusted command of the company to his adjutant, SS-Ostuf. Fechner.[21] Until January 21, 1944, the SS grenadiers held firmly on to their positions without giving up a meter of ground.

The other units of "Nordland" also began to pull back to the west, while, thanks to its mobility, the recon battalion under SS-Hstuf. Saalbach continued to shift to the hottest spots of the front, supporting the most-threatened units. On January 17, Saalbach was able to establish a new defensive line farther south with his recon group, 1.SS-Pi.Btl.11, and elements of 10.Lw. Fd.Div. Despite the cold and the intense fire from Soviet artillery and mortars, the positions were held with few losses.

Gruppe "Bunse" and the survivors of 2. and 3./SS-Pi.Btl.11 continued to defend themselves amid the ruins of the farm at Lewolowo (Levolovo) until the evening of January 17, when soldiers from the 61.Infanterie-Division arrived as reinforcements. That same day, it was necessary to abandon the position following another counterattack made by SS-Stubaf. Bunse himself, along with telephone operators, secretaries, drivers, and all the noncombat personnel of his staff.

On the "Danmark" Positions

Deployed farther west of the Oranienbaum pocket, the Germanic volunteers of the "Danmark" regiment were engaged in combat later. In the night between January 21 and 22, II./"Danmark," under SS-Stubaf. Walther, until then held in reserve, arrived to relieve SS-Hstuf. Wichmann's I./"Danmark" in its positions. After having been relieved, I./"Danmark" was to go in turn to relieve SS-Pz.Aufkl.Abt.11 in Djatlezy and on that occasion was reinforced by 10./"Danmark" and an antitank gun. Several units were shifted from the western sector of Oranienbaum to the more threatened eastern sector. During these moves, 8./"Danmark" was shifted to Dolgaja-Niva to free several batteries of SS-Art. Rgt.11 that had supported the tough fighting by the *Kampfgruppen* in the area of the breakthrough. Meanwhile, the Soviets continued their attacks to try to surround the German forces deployed farther south by employing a wide encircling movement. The armored vehicles of the "Nordland" recon battalion had to intervene continually by making rapid counterattacks in conjunction with Wehrmacht infantry units.

On January 22 the situation deteriorated unexpectedly, with a massive fresh Soviet attack against the defensive positions east of Witino, along the main supply line. SS-Ogruf. Steiner decided to commit the Dutch volunteers of the "Nederland" brigade to plug the gap that had just been opened. SS-Brigdf. Wagner sent Kampfgruppe Rühle, commanded by Hans Joachim Rühle von Lilienstern, consisting of three companies of I./SS-Frw-Pz. Gr.Rgt.48 and two companies of SS-Pionier-Bataillon 54. The Dutch volunteers occupied defensive positions on both sides of the village of Witino. During the night between January 22 and 23, the Dutch Kampfgruppe was hard pressed to push back against the repeated enemy assaults. SS-Hstuf. Rühle von Lilienstern personally led fully seventeen counterattacks to ease the enemy pressure and to repel the dangerous Soviet penetrations. The Soviets continued to launch attacks in an attempt to find gaps in the German defensive line. The situation on the morning of January 23, 1944, was as follows: in the area between Kapyloschka and Djatlezy were the grenadiers of I./"Danmark," a *Kampfgruppe* from 10.Luft.Feld.Div., and 1./SS-Pi.Btl.11.

SS grenadier armed with a machine pistol. *NA*

SS grenadiers giving aid to a soldier badly wounded in combat, January 1944

German grenadiers in a defensive position

A group of Sd.Kfz.250 half-tracks in battle

A group of SS grenadiers ready to attack, January 1944

A 20 mm antiaircraft gun engaged against ground targets

German grenadiers with an MG42 in combat

Farther south were the grenadiers of I./"Norge," and at Witino was Kampfgruppe Lilienstern. Still farther south was a *Kampfgruppe* of SS-Pz.Aufkl. Abt.11 in support of 61.Inf.Div.

New Defensive Fighting

Between January 23 and 24, defensive combat intensified all along the front line. In particular, Soviet attacks concentrated mainly against the I./"Danmark" positions, with the enemy's intent being to continue on toward Woronino, Bor, and Tsceremykino. The Soviet attacks were made with tank support and with artillery and mortar fire. The I./"Danmark" grenadiers managed at great sacrifice to hold their positions, suffering heavy losses. All the attacks against Witino were also repulsed. The Soviets continued to probe for weak points in the defensive line. At Chulgusi, south of the main supply line, a new concentration of Soviet forces ready to attack was spotted. SS-Pz.Aufkl.Abt.11, deployed in the Bol-Chapino-Wolgowo area, was given the following order: "Eliminate enemy concentrations in the Chulgusi area." SS-Hstuf. Saalbach organized his forces into two attack groups. The Gruppe "Nord," consisting of the 1., the 4., and the 5./SS-Pz.Aufkl. Abt.11, led by Saalbach himself, assembled at Wolgowo. The Gruppe Süd, consisting of 2. and 3./SS-Pz.Aufkl. Abt.11, under SS-Hstuf. Heckmüller, assembled at Torrossowo. After a brief preparatory fire, the two groups attacked, pushing toward Chulgusi; Gruppe Süd was engaged in tough fighting and was not able to make any forward progress until Gruppe "Nord" also entered into action. The 2./SS-Pz.Aufkl.Abt.11 suffered the loss of an armored car to antitank fire. The commander of 5./ SS-Pz.Aufkl.Abt.11, SS-Ostuf. Schmidt, was wounded. The enemy troops retreated in great disorder to the forests farther east. The operation was successful, although it was not able to stem the enemy advance along the rest of the front. Faced with this difficult situation, division headquarters began to shift its logistics units in the rear farther west. On January 25, the Soviets came back to attack the I./"Danmark" positions in force. After having sought in vain to oppose these new enemy attacks, the

"Danmark" grenadiers were completely overwhelmed. The battalion commander, SS-Hstuf. Karl Wichmann, and two company commanders, SS-Hstuf. Heinz Henneke[22] and SS-Ostuf. Eduard Hein, were killed during the bitter fighting. A dangerous gap was thus opened, with the Soviets on the verge of surrounding the German positions. Danish Hstuf. Per Sörensen assumed command of the battalion and gave the order to withdraw toward Witino, where there were Dutch units. Sörensen placed himself in the lead, with 2. and 4./"Danmark," and SS-Ostuf. Fritz Sidon, commander of 9./"Danmark," protected the withdrawal with 1. and 3./"Danmark." At that time the Danish companies numbered only a few dozen men each. After tough and bloody fighting, the remnants of I./"Danmark" finally reached the positions of the Dutch Kampfgruppe at Witino. SS-Hstuf. Rühle von Lilienstern deployed his grenadiers south of the village to fend off the continuous enemy attacks. These positions were held until January 27, in order to cover the withdrawal of other III.SS-Pz.Korps units to the west. In fact, on January 26, SS-Brigadeführer Scholz had received an official order to pull his units westward, toward Jamburg, on the Luga River. Although he had been wounded, SS-Hstuf. Rühle von Lilienstern remained in command of his battalion until he also was ordered to pull back to Jamburg. The Danish volunteers, led by Sidon, covered the retreat of the Dutch Kampfgruppe. For his exemplary conduct in the field, following the award of the Iron Cross First Class on January 22, 1944, SS-Hstuf. Rühle von Lilienstern was decorated with the Knight's Cross on February 12, 1944.

On January 25, Kampfgruppe Heiling, consisting of the remnants of 10.Lw.Fd.Div. and 1./SS-Pi.Btl.11, under Rittmeister Heiling, withdrew. The Soviets launched massive attacks on the afternoon of the next day. Heiling held a meeting with his company commanders, and SS-Ustuf. Arera,[23] commander of 1./SS-Pi.Btl.11, proposed an immediate disengagement under cover of darkness. As soon as it became dark, the men began to march, with the SS engineers in the lead. The snow seriously impeded progress and slowed down the withdrawal. Along the road, Heiling's column joined up with other surviving elements of other German units, and together they successfully continued their march westward.

Tank Attacks

The men of SS-Panzer-Aufklärungs Abteilung 11 continued to cover the withdrawal of their comrades; SS-Stubaf. Rudolf Saalbach's armored vehicles had gathered outside the village of Gubanizy, a few kilometers south of Klopizy, where the III.SS-Pz.Korps commander, Steiner, had set up his command post. The Soviet advance tank elements, followed by much infantry, attacked at dawn on January 26 in that very area. The 5.Kompanie, led by SS-Ostuf. Georg Langendorf,[24] was the only unit of the "Nordland's" recon battalion to have effective antitank weapons, among which was a platoon equipped with 75 mm antitank guns and eight SdKfz 251/19 half-tracks equipped with a 75 mm antitank gun. The Soviet tank force consisted of about sixty tanks, among which Langendorf recognized some of the older type of T-34. The antitank gun layers quickly got the first of the tanks in their

German defensive position with an MG34, January 1944

Sd.Kfz.250/1 armed with an MG34 in combat

Two German grenadiers in a defensive position with an MG42. In the background is a StuG.II, January 1944.

sights. The first enemy tank group that was approaching, consisting of seven tanks, was targeted by the fire of the German Paks; within a few minutes, six tanks were knocked out. When the second wave of enemy tanks attacked, the action was joined by the Stummels, the company's half-tracks armed with 75 mm guns; Dutch SS-Rottenführer Kaspar Sporck,[25] with his antitank half-track, threw himself against the enemy without a moment's hesitation. Along his path, fully eleven enemy tanks were knocked out and another four seriously damaged. Within a few days, Sporck was awarded both classes of the Iron Cross (January 30 and February 7, 1944), while awaiting the Knight's Cross. The Soviet offensive thrust against Gubanizy turned into a real slaughter of enemy tanks: forty-eight were destroyed by 5./SS-Aufkl.-Abt.11.

The Knight's Cross for Georg Langendorf

For having distinguished himself in combat, SS-Ostuf. Langendorf was awarded the Knight's Cross, officially presented on March 12, 1944. The following is the proposal written by SS-Hstuf. Saalbach: "Operating as part of Kampfgruppe Wengler, SS-Panzer-Aufklärungs-Abteilung 11 was engaged in defending the important crossroads at Gubanizy, northwest of Volossovo.

"On January 26, 1944, an attack was made against the city by fifty-six Soviet tanks, many of which were T-34s. Accompanying them was a battalion consisting of 350 men. Untersturmführer Langendorf, commanding the heavy company, had to defend the area northeast toward Torosowo with his antitank platoon. Despite not having any artillery available and the fact that our infantry had shifted to positions in the rear, Langendorf, on his own initiative, ordered his men to move their guns forward so as to be able to face the attack in an effective manner. Two assault guns that had very little ammunition disengaged after a brief

SS-Hstuf. Per Sörensen

An SdKfz. 251/9 of the "Nordland"

SS-Hstuf. Rühle von Lilienstern

exchange of fire. Thus, it was up to Langendorf's antitank platoon to face the main force of the Soviet attack. Thanks to his personal efforts, Langendorf and his gun platoon were able to destroy twenty-four tanks in two hours, fifteen of which were T-34s. Another six Soviet tanks were destroyed by Langendorf's defensive antitank rounds. Eight Soviet tanks were destroyed by the assault guns.

"After having destroyed the first wave of tanks, Langendorf deployed his armored half-tracks and personally led them to the southwestern outskirts of the city, following the advance of other enemy tanks. Once again, he repelled them, thus keeping the road open for reinforcements during the first phase of the battle. Returning to the northeastern perimeter, he scraped up the weak infantry elements for local defense against Soviet infantry and other waves of approaching enemy tanks. That day, Langendorf's antitank guns destroyed thirty-one enemy tanks (twenty-two of which were T-34s) and damaged another six Soviet tanks with their fire.

"On January 27, 1944, Langendorf successfully hit and destroyed another tank at Lagunovo. On January 29, 1944, another two enemy tanks were hit and then personally destroyed by Langendorf. Thus, in four days, Langendorf and the men of his company destroyed thirty-four enemy tanks and damaged another six. The total number of tanks destroyed at Gubanizy on January 26, 1944, made it impossible for the enemy to realize his intentions of pushing to Gubanizy and to reach Volossovo to take that city, an intention that was confirmed by declarations from prisoners. This made possible an orderly withdrawal movement to the west by our own forces."

A New Withdrawal

With the threat against Gubanizy now over with, the surviving elements of the "Nordland" recon group were shifted farther south, in the area of Volossovo, through which the important railway line that linked Jamburg with Narva passed. There for some days a *Kampfgruppe* of 227.Infanterie-Division, led by Oberst Maximilian Wengler, commander of Gren.Rgt.366, had been fighting. SS-Pz.Aufkl.Abt.11 remained in that area continuing to throw back enemy attacks. To reinforce the battalion's companies, the Germanic volunteers who returned to the

SS-Rottenführer Kaspar Sporck

SS-Ostuf. Georg Langendorf

SdKfz. 251/9 half-track

German grenadiers and a Tiger tank on the Oranienbaum front

German grenadiers and half-tracks in combat

A "Nordland" motorized column in a difficult withdrawal in the snow and impassable tracks. *NA*

Volossovo station from leave or from convalescence were assigned to the unit. Also engaged in that area were the Tiger tanks of schwere Panzer-Abteilung 502, led by Major Willy Jähde. On January 27, the Soviets made fresh attacks against the Gubanizy-Volossovo front but were thrown back. The German units slowly continued their withdrawal to the west. In the end, even the Volossovo position had to be abandoned. The vehicles of 5./ SS-Pz.Aufkl.Abt.11 covered the withdrawal of Kampfgruppe Wengler and of the Tigers, which were loaded aboard special flatcars at the Volossovo railway station. Then, in turn, the SS units pulled back to the west.

By late afternoon of January 26, 1944, all of the units of III./(germ.)SS-Pz.Korps had abandoned their positions in front of the Oranienbaum pocket. Steiner moved his command post from Klopizy to Opolje, east of Jamburg. The withdrawal orders were also transmitted to 4.SS-Pz. Gren.Brigade "Nederland" and to Kampfgruppe Küste. The front was no longer to the east, but to the south, as SS-Ogruf. Steiner told his chief of staff, SS-Staf. Ziegler: "The attack front has turned exactly like a door on its hinges." Care had to be taken to avoid having the withdrawal turn into a general rout. One after another the various units reached their new positions: the batteries of the "Nordland" artillery regiment were emplaced in the area between Ratchina and Osakova, from where they continued to shell Soviet columns. Covering the retreat of units that had remained farther back were the engineers of 16./"Norge," led by SS-Hstuf. Egil Hoel, busy blowing up all the materiel that could not be transported. Most of the Panther tanks that had been dug in to be used as fixed artillery positions could not be salvaged, and it was necessary to blow them up with dynamite charges. There were many fires on the snowy plains.

At Kirova, the "Nordland" commander, Scholz, had delayed leaving his command post, and some enemy forward elements had surrounded it. Likewise, half of 7./"Norge" had been cut off. Norwegian SS-Ustuf. Knapp made a quick counterattack with the rest of 7./"Norge," freeing Scholz, who was then able to continue to organize the withdrawal of his units to the west. There was no trace of the rest of 7./"Norge"; killed or captured, the tragic fate was the same as that of so many other soldiers of the division.

"Danmark" units also were able to withdraw. III./"Danmark" abandoned its positions and marched on foot for 30 kilometers toward Kyerstovo, while II./"Danmark" accompanied SS-Pz. Gren.Rgt. "Norge" through Gorbovitsy and Kirovo and then to Byegunitsy. The "Danmark" regimental staff pulled back toward Zaozyorye. The withdrawal of these battalions was covered by 16.(Pi)/Kp./"Danmark." This company established contact with the regimental staff during the night of January 27. Soon after, the engineers were busy protecting the bridge at Lamokha.

Even the few tanks of SS-Pz.Abt.1 "Hermann von Salza" were busy protecting the retreating columns. During a recon at Kaporje, a direct hit fired by a Soviet tank hit the tank of SS-Hstuf. Paul Holtkamp,[26] commander of 1./SS-Pz.Abt.1, which quickly caught fire. Holtkamp himself was killed, along with all of his crew. A few days earlier, SS-Ustuf. Herbert Smidichen, also of 1./SSPz.Abt.11, was also killed during defensive fighting at Biegunizy.

The retreat of the "Nederland" brigade units and of Kampfgruppe Küste began on January 28. Kampfgruppe Küste was able to leave with all its weapons and equipment. Most of the static coastal batteries had to be destroyed. Since January 26, some elements of the *Kampfgruppe* and some 20 mm flak guns had been sent to protect the bridge at Keikino, the only bridge still intact between the Gulf of Finland and Jamburg. The Dutch volunteers marched in the cold and snow through dense forests, dogged by incessant Soviet artillery fire. Arms and equipment were loaded aboard akjas, the boat sled used by Nordic peoples to transport materiel over snow. The engineers were busy mining roads to slow down the advance of Soviet units that were following closely. SS-Panzer-Jäger-Abteilung 54 of SS-Stubaf. Knud Schock[27] went to reinforce the rearguard forces before pulling back with its assault guns to the south, crossing the Luga River at Jamburg.

SS-Ostuf. Kuhne's recon company busied itself covering the flanks and maintaining contact with various other units. When they arrived in the Kotly area, the Dutchmen were attacked by Soviet forces. SS-Hstuf. Karl Heinz Ertel, Collani's aide-de-camp, was seriously wounded as he tried to get the last men of the "de Ruyter" to

Groups of withdrawing German grenadiers moving over snowy ground

Difficult move of a wounded soldier to the rear during the withdrawal

A 37 mm flak gun engaged in antiaircraft defense. *Cremin*

withdraw. An isolated flak gun of 14.Kompanie of the same regiment managed to keep the Soviets at bay and keep the road to the west open. The Dutch volunteers continued to fight as a rearguard against units of the Soviet 47th Army. As soon as the last men of Kampfgruppe Küste (the SS-Panzer-Korps unit defending the coastal sector) had crossed the Luga River at Keikino, the Dutchmen took up new defensive positions in a semicircle around the city. Placing himself at the head of a squad of engineers, SS-Hstuf. Günter Wanhöfer made it his business to destroy the bridge north of Padoga, thus cutting the Krikkowo-Jamburg road to enemy heavy vehicles. Throughout the retreat and formation of the new defensive line along the river, the "Nederland" brigade held the Keikino bridgehead. On January 30, 1944, the last men of the "General Seyffardt," led by SS-Ostubaf. Jörchel, crossed the Luga.

German troops withdrawing on the Oranienbaum front in January 1944, while crossing a still-intact bridge over a water course. In the right foreground is a knocked-out Soviet tank.

An MG34 on the Oranienbaum Front, January 1944.
Michael Cremin

CHAPTER IV

THE LUGA FRONT

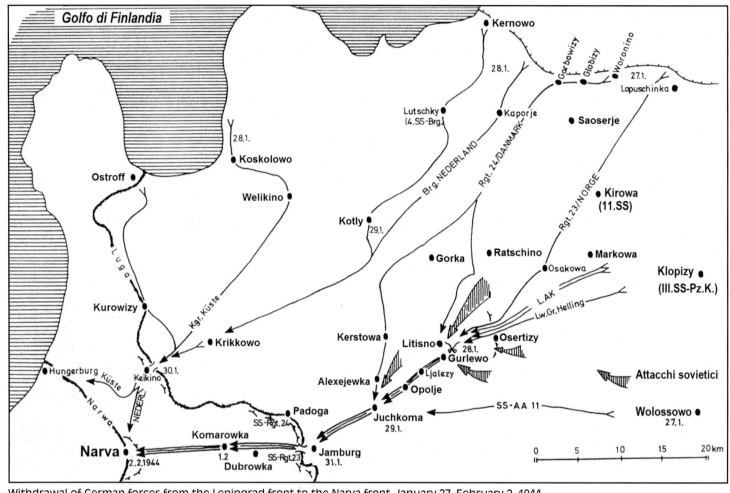

Withdrawal of German forces from the Leningrad front to the Narva front, January 27–February 2, 1944

By the end of January, all the III.SS-Pz.Korps units were to take up positions along the new defensive line, which followed the course of the river Luga. Field Marshal Walter Model, responsible for all of the northern front, ordered SS-Ogruf. Steiner to hold those positions for as long as possible in order to allow other German units to fall back to the west. While most of the "Nordland" divisional artillery assembled in the Ratschino area, continuing to fire with all its guns to cover the withdrawal, the grenadiers of the "Danmark" and "Norge" regiments dug in in the villages of Begunizy and Gomontovo; the companies were severely reduced in their manning after the heavy losses they had sustained in the fighting of the previous days. The 5./Bttr./ SS-Art.Rgt.11, under SS-Ostuf. Björn Binnerup, on the afternoon of January 28, fired more than six hundred rounds from his position at Osakowa, while III./SS-Art.Rgt.11, which had dislocated its two batteries east of Ratschino, continued to fire against the advancing enemy columns to the north and east.

German soldiers on the march, January 1944

Rearguard Actions

The remnants of I./"Norge" withdrew to the north, parallel to the main supply line. The division commander followed this battalion continuously, guiding it through the forests and swamps. The survivors of 10.Lwf.Fd.Div., including the Bataillon Heiling with 1./SS-Pi.Btl.11 and 1.Bttr./SS-Art. Rgt.11 under SS-Ostuf. Matt,[1] were engaged south of the main supply line. The Batterie von Matt, pulling out of its blocking positions, stopped numerous Soviet attacks. Soon after, the battery managed to pull back without leaving a single gun behind, thanks also to the covering action by 1./SS-Pi.Btl.11. Another Soviet attack from the northeast in the Ragowiczy sector threatened the withdrawal of III./"Danmark," which at that moment was located in Kerstovo; in order to fend off the threat, SS-Stubaf. Neergaard-Jacobsen sent 9./"Danmark" to Ssergowizy, 2 kilometers east of Kerstovo. The "Danmark" company set out on its march but disappeared completely, without leaving a trace. SS-Stubaf. Neeregaard-Jacobsen sent his aide, SS-Hstuf. Erik Herlov-Nielsen, to try to find the company: "Try to make contact with 9.Kompanie and return to inform me." The Danish lieutenant set out over the immense snow-covered plain to find his 9.Kompanie comrades but found no one, other than a Soviet patrol that captured him.

The artillery regiment units also were ordered to withdraw to the main supply line, and SS-Ostubaf. Karl sent runners to his three group commanders to organize the withdrawal to the west according to preestablished plans. There were no problems with the I and II groups. Only the III group was attacked by the Soviets during the withdrawal, registering the loss of four guns.

On the evening of January 28, the German defenses were anchored around the villages of Kerstovo and Opolje. During the day, 16./"Norge" had reached Ljalizy and had been attached to an army unit. The village of Ljalizy was attacked by strong Soviet units, which also surrounded the blocking positions on both sides of the main supply line. The Ljalizy position was held thanks to an immediate counterattack. The village of Gurlovo, 3 kilometers farther east, remained in Soviet hands and constituted a serious threat to the German troops still east of it. SS-Brigadeführer Scholz thus decided to mount a counterattack to retake the village of Gurlevo, committing 7./"Danmark," under SS-Hstuf. Heinz Hämel, reinforced by the motorcycle platoon of SS-Ustuf. Kaj-Albert Bertramsen and two assault guns. Scholz's orders to Hämel were precise: "'You need to absolutely retake Gurlovo. Many of our comrades are surrounded. You are their last hope!" After two hours of intense fighting, Gorlovo was retaken by the Germans and SS-Hstuf. Hämel stayed on to defend it, awaiting the passage of other retreating units.

German troops retreating from the Leningrad front, 1944

A group of grenadiers during a break, January 1944

German grenadiers riding on an assault gun, January 1944

The Knight's Cross for Heinz Hämel

For valor shown during the January 1944 fighting, on April 24, 1944, SS-Sturmbannführer Albrecht Krügel proposed that Hämel be awarded the Knight's Cross, a proposal that was seconded by the III.SS-Pz.Korps commander, SS-Ogruf. Felix Steiner, four days later, on April 28, 1944. The award was officially presented on June 16, 1944. Following is the text of the proposal: "In the afternoon of January 28, 1944, pursuing enemy forces were able to cut the road near Gurlevo. By doing this they cut off a motorized column located on a road farther east (read the attached combat report by the commander of III./SS-Pz.Art. Rgt.11). On the afternoon of that same day, 7Kp., 8.Kp., and elements of 5./SS-Pz.Gren.Rgt. 24 'Danmark,' led by SS-Hauptsturmführer Hämel, were assembled for combat at Kerstowo and later were moved to Ljalizy. There they were attached to Kampfgruppe 4 Sturmgeschütze. After having arrived at Ljalizy, Kampfgruppe Hämel was given the mission of seizing Gurlevo and guiding the trapped column to the east of the city to save it. Gurlevo was occupied by an enemy force of about a battalion, supported by heavy weapons (see sketch for the enemy situation). The operation was to be conducted without the support of our own artillery.

"At 0030 on 10.29.1944, Kampfgruppe Hämel advanced toward Gurlevo along both sides of the road. During the nighttime fighting, at first the attack made good progress, bringing the SS units as far as Gurlevo. Supported by assault guns, the western part of the village was captured. However, because of the losses sustained, as well as the arrival of enemy reinforcements from the south, the attack was on the verge of not being able to achieve its objective. In order to carry out his mission and guarantee that the attack could continue, SS-Hauptsturmführer Hämel decided to recall the forces that had been deployed for flank security to the north and to use them to give the attack greater impetus. In doing so, he ran the risk of exposing his flank to enemy attacks from the north, but he decided to carry out his mission at all costs. The continuation of the attack, which saw Hämel personally leading the attacking units from the front, made it possible to reach the outskirts of the village of Gurlevo and to reestablish contact with friendly units that had been cut off. This was possible all thanks to the exemplary conduct of the commander and his courage. With Gurlevo firmly in our hands, the *Kampfgruppe* ensured the safety of the column that had been trapped in Gurlevo. Elements of the column included the staff of 10.Luftwaffe-Feld-Division, II./Art.Rgt.10, and 7./-Pz.Art.Rgt.11, as well as of several resupply columns."

The Retreat Continues

On the afternoon of January 29, SS-Art.Rgt.11 and SS-Pz.Gren. Rgt.23 "Norge" were still east of the Luga River, and all the escape routes that led to the west had already been seized by Soviet advanced elements. Behind them were also other army units. Elements of SS-Pz.Aufkl.Abt.11 coming from the southeast reached the main resupply line, which was now blocked. The men had to fight to open the road to Jamburg. Meanwhile, strong enemy units had already shown up on both sides of Opolje; that village had been under Soviet artillery fire since

SS-Hauptsturmführer Heinz Hämel

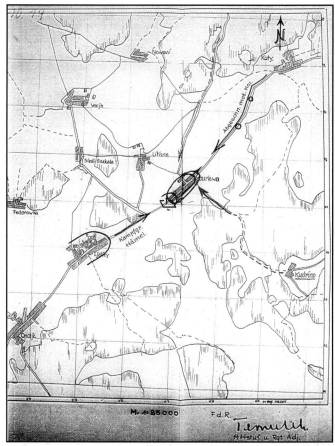

Map attached to the proposal for the Knight's Cross for SS-Hstuf. Hämel, with "Danmark" movements and places involved in the fighting. *BDC*

SS soldiers in a defensive position, January 1944

morning. At the last moment, all the wounded who had been amassed in the local church were picked up and moved toward Narva. The withdrawal of the units from Opolje was covered by SS-Stubaf. Lohmann's III./"Norge" and by the "Nordland" assault guns. During these covering actions, SS-Hstuf. Röntzsch, commander of SS-Pz.Jg.Abt.11, was killed while he was outside his assault gun making a terrain reconnaissance. Command of the unit passed to Hauptmann Schulz-Streek.

The "Nordland" artillery batteries had in the meantime taken up new firing positions on both sides of Jamburg. East of Jamburg, the "Norge" regiment established a bridgehead on the Luga River. The regimental command post was set up in the western part of the city. South of the city and west of the Luga were 16./"Norge," the remnants of I./"Norge," and other army formations. The "Danmark" regiment's command post was temporarily set up in Padoga; III./"Danmark" managed to get to the north of Jamburg, and II./"Danmark" even farther north. The 16./"Danmark" engineers continued to act as a rearguard, engaged in blowing bridges and mining roads. On January 30, units of the "Nederland" crossed the Luga in the Keikino area.

Meanwhile, Soviet units had already crossed the river south of Jamburg, threatening to surround the forces defending the city. In order to parry this new threat, Model ordered Steiner to counterattack and to establish a bridgehead on the eastern bank of the Luga, right in the middle of the Soviet lines, a practically impossible mission. In that season the river was completely frozen, allowing the Soviet infantry to cross it without problem. Steiner considered that the defensive line along the Luga could not be held for long because the Soviets had already crossed the river with their 8th Army farther south.

On January 31, the Soviets attacked the Jamburg bridgehead, but the men of the "Norge" held their positions firmly.

Enemy attacks then shifted against the "Danmark" positions; furious fighting erupted around Padoga, where the grenadiers of II./"Danmark" managed to fend off all the attacks. A few hours later, a dangerous new penetration threatened to break through the entire regimental front; 5./"Danmark," led by SS-Hstuf. Walter Seebach,[2] was ordered to launch a counterattack against the new enemy bridgehead. Seebach gathered his men and went on the attack: the Soviet soldiers defended themselves doggedly, but in the end, they were forced to give up the position after having taken heavy losses. But the "Danmark" grenadiers also took many losses, among them Seebach himself, being badly wounded during the fighting.

The Knight's Cross for Walter Seebach

Seebach survived his serious wounds and, for valor shown in combat during that last action, was proposed for the Knight's Cross, which was officially conferred upon him on March 12, 1944. Following is the text of the proposal written by SS-Ostubaf. Westphalen, commander of SS-Pz.Gr.Rgt. "Danmark": "Beginning on May 1, 1943, as regimental adjutant, Seebach was heavily engaged in the formation and training of the unit, and because of this, from the early days of January he was assigned the command of 5./SS-Pz.Gren.Rgt. 24 'Danmark.' These soldiers had fought well against partisan bands in Croatia, at Hrastovica, where the company was brought up to strength with the arrival of forty recruits from corps level. It was thanks to the capabilities and determination of Obersturmführer Seebach, whose men, in the space of ten days, had achieved a high degree of training, which would then be put to the test when the unit, on January 15, 1944, was surrounded in the Oranienbaum pocket. Seebach transmitted his own determination and warrior spirit to the young boys of the company, who soon showed their valor in the field during the fighting during the withdrawal.

"On January 30, 1944, Seebach led his men from their positions at Opolje and Kerstovo to new positions on the river Luga. Thanks to his energetic leadership, around 0600 on January 30, 1944, he reached and occupied new positions with his 5.Kp., despite strong enemy pressure and without taking many casualties.

"On January 31, around 1630, the enemy initiated offensive action in the sector held by 5./SS-Pz.Gren.Rgt.24 'Danmark.' The attacks were made by soldiers of two Soviet regiments in successive waves, which continued until the first light of dawn on February 1, 1944. At least eight consecutive attacks were made. The position was held for the entire day. This was thanks above all to the leadership and valorous behavior of SS-Obersturmführer Seebach, who reacted constantly to the enemy's daring attacks. At 2030, Seebach was wounded by several pieces of shrapnel in one of his feet (this was his seventh wound since the beginning of the war). Despite his wound, he continued to personally lead his company, with someone helping to hold him up, and he led his men in a successful counterattack. It was not until his wound became worse, because he paid no heed to it and, while moving, bumped and broke a malleolus, did he decide to have himself brought to an aid station. Before being evacuated, it was necessary to wait for the arrival of a new company commander designated by the regiment. The extraordinary valor shown by Seebach and his strong physical resistance were passed on to the rest of the company, which fought with daring and vitality. The battalion's other units were inspired by the exemplary behavior of Seebach's company, offering strong resistance against the enemy.

"In this way, the regiment's positions were held until the early hours of the morning of February 1, thus avoiding the rupture of the front by the enemy. This tactical success should be attributed above all to SS-Obersturmführer Seebach, and this allowed the division to withdraw in an orderly manner from the Jamburg bridgehead and prevented a premature breakthrough on the Luga front, which would have influenced the overall situation in a dramatic manner."

Seebach received the Ritterkreuz while he was convalescing in the hospital. Having accumulated another twelve days of hand-to-hand fighting, on March 16, 1944, he was also awarded with the hand-to-hand combat badge in gold.

The Battle Continues

Enemy attacks continued on into the next day, February 1, when the Soviets threw in fresh and numerous forces, in particular against the positions of III./"Danmark." SS-Stubaf. Neergaard-Jacobsen had been wounded during the withdrawal but had refused to be evacuated, to continue to command his compatriots. Soviet pressure fell mainly on the positions held by 9. Kp./"Danmark" and the remnants of 10.Kompanie. SS-Stubaf. Neergaard-Jacobsen pulled together all his reserves and threw

SS-Hstuf. Walter Seebach with the Ritterkreuz

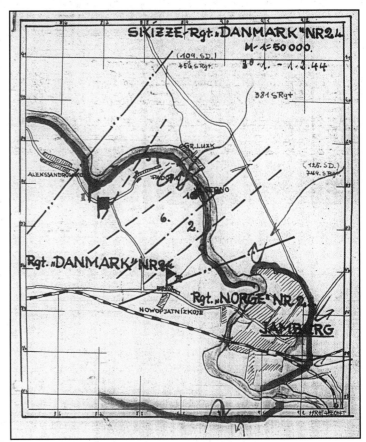

Map attached to the proposal for the Knight's Cross for SS-Ostuf. Walter Seebach. *BDC*

SS soldier observing enemy positions from a trench. *NA*

SS-Ustuf. Bent Worsöe-Larsen

German soldiers in a defensive position in the Jamburg area, 1944

them into the battle. SS-Ostuf. Bent Worsöe-Larsen,[3] commander of 11.Kp./"Danmark," fell to enemy fire while leading his men in a desperate counterattack. Neergaard-Jacobsen was also wounded again and was forced to be moved to an aid station. The counterattack by the Danish volunteers ran completely aground; the Germanic volunteers of 9. and 10.Kp. were, however, able to withdraw and join their comrades of 11.Kompanie, shifting to the western bank of the Luga. Hot on the heels of the Scandinavian volunteers, the Soviets themselves crossed the river, thus managing to establish a dangerous bridgehead on its western bank.

Farther south, in the Jamburg area, since January 31 the men of the Norge regiment were busy fending off repeated Soviet attacks, paying a heavy price in blood; the 16./"Norge" engineers, under SS-Ustuf. Josef Schirmer,[4] entrenched in a forward position, were particularly hard pressed in tough defensive fighting. Schirmer's men were able to keep the Soviets at bay, thanks in part to a 20 mm antiaircraft gun of 14./"Norge," which was well sited on a small hill that dominated all the surrounding area. As soon as darkness fell, SS-Ustuf. Schirmer moved to check the positions held by his platoons, in particular stopping at those of his third platoon, which was deployed farther south and thus was particularly threatened. When the officer returned to his command post, he met several soldiers of I./"Norge" who were withdrawing; according to them, the battalion had been ordered to pull back to the railway line. But Schirmer had received no such withdrawal order and thus decided to remain in his positions with his company. In order to get a better picture of the situation, he returned to his third platoon's positions, led by SS-Uscha. Hokkerup. Hokkerup reported that he had lost all contact with I./"Norge" farther south and that the Soviets had probably been able to break through. SS-Ustuf. Schirmer then decided to mount a counterattack with the third platoon, retaking the abandoned position. Following a brief but intense firefight, the platoon pulled back. In the meantime, other Soviet units had worked around the southern flank of 16./"Norge" and had reached the company command post. SS-Ustuf. Schirmer thus decided to return to his command post, a bunker made from tree trunks, clashing with the Soviets. The position changed hands several times but in the end was held firmly in the hands of the Germanic volunteers. Meanwhile, Danish SS-Ustuf. Christen Dall[5] of 13(IG)Kp./"Norge," the company was equipped with 150 mm infantry support guns. Schirmer, Dall, and their men returned to the command bunker, which was now surrounded by the Soviets. Dall then asked Schirmer if the telephone was still working, and then made contact with his company.

"This is Dall; I need covering fire immediately!" said the Danish officer. "On what target, *Untersturmführer?*" was the response.

"The 16th Company command post," responded Dall.

"But aren't you in it?" answered the 13(IG)Kp./"Norge" gunners.

"Yes, but the Soviets are on top of us—shoot now!" screamed Dall.

Solidly built of tree trunks, covered with dirt and snow, the bunker should have held. A few minutes later the first rounds could be heard, then the first 150 mm rounds began to hit. The noise was hellish. With each impact, the command post shook terribly, but the bunker took it well. On the outside the situation was decidedly worse for the Soviets. When the bombardment ceased, Schirmer and Dall were the first to come out; the Soviets had been scattered and there were many lifeless corpses of enemy soldiers on the ground. Schirmer decided to set up a new defensive front farther south, to face any new enemy attacks. At dawn on February 1, 16./"Norge" was again subjected to strong enemy pressure. The Soviets had brought up heavy guns in front of the positions occupied by Schirmer's engineers and by the crew of a 14./"Norge" flak piece. The 13./"Norge" heavy infantry guns had to be called upon to disperse the Soviet columns that were concentrating in the valley.

The Abandonment of Jamburg

On February 1, Jamburg was abandoned and the bridge over the Luga was destroyed. To cope with the dangerous penetration, managing to fend off enemy forces at Komerowka until late evening. south of Jamburg, II./"Danmark" was shifted behind the "Norge" regiment and engaged south of the main supply line. The 16./"Norge" was also moved to those positions, managing to fend off enemy forces at Komerowka until late evening. The men of the "Norge" and "Danmark" had to withdraw toward Narva, and III./"Norge," under SS-Stubaf. Lohmann, was designated as the rearguard, repeatedly holding back against Soviet attacks. Three times, Lohmann's grenadiers were forced to make furious counterattacks to ward off the enemy forces and to allow other friendly units to withdraw in good order. SS-Stubaf. Lohmann was able to repel a furious enemy attack near his command post, gathering all available personnel from his staff. Lohmann was himself wounded during the bitter close-in fighting.

The Knight's Cross for Hans Lohmann

For his battalion's exceptional conduct in the field, SS-Stubaf. Lohmann was proposed for the Knight's Cross, which was officially awarded on March 12, 1944. Following is the text of the proposal written by his regimental commander and countersigned by SS-Brigdf. Scholz and SS-Ogruf. Steiner: "On

A group of German grenadiers marching, 1944

German grenadiers on the Jamburg front, 1944

Retreating German troops, January 1944

SS-Stubaf. Hanns Heinrich Lohmann

January 31, 1944, III./SS-Pz.Gren.Rgt. 'Norge,' under the command of SS-Sturmbannführer Lohmann, was in position at the Luga bridgehead in the eastern sector of Jamburg. The withdrawal from the bridgehead that had been ordered took place the following night after a tough defensive battle that was successfully carried out by friendly forces. Following the evacuation of the bridgehead, SS-Stubaf. Lohmann had been given the mission to occupy new defensive positions on the western bank of the Luga. Inserting his battalion between Kramer's battalion and Kampfgruppe Vogt, he would substantially reinforce the defensive line that until that time had been held by Kampfgruppe Stoffers. At the beginning of the withdrawal of Lohmann's unit from the bridgehead, the following situation in the southern part of the western bank of the river obtained.

"Throughout the day the enemy had transferred numerous forces to the western bank of the river Luga, south of Saretschje. Several attacks were made against the flank of II Battalion, which was in position near the paper mill and Saretschje, but were successfully repulsed (in part by counterattacks) by the battalion. Nevertheless, the arrival of further enemy reinforcements made it necessary during the evening hours of 01.31.1944 to pull II Battalion back to a new blocking position along the Luga River and the swamp at Pjatnitzkij.

"Around 0430 on February 1, 1944, Lohmann and his battalion were still falling back. The 9. and the heavy company were in the eastern part of Novo Pjatnitzkoje, while 10. and 11.Kp. were in the western part of Jamburg. Having heard that the enemy had already pushed farther west with overwhelming forces, overrunning the II Battalion blocking positions and with advance forces that had gotten to within 300 meters of the road, on his own initiative SS-Sturmbannführer Lohmann threw his battalion into the counterattack. During the march he encountered elements of II Battalion that had pulled back, and he engaged the enemy.

"III Battalion conducted a quick surprise move with 9. Kompanie, which advanced past Hill 25.2 to the southeast, and 10. and 11.Kp., which moved to the south. In tough nighttime fighting, in which Sturmbannführer Lohmann distinguished himself by his personal courage, the enemy was driven back with extremely heavy losses. This continued until the old positions were once again under our control.

"It was thanks only to the great personal courage of Sturmbannführer Lohmann, a man who inspired his troops and who prevailed in the decisive moment of the close-in fighting, and thanks to his example, that this counterattack ended in success. The great energy and absolute determination of the commander of II./SS-Pz.Gren.Rgt. 'Norge' ensured that the enemy attempt to cut off our troops still in the bridgehead on the western bank of the river was thwarted. In addition, the enemy suffered the loss of a great amount of light and heavy infantry weapons, as well as part of his attacking forces. For this reason, the subsequent withdrawal planned by the division at Dubrowka was able to be carried out according to plans and with a minimum of losses."

Toward Narva

With the Soviets now on and past the Luga-Linie, the German headquarters was forced to order a new withdrawal to the west, this time along the source of the Narva River: "The Soviets have gotten past the positions along the River Luga. The new main line of resistance must be established along the course of the Narva River." That river had always, historically and geographically, marked the boundary between Estonia and Russia. The new defensive line, designated as the Panther line, was anchored on two natural defensive barriers, represented by the Narva and the Velikaya Rivers and by lakes Peipus and Pskov. Fortification works had begun since September 1943 but were far from being completed. The men of the "Nordland" and "Nederland" thus began a new withdrawal. Once again it was the SS corps' recon troopers that covered the German retreat, and once again it was the Dutch Rottenführer Kaspar Sporck who distinguished himself in combat, destroying numerous enemy vehicles, to cover the retreat of the German columns to the west.

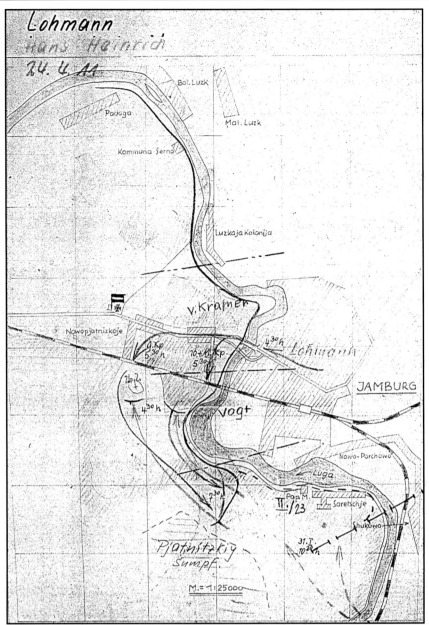

Map attached to the Ritterkreuz for Lohmann

A group of German grenadiers on the attack, accompanied by a signals squad, January 1944

The Sd.Kfz. 215/9 Stummel of SS-Rottenführer Kaspar Sporck

German motorized forces retreating from the Jamburg front, 1944

A Tiger tank of SS-Pz.Abt.502, stopped for a check by its crew, during the withdrawal toward Narva, January 1944

CHAPTER V
THE NARVA FRONT

A panorama of Narva seen from the river in a photo taken before the war. On the left bank is the Hermannsburg fortress, and on the right is the Ivangorod fortress.

German motorized units arriving in Narva, February 1944

Following the collapse of the German defensive front in the Leningrad area, German forces had withdrawn to the west, first establishing a temporary defensive line along the course of the Luga River, then deploying along the course of the Narva River: around the city of the same name, the forces of III.(germ.) SS-Panzer-Korps had taken up defensive positions, preparing to repel any enemy attacks. Narva constituted an obligatory choke point to be able to move from east to west, considering that all the region farther south, between the city and Lake Peipus, was covered by thick forests and immense swamps and thus was difficult to cross by military forces that were either horse drawn or motorized. The city of Narva had been founded in the thirteenth century by the Danes and had been transformed into a fortress by the Teutonic Knights as a bulwark against the Russians. The city was only about 10 kilometers from the Baltic Sea. At Narva, on the western bank of the same-named river, rose the Hermannsburg fortress, built by the Teutonic Knights, while on the eastern bank, right opposite it, was the Ivangorod fortress, built by Russian grand duke Ivan III.

For centuries, the Germanic and Slavic peoples had clashed in this area, and thus, in 1944, Narva continued to represent the bulwark of European civilization against the barbarians coming from the east. This time, defending the city were military formations of all types: Estonian volunteers, German soldiers of the Wehrmacht, Luftwaffe, and Kriegsmarine infantrymen, but above all, the Germanic volunteers of the Waffen-SS, coming from all parts of Europe. German propaganda made prodigious efforts to represent the defense of Narva at the battle of the European SS troops.

General Johannes Friessner

Generalfeldmarschall Walther Model

SS-Obergruppenführer Felix Steiner

Armee-Abteilung Narwa

III./SS-Panzer-Korps was initially subordinated to LIV.Armee-Korps (General der Infanterie Otto Sponheimer), detached as of February 4 from 18.Armee and subordinated directly to Army Group North (Heeresgruppe Nord). By Hitler's order, all available forces in the area were sent to the Narva bridgehead, forces that were used to form the so-called Sponheimer Gruppe, which on February 23 was renamed as Armee-Abteilung Narwa, following replacement of Sponheimer by General Johannes Freissner, with the task of controlling all military forces north of Lake Peipus. On February 22, his forces, by order of Heeresgruppe Nord (Generalfeldmarschall Walther Model), were arrayed as follows: III./SS-Panzer-Korps, under SS-Obergruppenführer Felix Steiner, north of Narva and in the bridgehead on the eastern bank of the river; XXXXIII.Armee-Korps, under General der Infanterie Karl von Oven, in the bridgehead at Auvere south of the city; and XXVI.Armee-Korps, led by General der Infanterie Anton Grasser, in the sector between the bridgehead at Auvere and Lake Peipus.

Composition of Armee-Abteilung-Narva

(as of March 1, 1944)

XXVI.Armee-Korps
11.Infanterie-Division
58.Infanterie-Division
214.Infanterie-Division
225.Infanterie-Division
3 Estonian Border Guard Regiment

XXXXIII.Armee-Korps
61.Infanterie-Division

170.Infanterie-Division
227.Infanterie-Division
Panzergrenadier Division "Feldherrnhalle"
"Gnesen" Grenadier Regiment

III./SS-Panzer-Korps
11.SS-Panzergrenadier Division "Nordland"
4.SS-Panzergrenadier Brigade "Nederland"
20 Waffen-Gren.Div. der SS (Estonische Nr.1)

Corps units
Eastern sector, coastal defense
"Reval" Estonian regiment
29th Estonian police battalion
31st Estonian police battalion
32nd Estonian police battalion
658 Ostbataillon (Estonian)
659 Ostbataillon (Estonian)
113th Artillery Command
32nd Engineer Command
502.Schwere.Panzer-Abteilung
752.Panzerjäger-Bataillon

Steiner's SS corps thus consisted of the 11.SS-Pz.Gr.Div. "Nordland," the 4.SS-Pz.Gr. Brigade "Nederland," and the new 20.Waffen-gr.Div. der SS (Estnische Nr.1). On their side, the Soviets fielded three full armies: the 47th Army in the north; the 2nd Shock Army, under Lieutenant General Ivan Fedyuninsky, in the center; and the 8th Army, under Lieutenant General Filip Starikov, in the south. In early March, the 59th Army, commanded by Lieutenant General Ivan Kornikov, replaced the 47th, shifting however to the south of Narva, while the 2nd Shock Army deployed north of the city.

SS Unit Deployments

Bit by bit, the SS units took positions along their new defensive line, while the engineers were busy reinforcing the line, digging trenches, building antitank obstacles, and laying minefields. The grenadiers of I Battalion "Danmark," under SS-Hstuf. Per Sörensen, were dug in along the Jamburg-Narva road in hastily dug trenches, having as heavy armament only a few machine guns and several antitank guns. Farther north, to their left, were the Dutch volunteers of the SS "Nederland" brigade, between the fortress of Ivangorod and Lilienbach's position with the "General Seyffardt" regiment in the Popovka area and the "de Ruyter" from Lilienbach as far as the main road to Jamburg. South of the Dutch positions, the other two battalions of the "Danmark" took up positions, while the "Norge" grenadiers took up positions even farther south, hidden in the forests along the Narva River, along with police units and the *Kampfgruppen* of 61., 170., and 225.Infanterie-Division. In the medieval castle of Hermannsburg, on the western bank of the river Narva, SS-Ostubaf. Friedrich Wilhelm Karl, the "Nordland" regimental artillery commander, set up his command post and his observers, emplacing his guns not far from the river, in the suburbs of the besieged city. Kampfgruppe Küste, led by Danish SS-Brigadeführer Christian Peder Kryssing, deployed along the coast with its command post at Auga; its sector was defended by an Estonian police battalion at Mereküla, with a coastal battery farther east, while another coastal battery was south of Mereküla. The Marine Bataillon Honschild was at Hungerburg, and farther south was Marine Bataillon Schneider. The Estonian SS units were deployed to the south, protecting the southern flank. The only armored units were several Tiger tanks of Schwere Panzer Abteilung 502, under Leutnant der Reserve Otto Carius, along with the few surviving assault guns of "Nordland," "Nederland," and 1.SS-Panzer-Abteilung 11 "Hermann von Salza." The other crews of SS-Pz.Rgt.11 "HvS," who were without tanks while awaiting the delivery of new ones, were organized as infantry troops under the command of SS-Stubaf. Paul-Albert Kausch, taking positions in foxholes and trenches dug along the western bank of the river, between Kudruküla and Riigi, north of Narva.

Leutnant Carius was ordered to report to SS-Brigdf. Scholz. He found the "Nordland" division command post in an old bus on the eastern bank of the river, a few hundred meters from the front lines. "Old Fritz" soon pointed out the gravity of the situation to Carius: "This famous Panther Line that we have to defend in reality exists only on paper. But it is necessary that my men reinforce it and that your tanks help me hold it."

Leutnant Carius then decided, in agreement with SS-Brigdf. Scholz, to displace his Tigers onto the western bank of the river. He would have had to cross the bridge to intervene in the most-threatened sectors. Just at the moment when his tanks were getting ready to move to the new positions, Feldmarschall Model showed up.

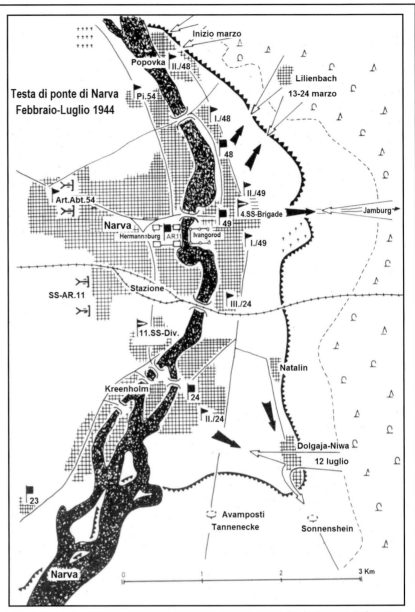

The Narva bridgehead with the location of various units between February and July 1944, with the locations involved in the fighting

SS-Brigdf. von Scholz, *second from left*, near his command post, speaking with his staff officers, February 1944

Assault guns in the Narva bridgehead, February 1944

A Panther Ausf.D of SS-Pz.Abt.11 "HvS" in the Narva sector. The Panthers that equipped the unit were defective tanks ceded by I./Pz.Rgt.24.

Leutnant Otto Carius (*left*) in front of Oberfeldwebel Rudolf Zwetti's Tiger (*right*)

"Who's in command here?" he yelled in a highly irritated manner.

Leutnant Carius stepped forward. Model fixed him with an icy state, then began to shout: "What are you doing on the western bank? Your mission is to block all attacks. And that happens on the other bank!"

Then he gave a final peremptory order to Carius: "I will hold you personally responsible that no enemy tank breaks through. None of your Tigers must be lost to enemy fire; we need every gun here!"

The Tigers thus crossed the river and took up positions amid the ruins of the eastern suburbs of Narva. The following days they were engaged in fighting between the positions of Narva and Hungerburg.

Early Attacks

In early February, units of the Soviet 47th Army were able to establish a bridgehead between Hungerburg and Narva. At Kudruküla, the Soviets were able to break though the defensive front along the river The reserves of Kampfgruppe Küste, led personally by SS-Brigdf. Kryssing and supported by three tanks, counterattacked and eliminated the dangerous penetration. After that attack, the Hungerburg front was split into two commands. The coastal sector was assigned to Kampfgruppe Küste, while the Hungerburg-Narva sector was assigned to Kampfgruppe Berlin, led by Generalleutnant Berlin, commander of 227.Infanterie-Division. The night following the elimination of the Soviet bridgehead at Kudruküla, the remnants of 7./"Norge" (around twenty men), led by SS-Ustuf. Arne Hanssen, reached the river Narva and friendly lines. For fourteen days they had marched in enemy territory.[1]

During the night between February 2 and 3, the Soviets attacked in the Kudruküla-Riigi area, where Kausch's "tank infantry" was in position. In particular, the Soviets broke through in the boundary between Kampfgruppe Kausch and Kampfgruppe Wengler of 227.Infanterie-Division. The recon platoon of SS-Pz.Abt.11 "HvS," which was the reserve platoon, under SS-Unterscharführer Stöckel, launched an immediate counterattack, pushing back the Soviets. On February 8, the Soviets returned to attack in the Riigi sector but were once again thrown back by the SS-Pz.Abt.11 "HvS" recon platoon.

Two days later, the Soviets again attacked with larger forces, first bombarding the German lines with artillery, then with airstrikes, and finally flooding the whole Narva front with infantry and tank units. It was a real hurricane of steel and fire that ran up against the strenuous resistance of the European volunteers. The fire of the guns of SS-Artillerie-Regiment 11 and the artillery group of the SS Polizei-Division, which was now permanently assigned to the Dutch brigade as I./SS-Art.Rgt.54, commanded by SS-Stubaf. Joseph Rüschoff, was able to effectively deal with the enemy offensive, throwing the Soviets back to their positions. Having taken heavy losses, for a few days the Soviets suspended any offensive actions in order to reorganize their ranks and wait for fresh reinforcements. Within the SS corps the brief pause was used to quickly reorganize the units.

The remnants of the two Luftwaffe field divisions (9. and 10.Luftwaffe-Feld-Division), decimated and with no cadre, were sent to reinforce the "Nederland" and "Nordland" units. Despite the forced transfer, the Luftwaffe infantrymen were able to adapt very well and very quickly to the combat spirit and to the iron discipline of the Waffen-SS. The brief pause also allowed the Germans to transform Narva into a real and true fortress: night after night, the SS engineers were busy erecting palisades, stringing kilometers of barbed wire, and building trenches and bunkers.

Despite the relative calm along the rest of the Narva front, on February 11 the Soviets attacked in the northern sector, between Riigi and Ssivertsi, which was defended by units of the German army; at least three thousand Soviet infantrymen were able to get onto the western bank of the river, establishing a bridgehead between the woods southeast of Riigi. The men of Kampfgruppe Wengler of 227.Infanterie-Division, under Oberstleutnant Wengler, managed with great sacrifice to contain expansion of the bridgehead. The recon platoon of SS-Pz.Abt.11 "HvS" was also engaged in this defensive fighting; about fifty Soviet infantrymen attacked the German positions but came under fire of SS-Uscha. Stöckel's scouts. Most of the enemy soldiers were killed or wounded, and only about a dozen of them were able to withdraw. The Soviets responded with heavy artillery fire, which took some victims, among them SS-Uscha. Moser. At the end of the day, SS-Uscha. Stöckel sent a brief report to SS-Stubaf. Kausch: "Our young soldiers held their positions well."

20 mm flak gun on the Narva front, February 1944

Survivors of 7.Kp./"Norge" who managed to withdraw to Narva

"Nordland" grenadiers on the Narva front, February 1944

A German grenadier armed with a Mauser rifle, trying to stop an enemy infantry attack from his defensive position

SS-Pi.Btl.54 demolition squad placing explosive charges under the Ivangorod castle on the eastern bank of the river, to prevent it from being occupied and used by the Soviets as a base for their attacks. *NARA*

German grenadiers in a defensive position at Narva, February 1944

The Battle for Ssivertsi

In anticipation of quickly mounting counterattacks, the hamlet of Paklamae, situated on a small hill, was chosen by SS headquarters as a base, where the "Nederland" artillery forward observers arrived, whose batteries were sited a kilometer farther south. While the army grenadiers continued to be engaged defending their positions in Riigi, trying to close the gap at Ssivertsi and to throw the Soviets back to the eastern bank of the river Narva, the Dutch volunteers of the SS "Nederland" brigade's engineer battalion, led by SS-Hstuf. Günter Wanhöfer, were called into action. Thrown into a ferocious counterattack, the Dutch volunteers were soon engaged in furious hand-to-hand fighting in the Ssiversti cemetery, attacked repeatedly by Soviet infantry.

Before managing to wrest several positions from the enemy, the SS engineers soon found themselves subjected to massive Soviet counterattacks that threatened to overrun them. By Steiner's order, all available forces were sent to the area affected by the penetrations. The first step was the formation of a combat group under SS-Stubaf Albrecht Krügel, formerly the commander of II./"Norge," by pulling together the two engineer companies of the "Norge" and "Danmark" regiments, the grenadiers of 11./"Norge" (led by SS-Ostuf. Sandborg),[2] and a motorcycle recon platoon from Norge under SS-Oscha. Wienke. As soon as they reached Ssivertsi, the German reinforcements were met with violent fire from Soviet artillery that was sited on the eastern bank of the river. Once the maelstrom of fire was over, the Soviet infantry went on the attack, crossing over the frozen surface of the river and moving against the Ssivertsi cemetery. The Norwegian, Danish, and Dutch engineers fought hand to hand with their enemies, fighting like devils among the devastated tombs, with grenades, bayonets, and daggers. The position changed hands several times after a series of furious attacks and counterattacks and with heavy losses on both sides. Throughout the day of February 12, Soviet artillery continued incessantly to bombard the German positions along the river Narva and in particular the Ssivertsi cemetery, where the SS engineers of the "Nederland" brigade and "Nordland" division held on doggedly.

In order to completely remove the Soviet threat from the Ssivertsi area, a new counterattack was planned for the following day, with support provided by a company of assault guns of SS-Panzer-Jäger-Abteilung 54, commanded by SS-Stubaf. Schock,[3] with 14 Sturmgeschütz III and artillery from the SS "Nederland" brigade. Furnishing further fire support was a platoon of 120 mm heavy mortars, which would impede the arrival of any enemy reinforcements.

During the night, the grenadiers and engineers marched toward the Ssivertsi cemetery northwest of Narva, followed by the assault guns that were held back as a covering force. It was, however, the StuG guns of the "Nederland" to be the first to attack the Soviet positions,

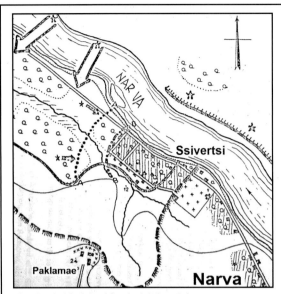
The Soviet bridgehead at Ssivertsi

German grenadiers preparing to attack, February 1944

A group of Waffen-SS NCOs in the sector north of Narva

A "Danmark" regiment soldier in combat

as they soon found themselves facing a massive barrage fire by enemy antitank guns. At the same time, the SS grenadiers and engineers in turn tried to break into the enemy defenses but, after having advanced only a few meters, also ended up under fire from enemy heavy weapons. At that point, the attack could be considered completely stalled: SS-Stubaf. Schock, after having lost several assault guns during the clashes, tried to reorganize his ranks and to incite his men to resume the attack. Having gotten out of his vehicle, while imparting new dispositions to his unit commanders, Schock was mortally wounded by a stray Soviet bullet. With the commander having fallen, the surviving assault guns pulled back in all haste in order to escape the murderous Soviet antitank fire. The other units engaged in the attack against Ssivertsi were luckier, managing to make a deep advance and to wrest several positions from the Soviets. Particularly caught up in the fighting were the 7./"Danmark," under SS-Ostuf. Landmesser,[4] and the 16./"Norge," under SS-Ustuf. Schirmer. SS grenadiers and engineers continued to attack the enemy bridgehead, increasing the clashes in the village of Ssivertsi. Even though he was wounded twice, SS-Ostuf. Landmesser remained at the head of his men. It was not until late evening that the fighting ceased for a few hours, giving the soldiers a moment's break and allowing the dead and wounded to be collected. Along with reinforcements, the "Nordland" commander, SS-Brigdf. Scholz, also arrived, who, after having personally taken stock of the situation that his men and those of the "Nederland" were in, decided to break off any further offensive action and to have them relieved by army units as soon as possible. A fresh Soviet assault the following morning, however, kicked off new bloody clashes, during which SS-Stubaf. Krügel was badly wounded and evacuated to the rear. Command of the *Kampfgruppe* then passed to his adjutant, SS-Hstuf. Michael Thöny,[5] and under his leadership, with a last desperate attack, Ssivertsi was definitively taken from the Soviets.

SS-Hstuf. Knud Henrik Ernst Schock

An SS-Panzer-Jäger-Abteilung 54 assault gun on the Narva front

Assault guns attacking an occupied village

An MG42 machine gun providing fire support

The Estonian Volunteers in Action

With the situation in the Ssivertsi area stabilized, another enemy island of resistance had to be eliminated, that of Vepsküla. A first attack by an assault group from 11/"Norge," led by SS-Oscha. Hollinger, was not successful, sustaining heavy losses, among them that of Hollinger himself, who was one of the first to be wounded during the attack. Some 150 mm howitzers from 13./"Norge" joined the action, and, later, artillery from the "Nederland" as well. Even though subjected to a downpour of fire, the Soviets held on firmly to their positions in Vepsküla, repulsing all attacks. In the end, the German headquarters decided to have the Germanic volunteers relieved by Estonian Waffen-SS volunteers. These began to arrive in the area beginning on February 20, 1944, with the Soviets still well dug in in their small bridgehead on the western bank of the river Narva. A bit at a time, the Estonian SS troops assumed control of the Hungerburg-Narva sector, allowing the German units to reorganize: SS-Frw.-Pz.Gr.Rgt. 46, led by Frw.-Staf. Juhan Tuuling, took up positions south of Hungerburg with its I. Bataillon (Stubaf. Ain-Ervin Mere) south of Kudruküla and its II.Bataillon (Hstuf. Rudolf Bruus) at Riigi. SS-Frw.-Pz.Gr.Rgt. 45, commanded by Waffen-Stubaf. Riipalu, occupied positions with its I.Bataillon (Hstuf. Paul Maitla) between Vasa and Vepsküla with its II. Bataillon (Hstuf. Ludvig Triik) from Ssivertsi as far as the northern outskirts of Narva, in contact with SS-Pionier-Bataillon 54.

Starting on February 24, all the units of the Estonian SS division were engaged in the general counteroffensive against the Soviet bridgeheads along the Narva front. The II./46, under Hstuf. Bruus, wiped out the Soviet troops in the Riigküla bridgehead. I Bataillon of the same regiment, commanded by Stubaf. Ain-Ervin Mere, was committed against enemy units deployed between Vaasa and Vepsküla; Soviet infantry had been able to make several penetrations between the German positions, threatening the collapse of the entire defensive sector north of Narva. On February 29, a young Estonian *Unterscharführer*, Harald Nugiseks,[6] who at that time was a platoon leader (*Zugführer*) in 1.Kp./46, took the lead of a small combat group consisting of his countrymen and threw himself into a desperate counterattack aimed at closing a gap opened by the enemy. Twice the Estonian volunteers were stalled only 50 meters from the Soviet trenches by massive barrage fire, but then, with a final charge marked by the use of many hand grenades followed by furious hand-to-hand fighting, the Soviet troops on the western bank of the Narva were surrounded and wiped out. For that action Nugiseks, twenty-two years old, was first awarded both classes of the Iron Cross and later, on April 19, 1944, with the Knight's Cross, becoming the second Estonian volunteer to receive it, after Alfons Rebane.

German grenadiers sheltering in a trench, February 1944

A group of SS grenadiers preparing to attack, February 1944

An Estonian mortar squad on the Narva front, February 1944

Estonian volunteers in combat, 1944

Harald Nugiseks in a 1943 photo

From left: Alfons Rebane, Nugiseks, and Haralt Riipalu

Frw.Staf. Tuuling decorates several Estonian soldiers, 1944

Memoirs of Harald Nugiseks[7]

"Our mission was to liberate the Vaasa and Vepsküla bridgeheads from the enemy. Initially there were thirty or forty of us, but enemy fire was so intense that half of that number fell in the field, some dead and some wounded, including our officers Jaan Lumera and Helmut Röömusar. At that time, a platoon leader, Röömusar, called me over to him and said, 'We still have twenty-two men; I'm about to die.' The battalion commander was Ain Ervin Mere, who was already thinking about withdrawing the platoon. When I found out that I had taken over command, he ordered me to 'Try again, if you can.' I then made the men pull back for a brief pause and to resupply our ammunition and hand grenades. We quickly resumed our attack and reached the Soviet trenches and got caught up in tough hand-to-hand fighting using entrenching tools, hand grenades, and bayonets. Riipalu pushed his men toward the houses of Vaasa, while with my men I attacked the trenches in front of the village, where the enemy was well dug in. If we had not captured hem, Riipalu risked being surrounded."

The Knight's Cross for SS-Stubaf. Albrecht Krügel

For actions in the Paklamae and Ssivertsi sectors, SS-Stubaf. Krügel was proposed for the award of the Knight's Cross, which was officially conferred upon him on March 12, 1944. Following is the proposal written by SS-Brigdf. Fritz von Scholz: "Following a successful enemy penetration outside the division's sector, SS-Sturmbannführer Krügel assumed command of a *Kampfgruppe* (formed by three companies), which went to occupy a blocking position that was hastily formed in front of it. At the head of this *Kampfgruppe*, he repulsed two enemy attacks from the area from which the penetration had occurred (Vepsküla-Vaasa-Foresta to the west of Vaasa) along the Paklamae-forest line a kilometer north of Germansberg.

"After the *Kampfgruppe* had been reinforced by two more companies and the enemy had been subjected to prolonged artillery fire, Krügel made an attack on his own initiative despite his orders. Made at night, this boldly led attack threw the enemy back to the opposite bank of the river Narva.

"In this manner, Krügel was able to eliminate the threat of enemy infantry to the Narva-Reval road and to prevent the conquest of the castle at Germansberg. If the enemy had been able to capture that castle, maintaining the bridgehead at Narva would have been extraordinarily difficult. Krügel destroyed the major part of the enemy's 131st Rifle Division during his defense and successive counterattacks."

Soviet Landing at Mereküla

In order to better exploit any breakthrough between Ssivertsi and Riigi, the Soviets planned to land troops on the coast west of Hungerburg, troops who would then link up with troops coming from Ssivertsi. At that time, defending the coast west of Hungerburg was an Estonian police battalion between Mummassaare and Mereküla, a coastal artillery battery with 100 mm guns and six 20 mm flak pieces for antiaircraft defense. The staff of 227. Infanterie-Division (Generalleutnant Berlin) was at Mereküla, a small fishing village. Marine Bataillon Hohnschild defended the sector west of Hungerburg, while Marine Bataillon Schneider was deployed to defend Hungerburg itself. Between Mereküla and Kiwisaare was a naval battery equipped with 150 mm guns. Headquarters of Kampfgruppe Küste was located in the small village of Auga. During the night between February 13 and 14, a small fleet of Soviet landing craft, protected by numerous destroyers, landed several infantry units on the coast near Hungerburg. The Germans reacted almost immediately, sending several elements of Marine Bataillon Hohnschild, which ended up being overwhelmed by superior enemy forces, but they were able to alert other units in the sector; artillery joined in the action, slaughtering the Soviet landing troops on the beach. SS-Stubaf. Paul Ranzow-Engelhardt, the Kampfgruppe Küste operations officer, scraped together some sixty men of his command at Auga and sent them to the area of the landings, while SS-Brigdf. Kryssing alerted all his units by phone. Shortly after, the headquarters of Kampfgruppe Berlin at Mereküla was surrounded by Soviet troops; Kryssing sent reinforcements, including elements of the "Nordland" recon battalion and some Sd.Kfz. 252/9 Kanonenwagen of 5.Kp. under SS-Ostuf. Langendorf, which attacked the Soviet forces from the southeast, annihilating them, thanks in part to support by several Stuka dive-bombers. Around 0900, other German units attacked the Soviet forces that had landed, while SS-Stubaf. Ranzow-Engelhardt arrived from the northeast with three tanks and about thirty men. At 1000 the Soviet landing force had been completely wiped out and the Soviets had suffered three hundred dead and about three hundred taken prisoner.

SS-Sturmbannführer Albrecht Krügel with the Ritterkreuz

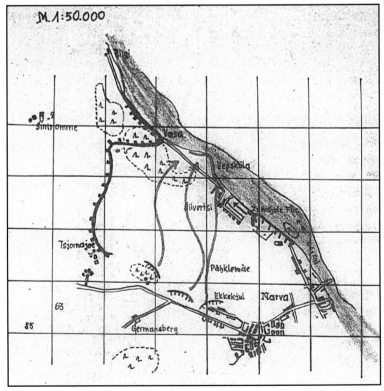

Map attached to Krügel's Ritterkreuz proposal

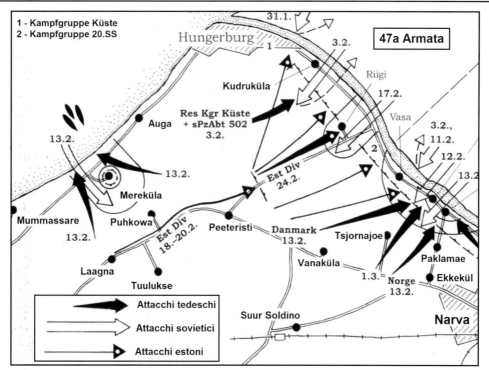

Situation in the northern part of the Narva bridgehead

A flak gun mounted on a half-track in defense of the coast

Half-tracks of SS-Pz.Aufkl.Abt.11 of Nordland on the Narva front

Soviet Attacks at Krivasso

While the positions around the bridgehead at Narva continued to hold fast, strenuously, southwest of the city, Soviet forces managed to establish a bridgehead in the Krivasso area in order to prevent any possibility of withdrawal by German forces as well as to hit them from the rear. The remnants of 170.Inf.Div. and elements of 227.Inf.Div. were forced to fall back after having been relieved in their positions by elements of Panzer-Grenadier-Division Feldherrnhalle, surviving units of 61.Inf.Div., and other combat groups. On February 24, the Soviets reached the railway line between the station at Vaivara and the local church (this penetration was referred to by the Germans as Westsack, or western pocket); defending the position were only two battalions of 61.Inf.Div. At the same time, other Soviet units had advanced along the road to Lipsu, reaching the railway line near the Auwere station (this penetration was referred to by the Germans as the Ostsack, or eastern pocket). In this way, the Wesenburg-Narva railway line was cut in two places, rendering the situation even more critical. In an attempt to push back the Soviet forces, the Tigers of 2./schwere-Paner-Abteilung 502 were sent to the area, four of them toward Krivasso (Westsack) and another two to Lembitu (Ostsack). "Nordland" was also ordered to pull together forces and led them immediately to the area; at dawn on February 25, SS-Ostubaf. Arnold Stoffers personally led a combat group from his "Norge" regiment in an attack southeast of the Vaivara railway station in order to hit the western pocket from the west. In the lead were the 10./"Norge" grenadiers, under Norwegian SS-Untersturmführer Stock,[8] who ended up against the Soviet main line of resistance and were subjected to a massive barrage fire. Most of the men were killed or wounded, among them Stock himself. SS-Ostubaf. Stoffers decided to continue the attack, falling himself to enemy fire that same day, along with many other SS grenadiers. He was posthumously awarded the Knight's Cross on March 12, 1944, mainly for previous actions on the Jamburg front. The counterattack against Vaivara was not successful, but nevertheless it served to block other offensive enemy thrusts in that sector, while other German units arrived to reinforce it, such as 13./"Norge," several army mortar units, and several armored vehicles from SS-Aufkl.Abt.11. Above all, it was the Tigers of 2./schwere-Panzer-Abteilung 502 that kept the Soviets at bay. Between March 17 and 22, the Tigers destroyed thirty-eight Soviet tanks, four assault guns, and seventeen antitank and antiaircraft guns. The Soviets responded with new attacks near Lembitu and Sirgala: the latter locality, defended by Estonian troops, was completely overrun, allowing the enemy to continue his advance through the thick forests of Riwimaa, a narrow and torturous path. Once again it was the grenadiers of the "Norge" regiment to be engaged in fighting to eliminate the dangerous enemy breakthrough. With fire support from the heavy infantry weapons of 8., 12., and 13./"Norge" and some elements of SS-Aufkl.Abt.11, the European volunteers were able

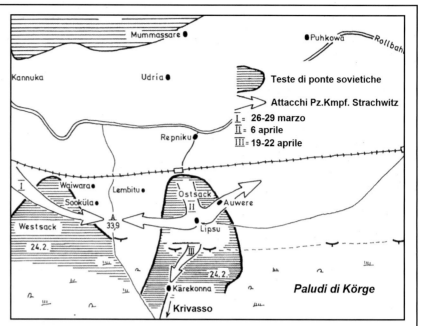

The Soviet bridgeheads north of Krivasso, February–April 1944

A Tiger of 2./schwere-Panzer-Abteilung 502, February 1944

A group of German grenadiers at the Krivasso front, 1944

Tigers of 2./schwere-Panzer-Abteilung 502 in combat

to catch the enemy units by surprise in the thick vegetation; the companies of II. and III./"Norge," led by SS-Stubaf. Albrecht Krügel, inflicted heavy losses on the Soviets, forcing them to return to their positions and thus returning Sirgala to German hands. During the fighting at Sirgala, SS-Ostuf. Dieter Radbruch, commander of 6./"Norge," was killed. The "Norge" grenadiers were relieved soon after by an army unit, in order to return to the Narva bridgehead.

PanzerKampfgruppe Graf Strachwitz

In order to eliminate the Soviet bridgehead at Krivasso once and for all, Generaloberst Lindemann, commander of Heeresgruppe Nord, designated General Hyazinth Graf Strachwitz as *Höheren Panzerführer* (high commander) of armored units of his army group. Thus, on March 26, 1944, Panzergruppe Graf Strachwitz, consisting of 170., 11., and 227.Inf.Div. and some armored units (among them the Tigers of 2./s.Pz.Abt.502 and some tanks of the Feldherrnhalle), attacked the flank of the Soviet 109th Rifle Corps south of the Tallinn railway line, supported by the Luftwaffe. The tanks led the attack with the infantry following, breaking through the enemy positions. At the end of the day, the Soviet 72nd and part of the 109th Rifle Corps in the Westsack bridgehead were surrounded. The rest of the Soviet rifle corps withdrew.

General Hyazinth Graf Strachwitz, *left*, giving final instructions to an officer for an attack, March 1944

SS-Ostuf. Dieter Radbruch

SS-Stubaf. Albrecht Krügel

A Tiger tank in combat, March 1944

As Strachwitz had foreseen, the next day the Soviets counterattacked but were repulsed. On March 28, two German armored thrusts penetrated the rifle corps' lines, splitting the bridgehead in two. The western half of the bridgehead was destroyed by March 31; the Soviets suffered around six thousand casualties. On April 6, the Panzergruppe made a diversionary attack against the Ostsack, held by the Soviet 6th and 117th Rifle Corps; the attack led the Soviets to think that with that action, the Germans intended to cut them off from the western flank. The actual attack was launched against the 59th Army and began with a heavy bombardment by dive-bombers. At the same time, 61.Infanterie-Division and Strachwitz's tanks broke through the 59th Army's defenses in depth, dividing the two rifle corps and forcing them to pull back into their fortifications. Marshal Govorov sent the 8th Army in as reinforcements, but his forces were driven back. On April 7, Govorov ordered his troops to go on the defensive. The 57th Army, having lost 5,700 men, was withdrawn from the bridgehead. Because of these successes, Strachwitz was awarded the Knight's Cross of the Iron Cross with Oak Leaves, Swords, and Diamonds on April 15, 1944. With the arrival of the spring thaw, the movement of German armored units was significantly slowed down by the state of the terrain, and thus the Soviet 8th Army was able to repel the next German attack, which lasted from April 19 to 24. The front in the Krivasso area remained stable for the following weeks, characterized only by action of the opposing artilleries.

A "Nordland" observer on the Narva Front, 1944. *Michael Cremin*

A "Nordland" soldier poses for a propaganda photo in a trench on the Narva bridgehead. *NARA*

Chapter VI
FIRE ON THE BRIDGEHEAD

The terrible effects of bombardment by artillery and Soviet airstrikes at Narva. *National Archives of Norway*

While enemy efforts were underway to break through the German lines around the bridgehead, Soviet artillery and aviation continued to incessantly hit the area around Narva with heavy bombardments, causing significant losses to III.SS-Pz.Korps in men and materiel and transforming the city itself into a heap of smoking ruins. Fortunately, most of the Estonian population had been evacuated, and thus civilian casualties were not high. Only the two medieval citadels remained standing, almost as bulwarks as witnesses to the undaunted will of the Germanic volunteers to hold out tenaciously against the Soviet attacks. After having hit the southern suburbs heavily, where elements of the "Danmark" regiment were located, the Soviets soon after concentrated on the area north of the city, making new infantry attacks against positions held by the Dutch volunteers of the "Nederland" SS brigade.

Engaged in furious hand-to-hand fighting, the SS grenadiers continued to hold their positions at great sacrifice; it was only at Lilienbach, a large hamlet northeast of Narva on the eastern bank of the river, that the Soviets were able to open a gap, forcing

SS grenadier in a defensive position at Narva

"Nordland" grenadiers in a defensive position, 1944

"Nordland" grenadiers moving in the trenches during fighting in the Narva bridgehead, March 1944

German soldier throwing a hand grenade

the Dutch troopers to withdraw in all haste in order to avoid being wiped out. In order to restore the situation, a new combat group was formed, pulling together volunteers from the two regiments of the "Nordland" under the command of SS-Hstuf. Thöny and sent in all haste to Lilienbach, where furious close-in fighting with Soviet soldiers soon broke out, with heavy losses. In early March 1944, SS-Flak-Abt.11, led by SS-Stubaf. Plöw, also arrived. Formed at the Arys training area in East Prussia, this unit consisted of three 88 mm batteries and one 37 mm flak battery. The railway convoy that was transporting this unit to the Eastern Front derailed, probably due to sabotage; most of the gunners were seriously wounded. The unit was then sent back to Arys and did not reach Narva until the beginning of March. SS-Brigdf. Scholz knew Plöw very well, having had him as a subordinate in the "Wiking" division during the fighting in Ukraine. The flak guns ensured protection of the bridge over the river, while the artillery and the 88 mm guns were also used in an antitank role.

New Soviet Attacks

After the failure of the Soviet attacks at Ssivertsi, Merküla, and Krivasso, the commander of the 3rd Baltic Front, General Leonid Govorov, changed tactics, attempting to sap German resistance with massive bombardments. Thus, during the night between March 6 and 7, Soviet aircraft bombed the Narva bridgehead heavily. A gigantic explosion shook the entire quarter along the river. The railway bridge had been mined with demolition charges by the engineers, and these had been hit by a bomb. The bridge collapsed into the bed of the Narva. Soviet bombs also hit the quarters of SS-Stubaf. Bunse's engineers at Petri square, causing many killed and wounded.

At dawn on March 7, Soviet infantry charged once again, supported by tanks. Bearing the brunt of attacks this time were the positions held by the Dutch grenadiers of SS-Frw.Pz.Gren.Rgt49 "General Seyffardt," located in the northern part of the bridgehead near Popowka: SS-Ostubaf. Wolfgang Jörchel sent all available men into the front line after the Soviets had managed to make several breakthroughs. Thanks to several counterattacks and barrage fire by heavy weapons deployed on the second defensive line, the Soviets were stopped, while artillery and 88 mm flak guns destroyed by direct fire all the supporting enemy tanks. Soon after, the Soviets attacked in the Lilienbach sector, where the grenadiers of SS-Freiwilligen-Panzer-Grenadier-Regiment 49 "de Ruyter" were deployed. Soviet infantry and their supporting tanks managed to break through. 9./"Danmark," under SS-Ostuf. Fritz Sidon, and the remnants of Kampfgruppe Thöny were grouped together and sent to the sector. A quick counterattack was mounted: SS-Ostuf. Sidon was badly wounded, while SS-Hstuf. Thöny continued to push his men forward. In the end, the Soviets were fended off and the main line of resistance reestablished. But the battle for Lilienbach was not over; the Soviets resumed their attack, using tanks, which were met by the Germanic volunteers at close range.

SS grenadiers in the Lilienbach sector

German grenadiers during a transfer march, March 1944

During the night, the Dutch volunteers were busy digging foxholes and trenches to better reinforce the defensive positions, which were soon completely surrounded by enemy forces. The position represented an important strategic objective for the Soviets, since it protected the entire northeastern sector of the bridgehead.

The Knight's Cross for SS-Oscha. Philipp Wild

The Soviets made an attack toward the bridge on the road that led to Jamburg, north of the main supply route. In order to stop the Soviet tanks, it was necessary to ask for the help of 1./SS-Pz.Abt.11 "HvS," commanded by SS-Ostuf. Rott,[1] whose Panthers clashed with the Soviet T-34s that had been sent to Lilienbach. One of his tank commanders, SS-Oscha. Philipp Wild,[2] was able to stop an enemy tank attack near the cemetery, and for that action he was later awarded the Knight's Cross on March 21, 1944, on the basis of the personal recommendation of the commander of the Dutch SS brigade, SS-Oberführer Wagner: "Strong enemy air formations bombed the bridgehead and city of Narva during the nights between March 6 and 8 with incessant attacks, each lasting ten to eleven hours. On March 8, 1944, at 0700, two and a half hours of intense artillery fire began, supporting an attack by the 63rd Guards Rifle Division. That attack was supported by fourteen tanks and made on a narrow front against the northeast pilaster of the bridgehead.

"Twelve tanks broke through the main line of resistance and advanced as far as the positions of SS-Frw.Pz.Gren.Regiment 48 'General Seyffardt.' In that critical moment, SS-Oberscharführer Philipp Wild (a member of 1./SS-Panzer-Abteilung 11) joined in the action with his Panther and in a very short time destroyed

Artillery observers sheltering in a trench, March 1944

SS-Oscha. Wild and SS-Ostuf. Rott of 1./SS-Pz.Abt.11

Loading ammo aboard a Panther of 1./SS-Pz.Abt.11 at Narva. SS-Ostuf. Rudolf Rotti is the second from the right, with the black jacket. To his right is Swedish SS-Ustuf. Per-Sigurd Baecklund, March 1944.

all the T-34 tanks that had broken through. As a result of his decisive intervention, he threw into disorder the enemy's plans to flank our positions in the Narva bridgehead. The destruction of the enemy tanks was also important. Because of their loss, the attacks underway by Soviet infantry, supported by tanks, were repulsed."

New Clashes at Lilienbach

Soviet attacks against Lilienbach did not slack off, and the grenadiers of SS-Frw.Gr.Rgt.49 "de Ruyter," who had in the meantime relieved the SS engineers, were heavily engaged in warding off enemy tanks and infantry, taking heavy losses; among those who fell were the II Bataillon commander, SS-Hstuf. Hans Burmeister. Finally, it was decided to abandon the position, which was deemed to be too exposed to enemy fire and attacks; the Dutch grenadiers pulled back to a new position known as "the devil's field" (Teufelwiese in German). Following the withdrawal of the Dutch volunteers, the Soviets quickly attacked their new defensive positions during the night between March 13 and 14. During the following hand-to-hand

Mechanics changing an engine on a Panther of 1./SS-Pz.Abt.11 in an improvised field repair shop at Narva, March 1944. *NARA*

A "Nordland" soldier observing enemy positions from the Hermannsburg fortress, on the western bank of the river Narva. Note on the left the bridge built by SS-Pz.Pi.Btl.11, christened the "Bunse bridge," in honor of the unit commander, SS-Stubaf. Fritz Bunse. *NARA*

fighting, many officers lost their lives, among them the new commander of II./"de Ruyter," SS-Hstuf. Walter Diener. When the situation became critical, SS-Ostuf. Helmut Scholz, the 7.Kompanie commander, after having collected a handful of courageous volunteers, immediately made a counterattack, managing to push the enemy back. The days that followed saw only local attacks along the entire defensive front, but with no notable results for the Soviets. On March 22, an unexpected intensification of Soviet artillery fire, in particular in the Lilienbach area and on the "devil's field," was a prelude to a new attack by enemy infantry, and the 5./"de Ruyter," under SS-Ostuf. Helmut Hirt, was literally overrun. SS-Hstuf. Carl Heinz Frühauf, the new commander of II./"de Ruyter," after having pulled together all the available men, combatants as well as noncombatants, led a desperate counterattack against the enemy, who had managed to pass through the first line of defense. Despite a strong enemy superiority, Frühauf was able to valorously lead his men in the attack and was thus able to retake all the positions that had been lost.

The southern sector of the bridgehead stayed relatively calm during the latest fighting. The positions of SS-Pz.Gren.Rgt.24 "Danmark" began south of the road that led to the cemetery, crossed the railway line, and continued on to the village of Dolgaja-Niva and terminated west of the river, including two small islands. SS-Pz. Gren.Rgt.23 "Norge" linked up with the regiment in the southern part of Kreenholm, on the western bank of the river. The "Nordland" artillery and logistic services were concentrated mainly in Kreenholm. The divisional headquarters were in the former Estonian barracks south of the railway station. The "Danmark" positions were slightly elevated, while the enemy positions ran parallel, about 800 meters east. Thanks to the work of the SS engineers, the position at Dolgaja-Niva had been turned into a fortress. About 400 meters away, a forward post had been set up, designated Sonnenschein (sunshine). South of Usküla, the "Danmark" regiment had established another forward post designated Tannenhecke (fir hedge).

Waffen-SS grenadier on the Narva front, 1944

SS grenadiers in the Narva bridgehead

SS-Brigdf. Fritz von Scholz

The Oak Leaves for Fritz von Scholz

During the defensive battles in the city of Narva, Fritz von Scholz's leadership had a strong impact on the combat spirit of his men. Because of his friendly and jovial manner in dealing with his men, he was playfully called "Papa Scholz" or "Alte Fritz" (Old Fritz). His visits to the front were frequent, and above all he worried much about the situation of his troops. For his excellent leadership of the "Nordland" division, Fritz von Scholz was awarded the Oak Leaves for his Knight's Cross on March 12, 1944, by proposal of Felix Steiner. Following is the text of the proposal: "SS-Brigadeführer Fritz von Scholz fought in the campaign on the Eastern Front, in the northeast sector, and was deeply engaged until today, since January 16, 1944, continuing to command the division, affirming himself by his method of employment and combativeness as an example to his troops. His division was able to block large numbers of enemy forces, impeding their advance along the main Kipen-Narva road. During this heavy and continuous fighting, there were several moments of crisis, which were always overcome in an exemplary manner by the personal intervention of the division commander.

"1. On 1.28.1944, the enemy attacked, advancing along both sides of the Kipen-Narva railway line, south of Osertizy, halting the remnants of 10.Lw.Feld.Div., scattering the 61.Inf.Div. and cutting the railway line, needed for movement to the west, north of Gurlevo. The Lohmann combat group of 11SS-Freiw.Pz.Gren. Div. 'Nordland,' which was at Osertizy, escaped the danger, but to the south the units of 10.Lw.Feld.Div., including the division staff, were surrounded by the enemy. The division commander, SS-Brigadeführer Fritz von Scholz, made a night counterattack from Ljalizy against Gurlevo, reaching the railway line and throwing the enemy back to the east, allowing the staff of 10.Lw.Feld.Div. to take the road to Ljalizy.

"2. On 2.1.1944, 11.SS-Freiw.Pz.Gren.Div. was withdrawn from Jamburg to Dubrovka. The enemy, with numerous forces, broke through the front in the north as well as in the south and attacked the railway line, clashing with elements of the division. SS-Brigadeführer Fritz von Scholz was the spirit of the resistance, knowing that what remained of 61.Inf.Div., of 227.Inf.Div., and of 10.Lw.Feld.Div. had to withdraw to the west to Narva, even though there was not much time to make that movement. Despite reiterated, strong attacks, supported by tanks, the men of the division prevented the enemy attack, in regimental strength, from breaking through the lines. The stubborn defense, made on both sides of Jamburg, Dubrovka, and on the sides of Komarovka, which resisted all attacks by superior enemy forces, created the premises for the orderly occupation of the Narva bridgehead and the assembly of forces adequate to occupy the northern positions in Narva itself.

"The resoluteness of the units of 11.SS-Freiw.Pz.Gren.Div. 'Nordland' enabled time to be bought to quickly bring Panz.Gren. Div. 'Feldhernnhalle' and other reinforcements into the area, allowing the remnants of 61. and 170.Inf.Div. and 10.Lw.Feld.Div. to shift in an orderly fashion to the western sector of Narva. The determination of the forces under the command of SS-Brigadeführer Fritz von Scholz created the premise for further fighting on the Narva front, even though the center of gravity and decisive factors on this front still have to be evaluated. The personal commitment and example of SS-Brigadeführer Fritz von Scholz and his strictness did in fact spur on his troops to high acts of heroism. He once again drew his young division with an exemplary force."

Transporting a wounded soldier to the rear. *Cremin*

A Norwegian grenadier of "Nordland." *NARA*

Festung Narwa

On March 23, 1944, Adolf Hitler officially proclaimed Festung Narwa, the fortress of Narva, an "elegant" way of ordering that it had to be defended at all costs, until the last man. That same day, German units under Oberst Graf von Strachwitz were engaged in a series of attacks to once and for all eliminate the Soviet bridgeheads southwest of Narva. At his disposition were Carius's Tigers and the rocket launcher batteries of SS-Vielfachwerfer-Bttr.521, under SS-Hstuf. Flecke. The German troops were able to throw the enemy forces from their positions, ensuring that the defensive line was held south of the bridgehead. With the arrival of spring at the Narva bridgehead, fighting slacked off, and SS-Brigdf. Scholz took advantage of that to reorganize his units as best he could. In view of the very high losses sustained and the gaps created in the various units of the division, the "Norge" and "Danmark" regiments were down to two battalions: the I./"Norge" and I./"Danmark" were disbanded.[3] SS-Hstuf. Fritz Vogt was repatriated to reorganize his I./"Norge," while SS-Hstuf. Sörensen was at the disposition of the "Danmark." Command of the "Norge" regiment passed to SS-Ostubaf. Fritz Knöchlein,[4] a veteran officer of the SS-"Totenkopf" division. The II./"Norge" came under the command of SS-Stubaf. Scheibe,[5] and III./"Norge" was assigned to SS-Hstuf. Gürz,[6] replacing Lohmann, who had been badly wounded.

SS-Pz.Abt.11, without its tanks, was transformed into Kampfgruppe Kausch, consisting of two infantry companies formed with the tank crews, two companies of SS-Pi.Btl.11, and two Estonian companies. In early April, the deployment of the units along the front line was also modified: the "Norge" regiment took up positions at Joala, south of Narva, on two islands in the river Mulgu, an affluent of the Narva. Southeast of the Narva bridgehead, the Danmark regiment anchored its resistance around the Dolgaja-Niva position and on the two outposts of Tannenhecke and Sonnenschein. On April 9, 1944, during a new Soviet artillery bombardment, SS-Ostubaf. Hermenegild Graf von Westphalen was seriously wounded following an explosion by a howitzer round while he was crossing the bridge over the Narva at Kreenholm.

Brought in very serious condition to an aid station, he was soon after transferred to the military hospital in Reval, where he died on May 28, 1944, due to his wounds. On April 23, 1944, he was awarded the German Cross in Gold. SS-Stubaf. Albrecht Krügel, former commander of II./"Norge," assumed command of "Danmark." At the same time, II./"Danmark" was taken over by SS-Hstuf. Heinz Hämel. On April 20, 1944, Fritz von Scholz was promoted to *SS-Gruppenführer*. The reorganization of Armee Abteilung Narwa was completed in late April: III.(germ.) SS-Panzer-Korps remained deployed in Narva, XXXXII.Armee-Korps (11., 58., and 122.Inf.Div.) was in the center, and XXVI. Armee-Korps (225., 170., and 227.Inf.Div.) was west of Narva.

Kampfgruppe Kausch was inserted between the positions of "Norge" and of 11.Inf.Div., with the mission of defending the road between Lipsus and Krivasso, one of the hottest points in the sector. Throughout the month of May, fighting in the Narva bridgehead waned in intensity, and the various units were able to catch their breath. The "Nordland" staff took advantage of the lull to organize awards ceremonies for the numerous soldiers who had distinguished themselves in combat. The following weeks were marked only by long-distance artillery duels and by recon patrols.

"Nordland" grenadier in a defensive position, March 1944

SS-Ostubaf. Fritz Knöchlein

On the left is a "Nordland" defensive position on the Narva front, April 1944. At right is a prewar photo of Hermenegild Graf von Westphalen, during his stay at the SS-Junkerschule at Bad Tölz.

Late April 1944: SS-Gruf. Fritz von Scholz, *center*, speaking with SS-Stubaf. Albrecht Krügel, commander of II./"Norge." On the right is SS-Stubaf. Fritz Knöchlein, the new "Norge" regimental commander. *NA*

Late April 1944: SS-Gruf. Von Scholz awarding Iron Crosses

SS-Gruf. Von Scholz

SS-Stubaf. Albrecht Krügel awarding Iron Crosses

An *SS-Hscha.* of SS-Pz.Abt.11

A decorated *SS-Hscha.*

A group of "Nordland" officers and soldiers with the Iron Cross awards

SS-Ustuf. Leo Anton Madsen

The Sonnenschein Outpost

On June 7, 1944, the Soviets made an attack against the Sonnenschein outpost, held by 7./"Danmark," completely overwhelming the positions and causing numerous losses among the Danish volunteers. The remainder of the company, under Danish SS-Ustuf. Leo Madsen,[7] somehow managed to fend off the first attack. The company consisted mainly of veterans of the former Freikorps "Danmark." Five days later, the Soviets resumed their attack, preceded by a heavy artillery bombardment against the rear area of the Germanic volunteers. The Sonnenschein outpost was completely isolated. The Soviet gunners used smoke shells that covered the entire landscape with an artificial fog. The clouds of smoke reached as far as the II./"Danmark" command post at Dolgaja-Niva. The "Danmark" commander, SS-Ostubaf. Krügel, asked SS-Hstuf. Hämel if he was still in contact with his 7./Kompanie, which was by now surrounded.

"No contact; I think the telephone line has been cut. Madsen has a flare gun and I think he'll use it," responded the officer. A few minutes later, the young Danish second lieutenant did in fact launch a flare to ask for help, considering that the remnants of his company were completely surrounded on the Sonnenschein outpost. SS-Ustuf. Madsen could not hold his position much longer, so he decided to attempt to break through to reach his battalion at Dolgaja-Niva. But by then it was too late; the Soviet grip had tightened around them. Under cover of the smoke and the noise of the explosions, the Soviets again attacked the 7./"Danmark" positions, giving rise to fierce hand-to-hand fighting. Two platoon leaders fell while leading their men, SS-Ustuf. Johannes Koopmann and SS-Ustuf. Arne Michaelsen. Only a small group of about a dozen men, led by SS-Uscha. Egon Christophersen,[8] continued to hold out like lions on the northern edge of the position. The Danish volunteers hugged the ground and greeted the Soviets with short bursts from machine pistols and some hand grenades. Ammunition started to run short, and the situation became even more desperate. The flare fired by Madsen at the beginning of the attack had been seen by the "Nordland" artillery regiment's observation post. The guns joined the action and sent a torrent of fire against the area east of Dolgaja-Niva, where the Soviets had amassed their troops. Meanwhile, at least two hundred Soviet infantrymen had already rushed through the gap that had been opened, and were able to gain more ground. Other Soviet units came out of the forest and moved against the hamlet. SS-Ostubaf. Karl's guns had adjusted their fire well, literally pulverizing the Soviet infantry, which disappeared amid the smoke and explosions. Nevertheless, nothing seemed to be able to stop the Soviets, who continued to attack despite the losses they were taking; they now were the owners of outpost Sonnenschein and were pushing into Dolgaja-Niva, where the fighting was house to house. The group led by Christophersen still held on, even though completely surrounded. Only a decisive infantry counterattack could restore the situation and close the gap that had been opened. Norwegian SS-Hstuf. Erik Lärum,[9] commander of 13./"Danmark," equipped with 150 mm howitzers, from his forward position had observed the fighting around Sonnenschein and, seeing the gravity of the situation, decided to abandon his howitzers momentarily in order to hasten to the aid of his comrades in difficulty. He placed himself at the head of a combat group, consisting of his gunners and the grenadiers of two companies of II. and III./"Danmark": 8. Kompanie, led by SS-Ustuf. Svend Birkedahl-Hansen, and 12.Kompanie, under SS-Ostuf. Paul Thorkildsen. In addition, Lärum requested mortar and artillery support from division headquarters; all the guns in the sector concentrated their fire on the Soviet positions around Dolgaja-Niva. Completely drowned in a torrent of fire, the Soviet soldiers were forced to find shelter to avoid being killed. Shortly after the artillery barrage, a counterattack was made with all available forces: SS-Hstuf. Herbert Meyer arrived with part of his 9./"Danmark" to take part in the attack against Dolgaja-Niva, while other elements of 8. and 16./"Danmark" showed up as reinforcements along with two StuG II assault guns. The "Danmark" grenadiers arrived shortly afterward in the trenches where the survivors of the Soviet attack had taken refuge, took about forty prisoners, and retook the ground that had been lost. Soon after, contact was made with their 7.Kompanie comrades, who were clustered around SS-Uscha. Christophersen: the Danish sergeant had not expected the arrival of reinforcements to make a counterattack to the north and south, with his handful of grenadiers managing to break the encirclement. SS-Hstuf. Hämel, who had gone up to the front line, reached the Danish NCO in the trenches, whom he knew very well from his time when he had commanded his company, in order to personally award him the Iron Cross First Class and to later recommend him for the Knight's Cross, the first Danish volunteer to receive it; the award was formally granted on July 11, 1944.

SS-Uscha. Egon Christophersen

A "Nordland" artillery observer. Note the Sonnenrad collar tab.

An SS grenadier with a machine pistol on the Narva front, 1944

In the meantime, the Soviets had also attacked Natalin and Usküla, managing to penetrate the "Danmark" positions. All the southern part of the bridgehead on the eastern bank, south of the road and the Narva-Jamburg railway line, was threatened. With the support of Nordland artillery, a new counterattack was made by the grenadiers of 7./"Danmark," part of 9./"Danmark," the engineers of 16.Kompanie, the special tank-killer platoon, and, most importantly, two assault guns. The Germanic volunteers were thus able to retake Dolgaja-Niva and the Sonnenschein outpost, where they discovered the burnt remains of their comrades. Of the twenty-five men of the small garrison, there were only two survivors. At the end of that day of June 12, the balance for the "Danmark" regiment was terrible: ninety men lost, either killed, wounded, or missing.

SS-Uscha. Egon Christophersen with the Ritterkreuz

"Danmark" grenadiers in a trench, 1944

A Waffen-SS anti-tank gun squad in combat, summer 1944. *Michael Cremin*

CHAPTER VII

THE ABANDONMENT OF NARVA

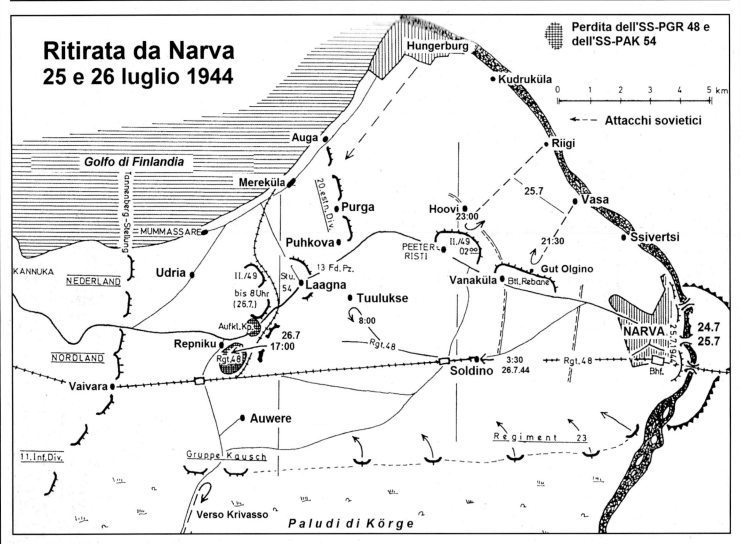

Ritirata da Narva
25 e 26 luglio 1944

Golfo di Finlandia

Perdita dell'SS-PGR 48 e dell'SS-PAK 54

0 1 2 3 4 5 km

← - - Attacchi sovietici

Hungerburg

Kudruküla

Auga

Riigi

Mereküla

Purga

Hoovi
23:00

25.7

Vasa

MUMMASSARE

Puhkova

PEETER-RISTI

II./49
02:00

21:30

Ssivertsi

KANNUKA

NEDERLAND

Udria

II./49

bis 8Uhr
(26.7.)

Stu.
54

13 Fd.Pz.

Laagna

Tuulukse

8:00

Vanaküla

Btl.Rebane

Gut Olgino

NARVA

24.7
25.7

25.7.1944

Aufkl.Kp.

26.7
17:00

Rgt.48

NORDLAND

Repniku

Rgt.48

Soldino

3:30
26.7.44

Rgt.48

Bhf.

Vaivara

Auwere

Regiment 23

11.Inf.Div.

Gruppe Kausch

Verso Krivasso

Paludi di Körge

Retreat from Narva, July 25–26, 1944

Following the offensive launched by the Soviets on June 22, 1944 (Operation Bagration), against Army Group Center, the German forces in Narva, and more generally in the Baltic region, risked being completely cut off. The Soviet offensive on the Karelia front further accentuated the threat, forcing the German headquarters to plan to abandon the Narva bridgehead, despite the fact that the Estonian city had become the symbol of resistance by the European volunteers against the Soviet forces. On July 11, 1944, the southern wing of 8.Armee was attacked by the 2nd Baltic Front south of Pleskau, causing the German forces to withdraw to a new defensive line long the Pleskau-Jakobstadt road. On July 24, the 3rd Baltic Front, numbering twenty divisions, attacked the Armee Abteilung Narwa positions, forcing the German forces there to withdraw to the west as well. The Soviets were able to establish numerous bridgeheads on the western bank of the river, with the intention of trapping the troops defending Narva; during the following night, the order was given for III.SS-Pz.Korps to abandon Narva and to pull back about 20 kilometers farther west, on the Blue Mountains,

An assault gun on the Estonian front

to a new defensive line called the Tannenbergstellung on the road that ran from Narva to Riga. Naturally, the withdrawal movement required time and, most of all, the sacrifice of several units that had to remain as the rearguard to cover the retreat of the other units.

A PzKpfw.V Ausf.A being towed by a Bergepanther during the evacuation of Narva. The branches used to hide it from enemy air reconnaissance are being removed, July 1944. *NARA*

"Nordland" soldiers evacuating the bridgehead, using the bridges still intact. *NA*

SS-Hstuf. Günther Wanhöfer

Final briefing for these "Danmark" soldiers before withdrawing

The Dutch units were engaged in that mission, and while the "de Ruyter" (under SS-Stubaf. Collani) was able to disengage, the "General Seyffardt" (under SS-Ostubaf. Benner) was surrounded by enemy forces and was wiped out. The "Nederland" units engaged in defending the withdrawal of other German units were reinforced with other units, among them II./SS-Frw.Gr.Rgt.47, led by Stubaf. Alfons Rebane, a coastal artillery unit from Hungerburg, and a Pak platoon of the 20.SS. Their mission was to defend the northern extremity of the bridgehead, from the center of Narva to Hungerburg. To the south were the "Nordland" units, reinforced by elements of SS-Pz.Abt.11 "HvS," the Gruppe Riipalu (the Stab of SS-Frw.Gr.Rgt.45), the reinforced 5./"Seyffardt," and a platoon from SS-Pz.Jäg.Abt.20.

SS-Ostubaf. Kausch's command post was also surrounded by Soviet riflemen. Kausch gathered his men and opened up an escape route while fighting, avoiding being captured. Until July 25, the units of III.SS-Pz.Korps, acting as rearguards, remained in the city: SS-Ostuf. Wanhöfer, commander of SS-Pionier-Bataillon 54, saw to blowing up all the bridges over the river Narva, and when the Soviets got to the banks of the river, they found not a bridge still standing. For his excellent action during the fighting at Narva, SS-Hstuf. Günther Wanhöfer was awarded the Knight's Cross on August 27, 1944.

Also on July 25, the second day of the Soviet offensive, in the area around Vasa north of Narva where the Estonian SS units were deployed, Soviet forces were able to make a dangerous breakthrough; with the Estonian units having abandoned the sector, the Germanic volunteers of the "Nederland" brigade were called in to close off the new dangerous breach at Hungerburg. The remnants of the four grenadier battalions of the "Norge" and "Danmark" withdrew in order along the railway line, and behind them the SS engineers were busy destroying bridges and crossings, while 5./"Norge" and, to the south, 7./"Danmark" remained as rearguards to cover the retreat.

"Danmark" troops withdrawing from Narva. *Tiquet*

The Tannenbergstellung

The defensive line along the Tannenbergstellung began at the Gulf of Finland and ran for about 3 kilometers through the plain cutting the Narva-Reval (Tallin) road as far as the Blue Mountains (in Estonian, the hills of Sinimäed), the fulcrum of the defensive system. Then it continued to the south, passing between the railway station at Auvere and that at Vaivara, following the Narva-Reval railway line. The German defensive deployment was thus concentrated on the Blue Mountains (Blauberg in German), a series of three hills called the Kinderheim (Orphanage), Grenadier, and 69.9 Höhe (Hill 69.9, or Hill of Love).

The staff and services of the "Nordland" division set themselves up in the woods of Repniku, along the Narva-Tallinn highway. The Dutch soldiers of the "Nederland" brigade, by now down to only a single regiment, were deployed in the northern portion of the Tannenbergstellung, between the coast of the Gulf of Finland and the Narva-Tallinn highway. Farther south were the Estonian volunteers of the 20.Waffen Grenadier Division, the engineers of the "Nederland" and the I. and II./"de Ruyter," the II. and III./"Danmark," and the 11.Infanterie-Division. The men of the Norge regiment had been placed in reserve. The Orphanage Hill was held by the Flemish volunteers of the "Langemarck," grouped in Kampfgruppe Rehmann,[1] whose antitank guns had been emplaced at the foot of the hill. On Grenadier Hill and Hill 69.9 were other elements of the Estonian SS division and two companies of SS-Pionier-Bataillon 11. The most-forward positions on both sides of the Narva-Tallinn road were held by II./"de Ruyter" on the northern side and by II./"Danmark" on the southern side. To reinforce the III.SS-Pz.Korps defense, the batteries of SS-Vielfach-Werfer-Batterie 521 were brought in, led by SS-Hstuf. Friedrich Flecke, equipped with half-tracks that mounted multiple rocket launchers similar to the Soviet Katyushas, capable of firing forty-eight rockets in two or three seconds. The unit took up positions behind the "Danmark" regiment, and its forward observer, SS-Uscha. Lerner, set up his observation post near headquarters of III./"Danmark."

The Soviets Attack

On July 26, the Soviets unleashed a hurricane of fire on the positions held by the European Waffen-SS volunteers. Soviet artillery particularly devastated the positions on the Kinderheim hill, and a shell hit the bunker where the Flemish *Kampfgruppe* command post was, killing the 1.Kp. commander, SS-Ustuf. Albert Swinnen, and the 2.Kp. commander, SS-Hstuf. Van Moll, and badly wounding SS-Hstuf. Rehmann. The commander of 3.Kp., SS-Ustuf. D'Haese, assumed command of the Flemish unit. Shortly after, a Soviet tank column, followed by infantry units, attacked the hill; fierce fighting ensued, which saw Flemish antitank guns and the SS grenadiers destroying the enemy tanks and repelling the Soviet infantry.

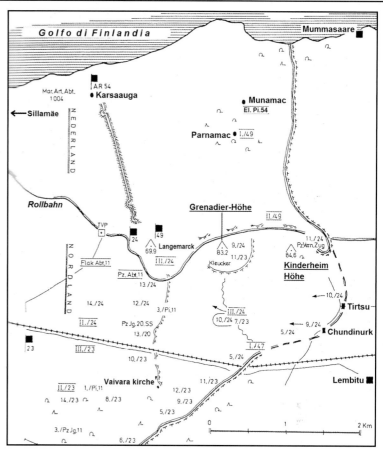

Deployment of German units on the Tannenbergstellung, 1944

SS-Vielfach-Werfer-Batterie 521 half-tracks on the Estonian front

SS grenadiers in a defensive position on the Tannenbergstellung, July 1944

Several positions held by the "Danmark" volunteers were overrun, as were those of the Flemish 2. and 3.Kp., leaving most of the eastern side of the hill in enemy hands. In the late afternoon, the Soviets resumed their attack with infantry and tanks south of the Narva-Tallinn road after having overrun the positions defended by a Kriegsmarine infantry company; a Soviet tank formation continued the attack toward the Kinderheim Höhe, while the infantry headed farther south. Fighting flared on the other two hills as well. SS-Gruf. Fritz von Scholz, the "Nordland" commander, sent all available forces to stem the Soviet offensive, which now seemed unstoppable, including the last of the Sturmgeschütz of SS-Stubaf. Karl Schulz-Streek, commander of SS-Pz.Jg.Abt.11 and Kausch's Panthers. Among the units sent in as reinforcements were a group of tank killers led by SS-Uscha. Mellenthin, equipped with individual German antitank weapons, such as the deadly *Panzerfaust* and *Panzerschreck*, who took up positions among the motorcycle riflemen of SS-Oscha. Albert Hektor of 7./"Danmark" and the grenadiers of 11./"Danmark," under SS-Hstuf. Trautwein.[2]

On July 27, beginning at dawn, Soviet artillery lengthened its fires, no longer hitting the first-line trenches but rather the rear area. Soviet infantry attacked soon thereafter in force and in serried ranks; the two units most directly threatened were Trautwein's 11./"Danmark," deployed along the highway, and SS-Ostuf. Hugo Jessen's 10./"Danmark," deployed near the village of Tirtsu. When the Soviets reached the 11./"Danmark" positions, SS-Hstuf. Trautwein had his men open fire, staying on the front line. The Soviets responded, hitting the Danish positions with their heavy weapons; among the first to fall to enemy fire was Trautwein himself, who was seriously wounded in the stomach. His grenadiers continued to hold their positions and to ward off the enemy attack, thanks in part to reinforcement by Mellenthin's tank killers. The Soviets resumed their attack with an armored formation consisting of about thirty tanks escorted by fresh infantry units that had come up from the rear. The *Panzerjäger* with their

And StuG.III of SS-Pz.Abt.11 on the Estonian front. *Charles Trang*

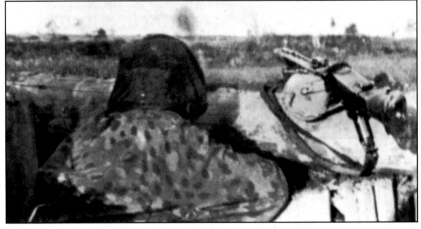

An SS defensive position with an MG42 in the Tirtsu area, July 1944

Waffen-SS grenadiers in a defensive position ready to face enemy tanks with a *Panzerschreck*

Waffen-SS positions on the Tannenbergstellung

Panzerfäuste, well hidden along the embankment that ran alongside the highway and in the folds in the ground, awaited the arrival of the enemy tanks and, when these were in range, opened fire, destroying many of them. For their part, the German grenadiers faced the enemy tanks with bunches of hand grenades, thrown at close range, with devastating effect. More than half the Soviet tanks were thus knocked out, and many others were seriously damaged. 11./"Danmark" also suffered heavy losses; following the wounding of its commander, the unit's command was assumed by SS-Ustuf. Kaj-Albert Bertramsen.

Soon after, massive attacks hit Chundinurk and the II./"Danmark" and III./"Norge" sectors. The Soviets moved from Auwere, Lembitu, and Sooküla. The two SS battalions managed to hold their positions, but contact was lost with 9./"Danmark" at Chundinurk. The Soviets had attacked the company led by SS-Hstuf. Herbert Meyer[3] from three sides. German artillery and heavy weapons of the regiment supported the company's defensive action with their fire, hitting enemy concentrations east of Tirtsu, Repniku, Auwere, Lembitu, and Sooküla. This stalled the enemy attacks.

On the left, a German soldier armed with a *Panzerfaust*, sheltering in a trench while awaiting enemy tanks. *On the right*, SS-Usuf. Kaj-Albert Bertramsen. Note the special collar tab with the Danish flag, authorized in April 1942 only for members of the reserve company of Freikorps "Danmark."

A Flemish Antitank Gun

After having gotten past the main line of resistance east of Kinderheim hill, the Soviet attack concentrated on the hill itself, held by Flemish volunteers of the "Langemarck." The Soviets preceded their attack with many tanks, which were quickly engaged by the 5.Kp./"Langemarck" antitank guns under SS-Ustuf. Marcel Laperre; one after another, the Flemish antitank guns were put out of action by enemy fire, and Laperre himself was wounded. A single 75 mm antitank gun was left at the foot of the hill, served by Flemish *Sturmmann* Remy Schriynen, partially hidden by the smoke of the battle, who had lost most of his gun crew. SS-Hstuf. D'Haese had ordered him not to be spotted and to open fire only at the last moment; from his position the Flemish corporal saw the Soviet tanks passing laterally in front of his position at short range, which was an opportunity not to be missed. Before being completely bypassed by the enemy tank column, he decided to act.

Schriynen loaded the gun and fired, loaded again and fired again, continuing to fire until he was out of ammunition, after having knocked out three Josef Stalin tanks and four T-34s and having damaged at least another pair. Spotted by the Soviet tankers, the Fleming's position was targeted several times before a Josef Stalin tank headed directly at it. The tank was hit at the last minute, but in the explosion, Remy Schriynen was thrown by the rush of air and was slightly bruised. For his heroic action, Schriynen was awarded the Knight's Cross and promoted to the rank of *Unterscharführer*. Despite Schriynen's success, the Flemish volunteers were forced to abandon their positions on the hill and withdraw to Grenadier Hill. Only II./"de Ruyter" continued to hold the positions north of the Kinderheim; SS-Hstuf. Frühauf had been badly wounded, and command of the battalion passed to SS-Ostuf. Helmut Scholz. The Dutch battalion's antitank unit had been able to destroy

Flemish Sturmmann Remy Schriynen

A Flemish antitank squad with a 75 mm Pak 40 engaged against Soviet tanks, July 1944

A "Langemarck" brigade antitank gun on the Tannenbergstellung

numerous enemy tanks. In an attempt to push the Soviets back, a counterattack was ordered, and to that end, SS-Ostubaf. Kausch sent a dozen assault guns under SS-Ostuf. Ernst-Richard Stübben,[4] commander of 3./SS-Pz.Abt.11, which decimated the enemy tanks.

Having been repulsed in the north, the Soviet attacks shifted to the Chundinurk area, with SS-Hstuf. Hans Meyer's 9./"Danmark" still holding the village without any contact with other units. The Soviet attacks also threatened the III./"Danmark" command post, located between Grenadier Hill and the railway line. SS-Stubaf. Kappus,[5] commander of III./"Danmark," asked for reinforcements. Only the remnants of 7./"Norge" showed up; when they arrived at the III./"Danmark" command post, they found it surrounded by Soviet troops. They immediately went on the attack, unleashing wild hand-to-hand fighting. After having joined up, Danish and Norwegian grenadiers dug in in a small woods farther north, attempting to establish contact with the other companies that were fighting on the front line.

The situation that II./"Danmark" found itself in continued to be critical: SS-Hstuf. Hämel decided to counterattack in order to disengage 9.Kompanie. He scraped together all the available men and attacked toward Chundinurk. Personally leading the assault, SS-Hstuf. Hämel was wounded. The attack advanced toward the 8./Kompanie position, which itself was surrounded. Contact was reestablished with friendly units engaged in Chundinurk.

"Danmark" grenadiers during the fighting on the Tannenbergstellung, July 1944. *Ullstein*

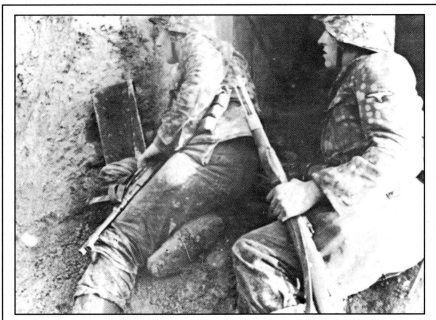

"Danmark" grenadiers in combat, July 1944

A "Danmark" machine gun team moves up to attack, July 1944

A difficult move of a wounded soldier to the rear, 1944

The Death of Commander Scholz

That same day, July 27, 1944, around noontime, SS-Gruppenführer Scholz went to the command post on Hill 69.9 to confer with the occupants there. The meeting was attended b SS-Ostubaf. Albrecht Krügel, commander of the "Danmark" regiment, and SS-Ustuf. Herwarth Arera, commander of 1./Kp./SS-Pi. Btl.11: "You have to send troops to reinforce the defensive line; the situation is serious, but we have to continue to hold the positions," Scholz ordered the two officers. After having presided over the organization of an emergency *Kampfgruppe* placed under command of SS-Ustuf. Arera, Scholz then went to inspect the positions held by SS-Hstuf. Erik Krislian Lärum's 13./"Danmark" in order to satisfy himself that the grenadiers on the front line were receiving adequate fire support. "Old Fritz," as his men affectionately called him, arrived at 13./"Danmark" just at the moment when a heavy enemy artillery bombardment began; a howitzer shell exploded close to Scholz, raising a cloud of smoke and scattering splinters in all directions. One of these fragments hit Scholz in the face, and his face quickly turned into a bloody mask. The commander lost consciousness and showed no signs of life, even though he had been administered first aid and brought to the hospital at the camp at Rakvere. The first to tend to his wounds was SS-Ostubaf. Franz Riedweg, the "Nordland" medical officer of Swiss origin: "The cranial trauma is serious; he has to be operated on urgently at the hospital in Weisenberg" were his first words. For Riedweg, old Fritz was not only a boss but most of all a friend, with whom from the beginning he had shared the idea of a European Waffen-SS and the inclusion of foreign volunteers in the German armed forces. Rather than transport Scholz in a vehicle, a train was chosen; a special carriage was prepared at the Vaivara station, where SS-Hstuf. Heinz Hämel, who had also been wounded, was accommodated. Throughout the trip, Hämel hovered over his commandant, whose condition appeared more serious by the hour. When the train arrived in Weisenberg, Fritz von Scholz had already passed away: the "Nordland" commander had died from his wounds. It was a great loss for the "Nordland" division, for the Waffen-SS, and for all the German armed forces.

On August 8, 1944, Scholz was posthumously awarded the Knight's Cross with Oak Leaves on the basis of a proposal written by Felix Steiner and sent to the Reichsführer-SS via telex.

Following is the brief text: "On 7.24.44, after two hours of pounding artillery fire, the enemy broke into the G.R.45 sector with tanks, with the center of gravity on both sides of the main road to Lipsu, penetrating to a width of about 1 kilometer and a depth of about 1 kilometer. The capture of the adjacent heights occurred because it was essential in order to continue the advance. SS-Gruppenführer Scholz personally brought troops to the front line, creating defensive positions that prevented a second breach in the front. After having set up positions of 4./SS-Panzer-Abteilung 11, the commander personally led a counterattack with 4./SS-Pz.Abt.11 and 2./Pi.Kp. on the hill, managing to repel the enemy and to seize the earlier main combat line. It was a success: the breakthrough hypothesized by the enemy did not occur, and infiltration by Soviet troops along the Narva road was prevented. The attack by the enemy's 120th Division, which had as its aim to expel III. SS-Pz.Korps from the Tannenberg position, ended up in failure."

Command of the "Nordland" was assumed by SS-Brigdf. Joachim Ziegler,[6] formerly the chief of staff of III.SS-Pz.Korps. He in turn was replaced in that post by SS-Ostubaf. Bockelberg, while SS-Staf. Erich von Bock und Polalch became the "Nordland" chief of staff.

New Counterattacks

In order to recapture Kinderheim hill, SS-Ostubaf. Krügel decided to mount a counterattack with the "Nordland" engineers, the 1.Kp. (of SS-Ustuf. Herwarth Arera), the 3.Kp. (under SS-Ustuf. Werner Schimpf), the I./SS-Frw.Gr.Rgt.47 (under Waffen-Stubaf. Sooden), and several assault guns. 1./SS Pi.Btl.11 was to attack from the north and 3./SS-Pi.Btl.11 from the south; if the two units could manage to make contact, that would mean that the front had been reestablished. The attack was to be signaled by firing three white flares: SS-Ustuf. Arera had split his company into two assault groups, led by SS-Uscha. Frommelt and SS-Uscha. Simanski. Around 2100, the two engineer companies assembled at the departure points while the Kampfgruppe Kausch assault guns began to move to the two sides of Kinderheim hill, where the last of the Flemish volunteers were already pulling back. Around 2300, the attack began, with Arera's men from the northern flank and Schimpf's from the south, as planned, but contact was not made between the two units. A signal flare was fired from the top of Kinderheim; the Estonian volunteers had reached the top after having overrun the Soviet defenders. When SS-Ustuf. Arera reached the southern slope of the hill, he saw some men approaching and, thinking that they were engineers from 3.Kp., called to them, but his answer was a hail of enemy fire. The SS engineers reacted quickly by tossing hand grenades. While trying to throw a grenade, SS-Ustuf. Arera was hit in the stomach. Two engineers carried him to the rear to the SS-Frw.Pz.Gren.Rgt.49 "de Ruyter" command post. Arera's engineers found themselves fighting against battle-hardened enemy formations, while Schimpf's men were stalled at the base of the hill, also engaged in bitter fighting. SS-Ustuf. Schimpf was killed while leading his men.

The Estonian volunteers were alone on top of the hill, continuing to ward off continuous Soviet attacks, but they couldn't hold out for long. Waffen-Stubaf. Sooden was himself killed during the fighting. A new *Kampfgruppe*, led by SS-Stubaf. Scheibe, commander of II./"Norge," consisting of the survivors of 5. and 6.Kp./"Norge" and those of a naval infantry battalion, was sent to aid the Estonians. Scheibe requested artillery support before attacking, but only a few rounds were fired, and when his men attacked the eastern and northern slopes of the Kinderheim, they were met by heavy enemy fire. Soviet artillery also opened fire on Scheibe's grenadiers, completely canceling their action. Scheibe was seriously wounded by a howitzer round, and the few survivors of the attack dug in along with the Estonian volunteers.

One of the last photos of SS-Gruf. Fritz von Scholz

Waffen-SS soldiers carrying a wounded soldier to the rear

SS-Hstuf. Heinz Hämel and SS-Gruf. Fritz von Scholz during the award ceremony for Hämel's Knight's Cross, spring 1944

Soviet infantry and tanks attacking German positions, 1944

SS-Ostubaf. Helmut von Bockelberg (*left*) meeting SS-Brigdf. Joachim Ziegler, the new "Nordland" commander

Observing enemy positions before an attack, summer 1944

In late afternoon of July 28, 7./"Danmark," consisting of some fifty men, reinforced by about twenty Flemish volunteers from "Langemarck," was involved in a fresh attack to try to recapture the Kinderheim Höhe. The Soviets, however, were not taken by surprise and greeted the SS grenadiers with a massive hail of fire, inflicting many losses on the attacking forces. Among the wounded was the company commander, SS-Ustuf. Madsen. Command of the company was temporarily assumed by SS-Oscha. Hektor, who was able to control the men and have them assume new defensive positions to meet the Soviet counterattacks. In the fighting that followed, the SS grenadiers were able to drive off all the Soviet penetrations and attacks, destroying seven tanks at close range and another three with antitank guns. For valor in the field, SS-Oscha. Albert Hektor, a platoon leader in 7./"Danmark," was recommended for the Knight's Cross, which was officially granted him on August 23, 1944.

Hills in Flames

At dawn on July 29, the third day of battle along the Tannenbergstellung, Soviet artillery began to hit the German positions very heavily: the two main targets were Grenadier Hill and the village of Chundinurk. The 9./"Danmark" grenadiers still held the village but were on verge of giving out, exhausted after having repelled numerous enemy attacks. Around ten in the morning, the Soviets made yet another attack against the position with infantry and tanks, and once again the Danish volunteers managed to hold, thanks to the supporting fire provided by two assault guns that had come up as reinforcements. Southeast of Lembitu, an enemy armored formation was stopped by the fire of SS-Hstuf. Flecke's Nebelwerfer batteries and by the "Nordland" divisional artillery's guns.

Farther north, the situation was even more critical, and after Kinderheim Hill was captured by the Soviets, fighting had shifted to Grenadier hill, farther west. After a heavy shelling by Soviet artillery, the Soviets attacked with numerous infantry formations supported by a concentration of tanks never seen before; the forward positions were overrun almost immediately, while others were simply bypassed, while the bitterest fighting naturally took place on Grenadier Hill. The completely isolated survivors of 10. and 11./"Danmark" continued to fight, attempting to reestablish contact with their regiment. Some of Mellenthin's men were alongside them, without any officers, all of whom had fallen in combat. Toward the highway, SS-Hstuf. Josef Bachmeier,[7] who had replaced SS-Stubaf. Scheibe at the head of II./"Norge," was fighting desperately against overwhelming Soviet forces, having under his command German soldiers and Norwegian, Dutch, and Estonian volunteers, entrenched on the western slope of Grenadier Hill. Other Soviet units pushed as far as Hill 69.9, getting close to the Dutch "de Ruyter" command post; after having tried up to the last moment to fend off the enemy, SS-Ostubaf. Hans Collani chose to commit suicide rather than to fall alive into the hands of the Bolsheviks.

SS-Oscha. Albert Hektor

Siegfried Scheibe with *SS-Ustuf.* rank insignia

German antitank squad in action

With the deterioration of the situation on Hill 69.9, the positions on Grenadier Hill risked being overwhelmed, and thus SS-Hstuf. Bachmeier had his men begin to withdraw. In order to restore the situation, corps headquarters threw in the last of the reserves and the last of the Panthers and StuGs still available. Kausch's tanks clashed with the Soviet tanks in the open area between the two hills, miraculously managing to cause the enemy attack to vacillate and then pull back.

Encouraged by the unexpected victory of Kausch's panzers, Bachmeier's grenadiers, still holding the western slope of Grenadier Hill, went on the counterattack, wresting several enemy positions on the hill. Farther south, near the railway line, elements of III./"Danmark" continued to fight to repel the continuous enemy attacks, split into small isolated groups and often completely surrounded, firing their last cartridges and throwing their last grenades.

Fighting continued until July 31, as reported in the Wehrmacht war diary: "On the Narva isthmus, the enemy has suspended his attacks because of heavy losses incurred. The following formations played an important role in the defense against the recent Soviet attacks: the 'Nordland' division, the 'Nederland' brigade, the 20th SS Division, the 11.Infanterie-Division, Kriegsmarine units." On August 2, 1944, the battle flared up again, with Bachmeier's men once again called on to valorously defend their positions. Some enemy penetrations were quickly eliminated with rapid and decisive counterattacks. On August 3, there was still fighting on Grenadier Hill; attacks and counterattacks followed in rapid succession, with the Soviets finally withdrawing. On August 5, the Soviets attacked the hill

"Danmark" radio operator

A rocket launcher half-track of SS-Vielfach-Werfer-Batterie 521

"Danmark" grenadier bandaging his wounded hand. This is undoubtedly a Danish volunteer, formerly of Freikorps "Danmark," judging by the Demjansk campaign badge on his left sleeve.

three times, with scant artillery supporting fire. All the attacks were repulsed. SS-Hstuf. Bachmeier was wounded in the fighting, and command of the forces defending the hill was assumed by SS-Ostuf. Otto Kleucker, commander of SS-Bewährungskompanie 103, the III./(germ.)SS-Pz.Korps disciplinary unit. That same day, Chundinurk, considered to be too exposed to enemy attacks, was abandoned by the "Danmark" volunteers, who pulled back to the western slope of Hill 69.9. Some days of quiet ensued, and it was not until August 12 that the Soviets resumed their attacks anew against the Tannenbergstellung positions, but the Germanic volunteers were still able to repel all the enemy attacks.

A group of the Waffen-SS soldiers transporting an antitank-gun, summer 1944. *Michael Cremin*

A "Danmark" machine gunner firing bursts from his MG42 against enemy infantry

Estonian volunteers with a *Panzerschreck*

SS-Hstuf. Josef Bachmeier

SS-Ostubaf. Paul-Albert Kausch

The Knight's Cross for Josef Bachmeier

For his excellent and valorous action during the defensive fighting in July 1944, SS-Hstuf. Josef Bachmeier was recommended for the Knight's Cross, which was officially awarded him on August 23, 1944. Following is the proposal written by SS-Stubaf. Krügel and countersigned by SS-Brigdf. Ziegler and by SS-Ogruf. Steiner: "SS-Hauptsturmführer Bachmeier, commander of II./ SS-Pz.Gren.Rgt. 23 "Norge," was in charge of the defense of Grenadier Hill between August 1 and 3, 1944. During that period, he repelled numerous attacks made every day by enemy forces in regimental or divisional strength. On August 3, 1944, after several hours of bombardment by Soviet artillery and the loss of contact with the regiment, he was able to eliminate all the enemy penetrations with counterattacks made on his own initiative. That same day, the enemy intended to break into the Tannenberg line with fresh troops. Nevertheless, that objective was not successful thanks to the courage of Bachmeier and his men. During the fighting, the enemy suffered heavy losses in men and materiel (including six tanks destroyed)."

The Knight's Cross for Paul-Albert Kausch

SS-Ostubaf. Paul-Albert Kausch was also proposed to receive the Knight's Cross by SS-Brigdf. Ziegler and SS-Ogruf. Steiner, which he was awarded on August 23, 1944. Following is the proposal: "On July 24, 1944, the threat of breakthrough by the Soviet 120th Rifle Division was avoided. During the attack, Kausch's command post was surrounded: protected only by soldiers armed with machine pistols, Kausch gathered together all the available men and led them in a counterattack. Thanks also to our armored attack in a nearby sector, the breach in the front was again closed. In this way the threat against the southern flank of the defensive front was removed. On July 28, 1944, Kausch decided on his own initiative and with merciless audacity to lead a group of assault guns and grenadiers in an attack against the enemy on a wide front. The enemy penetration was eliminated, and the threat to Reval by Soviet formations was impeded. On July 29, 1944, Kausch was wounded during a new attack."

CHAPTER VIII
DEFENSE OF THE BALTIC COUNTRIES

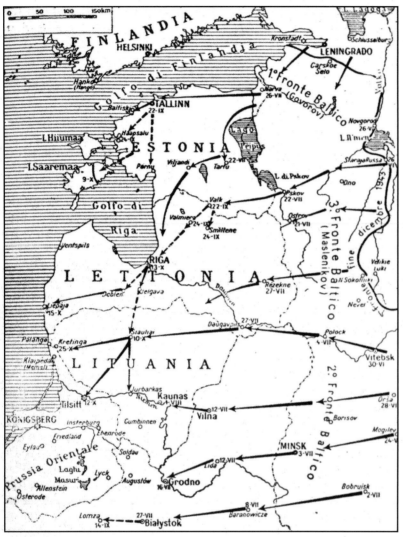

Soviet offensives on the Baltic front, summer–autumn 1944

A "Nordland" *SS-Ustuf.* with the EK II

While fighting was underway at the Narva bridgehead, the Soviets made an encircling attack from the south, toward Latvia and Lithuania, with the aim of capturing Riga, the capital of Latvia, and to cut the German defensive dispositions in the Baltic region in two. After having crossed the Neva River south of Lake Peipus and the city of Pleskau, the Soviet forces headed north to take the German forces still stationed on the northern Estonian front from the rear. The Germans were thus forced to abandon the positions that they had held since February 1944, in order to attempt to establish a new defensive line, oriented to the southeast, along the Pleskau-Jakobstadt railway line, with the city of Tartu (Dorpat in German) in the center. The Soviets lost no time in attacking this new German line of resistance, shifting their offensive to the northeast, between Lake Peipus and the small Lake Virz (Vörtsjärv).

Sd.Kfz.222 of 2./SS-Pz.Aufkl.Abt.11 in Estonia, 1944

SS-Untersturmführer of SS-Pz.Aufkl.Abt.11 on board his Sd.Kfz.250 armed with an MG42. *NA*

The "Nordland" Reconnaissance Group in Action

Heeresgruppe Nord was asked to transfer all available forces to the area of the breakthrough, and III.(germ.) SS-Pz.Korps decided to send SS-Panzer-Aufklärungs-Abteilung 11, led by SS-Stubaf. Rudolf Saalbach. The "Nordland" recon group was moved by train to Dünaburg (Daugavpils). Because the Soviet advance was very rapid, the unit was moved farther to the rear, to the northwest, to the Jakobstadt (Jekabpils), where it arrived on July 10, 1944. On July 14, it was decided to organize a combat group to restore contact between Heeresgruppe Nord and Mitte. The *Kampfgruppe* was placed under command of General der Kavallerie Philipp Kleffel and consisted of 61.Inf.Div., 225.Inf.Div., and SS-Pz.Aufkl. Abt.11. The *Kampfgruppe* went on the attack, and some of its elements were soon able to make contact with Heeresgruppe Mitte forces.

But the area was too vast, and this contact broke down almost immediately. Panzergruppe Saalbach, with its armored vehicles and half-tracks, proved to be an effective and extremely mobile force, engaged in the most-threatened points on the front. The SS troops carried out reconnaissance and rapid counterattacks and were used to close gaps in the defensive front. Kampfgruppe Saalbach soon became a sort of phantom unit, whose armored cars appeared unexpectedly, bringing death or confusion among enemy positions, then to disappear again. Soon after, they were in action again in another sector of the front.

Farther south, Soviet forces were continuing to advance, especially in the Polozk area. The Tiger tanks of Schwere-Panzer-Abteilung 502 sought to halt the enemy advance, managing to destroy numerous Soviet tanks. Other enemy tanks were knocked out from above by the Stukas of Major Hans Rudel. Nevertheless, on July 24, Dünaburg was captured by Soviet forces. A few days later, Soviet forces were able to reach the coast of the Gulf of Riga, not near the capital but a little more to the west, at Tukums, where the most-violent fighting on the Latvian front broke out. The last of the Wehrmacht's panzers were concentrated and thrown into a counterattack, led by Generalmajor Strachwitz, but in the end only about a dozen tanks and fifteen half-tracks were scraped together. Only after having received other reinforcements, among them the Panzer-Brigade-Gross, was Strachwitz able to attack and retake Tukums on August 20, 1944.

Kampfgruppe Wagner

Stalled in the south, the Soviets resumed their attack farther north, between Lake Peipus and Lake Virz, in the Dorpat (Tartu) Peninsula. A defensive line was hastily formed to contain the Soviets who were advancing from Pleskau (Pskov), south of Lake Peipus. In the Tartu area, the German headquarters decided to launch

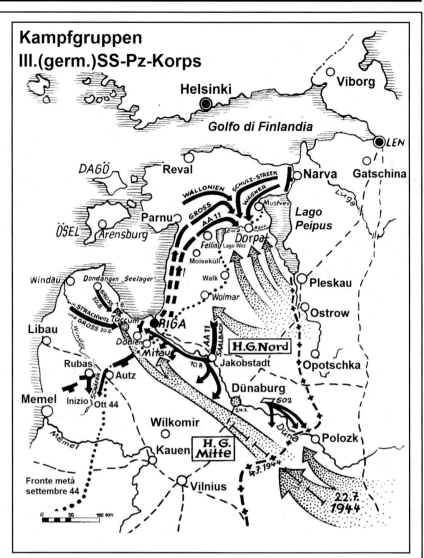

Movement of SS Kampfgruppe*n* between summer and autumn 1944

Panthers and German grenadiers on the Latvian front, summer 1944

Left, SS-Brigdf. Wagner (*left in photo*) in a "Nordland" defensive position, personally awarding Iron Crosses to several soldiers. *Right,* an SS-Rottenführer of SS-StuG.Abt.11. *NA*

a counteroffensive to cover the retreat of German troops toward Latvia and to contain the Soviet assault made south of Lak Peipus. SS-Ogruf. Steiner was ordered to send troops to the south to block the Soviet advance, and to that end, a *Kampfgruppe* was formed under SS-Brigdf. Jürgen Wagner,[1] the "Nederland" brigade commander, consisting of elements of the Dutch brigade (the rest of the brigade remained on the Tannenbergstellung, under Oberst Friedrich), I./ Waffen-Gr.Rgt.d.SS 45, the I. and II./Waffen-Gr.Rgt. 46, a combat group of the SS Wallonien assault brigade, Grenadier Regiment 23 of the 11.Inf.Div., SS-Panzer-Aufklärungs-Abteilung 11 (already transferred to the area), a company of SS-Pz.Jg.Abt.54, the II./SS-Art. Rgt.54, several army artillery groups and rocket launcher batteries, and the last of the "Nordland's" assault guns.

During the night between August 15 and 16, the units of the just-formed Kampfgruppe Wagner were withdrawn from their positions on the Tannenbergstellung and from the rear areas of III.(germ.)SS-Panzer-Korps. The combat group of the SS Wallonien assault brigade came directly from the Debica training camp, where the unit was being reorganized. Organized as a battalion with 452 men, commanded by SS-Hstuf. Georges Ruelle, it was later led by SS-Stubaf. Léon Degrelle.[2] Degrelle reached the Baltic front on August 8 to personally lead his Walloon volunteers in combat. On August 16, SS-Art.Rgt.54, led by SS-Hstuf. Quintus de Veer, left from the Jöwhi railway station in Dorpat, where the other units of the *Kampfgruppe* also arrived. On the basis of orders from the high command, the defensive line of Kampfgruppe Wagner was to run from Lake Virz to southeast of Lake Peipus; the course of the river Embach (Ema) that connected the two lakes was to have constituted the natural combat line if the Soviets had been able to get close to the Tartu area.

From the left, SS-Brigdf. Wagner, SS-Stubaf. Léon Degrelle, and SS-Ostuf. Karl Schäfer, Degrelle's German aide. *Munin Verlag*

Members of an Estonian border regiment in the Dorpat sector, 1944

Aerial view of Dorpat crossed by the river Embach, 1944

A German 105 mm howitzer engaged in battle

A 75 mm antitank gun in position on the Baltic front, summer 1944

Organization of the Defenses

At Tartu, SS-Brigdf. Wagner got together as many men as possible to reinforce his *Kampfgruppe*: among the civilian population, all men between the ages of sixteen and fifty were recruited and armed with whatever was at hand; Estonian paramilitary forces were called up; and the remnants of several German units were brought in, such as Grenadier Regiment 23, the III./Werfer-Regiment 3, and II./Artillerie-Regiment 58, which had already been involved in the defense of the sector. The first units of the *Kampfgruppe* took up positions south of Tartu, and several recon patrols were soon sent out throughout the area in order to intercept the Soviet advance elements in time. The two Walloon companies, numbering about three hundred men, were deployed along a line that ran from the road that led from Dorpat to Petseri, along Lake Peipus, to the road that ran from Dorpat to Valka toward the center of the town. II./SS-Art.Rgt. 54 emplaced its batteries on both sides of the city but on August 20 were moved farther forward by about 20 kilometers southeast in order to provide fire support to Estonian units and to 11.Infanterie-Division. The Soviets assailed the thin defensive line with massive forces. The Estonians, badly armed and equipped, were easily overwhelmed. The 1st Company of Füsilier-Battalion 11, led by Leutnant Bucholz, on the left wing, bore the brunt of the enemy attack. The commander of 4./SS-Art.Rgt. 54, SS-Ustuf. Günther Horstmann, quickly provided supporting fire, managing to throw the Soviets back. Soon after, the enemy returned to attack, employing greater forces. SS-Ustuf. Horstmann ordered his gunners to fire on the Soviets, once again stalling the Soviet attack. The Soviets answered with fire from their antitank guns, then resumed their attack. The German units were forced to withdraw to a new defensive line. II./SS-Art.Rgt. 54 displaced to new firing positions at Meliste. On August 19, SS-Brigdf. Wagner ordered SS-Stubaf. Degrelle to halt the enemy penetration in the Kambi sector, providing several assault guns in support. Two Walloon companies were engaged in capturing the village of Patska, after which they had to deal with successive Soviet counterattacks but were able to hold on to the position.

When enemy pressure became very strong, the Walloon volunteers pulled back to positions farther to the rear, continuing to repel the Soviet attacks. The Walloons did not abandon their position at Kambi until dawn on August 22, then joined other units of the *Kampfgruppe*. Meanwhile, the Soviets had gotten past Unikula and had taken Kuunja, southeast of Dorpat, reaching the gates of Nôo, where another group of Walloon volunteers led by SS-Ustuf. Léon Gillis was in position with its three 75 mm Pak guns and three 80 mm mortars. When Nôo fell on August 23, Gillis's Walloon group withdrew to the northeast, and this time the antitank guns were emplaced to defend the bridge over the river Embach at Voora. There the Soviets attacked with about a dozen Josef Stalin tanks; seeing those steel monsters, Gillis did

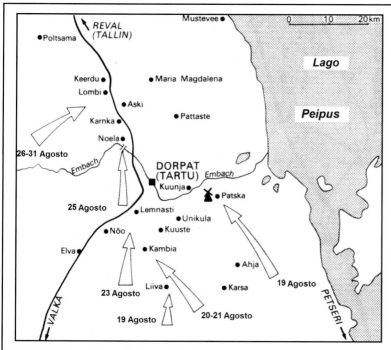

The defense of Dorpat, August 1944

Léon Degrelle on the march with his Walloons, August 1944

SS-Ustuf. Léon Gillis

A Waffen-SS 75 mm antitank gun in action

not lose heart and ordered his men to prepare to fire. The antitank gun crews waited until the first tank got to within about 30 meters from their positions, and then opened fire. The first tank was hit, going up in flames, then another tank was hit in the tracks and began to rotate on its own axis uncontrollably. Unexpected support came from a German artillery battery that was located not far from Valloni, whose fire added to the destruction of enemy tanks. Soviet infantry nevertheless attacked along with the surviving tanks. In short order, the three Walloon antitank guns were destroyed, and it was thanks only to the supporting fire of the German battery that the Walloons were able to pull back to new positions west of Dorpat and south of the crest of Em.

On August 24, Panzer-Brigade 101 and SS-Panzer-Brigade Gross moved against the positions at Elwa and Nôo, coming from Latvia. SS-Pz.Aufkl.Abt.11, led by SS-Stubaf. Rudolf Saalbach, with Kampfgruppe Graf Strachwitz, captured the village of Tamsa, farther north. Also on August 24, the Soviets reached the southern shore of Lake Virz, separating Armee Abteilung Narwa from 18.Armee. The next Soviet objective was now represented by the port of Pärnu on the Gulf of Riga. In the meantime, SS-Pz.Aufkl.Abt.11 was attached to Kampfgruppe Wagner, to be employed as a mobile quick-reaction force.

Half-tracks of 3.Kp./SS-Pz.Aufkl.Abt.11 on the march, summer 1944

SS-Stubaf. Rudof Saalbach

The Battle for Dorpat

The battle for Dorpat began on August 25; committed to its final defense were I./Gren.Rgt.33, the I./StuG.Brigade 393, and Estonian units, which were able to hold their positions until the afternoon. By 1800, the Soviets had taken Dorpat. SS-Unterscharführer Berthold Behnke of 5.Kp./SS-Pz.Aufkl.Abt.11, along with a handful of Germanic volunteers, continued to hold the Dorpat airfield with his Sd.Kfz.251/9 half-track armed with a 75 mm gun. The Soviets attacked with superior forces, but Behnke and the SS grenadiers drove them back. Once Dorpat had fallen, the Soviets crossed the river at Embach, establishing a bridgehead on the northern bank. SS-Stubaf. Degrelle had been ordered to set up a blocking position north of Dorpat along the Parna-Lombi-Keerdu line. The Walloon commander put all the available men on the front line, including noncombatants and wounded soldiers still able to hold a weapon. After having managed to scrape up around sixty men, Degrelle led them to the outskirts of Dorpat, where the presence of Soviet advance units had been reported. An initial attack was repulsed. Meanwhile, Degrelle had been able to find two artillery pieces that were hastily put in battery in the antitank role. Shortly thereafter he contacted Wagner via telephone to bring him up to date on the situation and to ask for reinforcements. Wagner answered, "Hold out at all costs. I'll send reinforcements as soon as I can." Degrelle

A short 75 mm gun mounted on an Sd.Kfz.252/9. The white stripes painted on the barrel indicate enemy tanks destroyed.

Léon Degrelle among his Walloon volunteers on the Estonian front, summer 1944

Walloon machine gunners in action

Walloon volunteers in combat on the Estonian front, 1944

SS grenadiers checking the smoking wreckage of a destroyed tank

moment that they were about to overrun the enemy defenses, a squadron of Stuka dive-bombers came on the scene to repel them anew. Many enemy tanks were destroyed on the ground, while Soviet infantry was forced to shelter in the nearby forest. Soon after, some Tiger tanks arrived to bolster the defenses. For this exemplary conduct of defensive operations at Dorpat, on August 27, 1944, Degrelle was awarded the Oak Leaves for his Knight's Cross.

SS Units in Action

At the same time, the vehicles of SS-Pz.Aufkl.Abt.11 continued to be busy in the hotspots on the front line as a quick-reaction force. Thus, on August 26, SS-Standarten-Oberjunker Walter Schwarck, a platoon leader in 5./SS-Pz.Aufkl.Abt.11, was informed that the crews of two flak guns and two 105 mm howitzers deployed in a defensive position had been surrounded in the village of Haage, running the risk of being overrun at any minute. His recon troopers jumped into their half-tracks armed with 75 mm guns and quickly moved to the position freeing their comrades. The "Nordland" assault guns were also hard pressed in the Dorpat area; initially there were seven StuGs from SS-Pz.Abt.11 and six StuGs from SS-Pz.Jg.Abt.11, commanded by SS-Hstuf. Schulz-Streek. But soon, no one was left: SS-Hstuf. Hans-Karl Becker was the only officer left alive. Among those killed were SS-Ustuf. Heinz Stamm, commander of 2./SS-Pz.Abt.11, and SS-Ustuf. Ernst-Richard Stübben, commander of 3./SS-Pz.Abt.11.

During the final days of August, the Walloon volunteers continued to hold their blocking positions along the Pärnu-Lombi-Keerdu line, repelling all the Soviet attacks at great sacrifice. Degrelle's men were cited three times in the order of the day of III.(germ.)SS-Pz.Korps. When the fighting was over, SS-Ogruf. Steiner awarded more than two hundred Iron Crosses to the Walloon volunteers. Léon Gillis was awarded the Knight's Cross. A few days later, what was left of the Walloon battalion was transferred to Germany.

replied, "As long as I'm alive, the Soviets won't get through." After having managed to scrape together around another forty volunteers, Degrelle organized his hundred men into two combat groups, positioning them on both sides of the road that led to Dorpat, and at the same time sent out recon patrols to determine the enemy's movements in a timely manner.

The Soviets came back to attack in force, putting the resistance of the extreme defenders of Dorpat to the test, but just at the

SS-Stubaf. Degrelle awards the Iron Cross to a wounded soldier.

An assault gun in ambush

Führer headquarters, August 27, 1944. SS-Stubaf. Léon Degrelle receiving the Oak Leaves for his Knight's Cross, directly from Adolf Hitler, in the presence of SS-Ogruf. Felix Steiner.

Waffen-SS grenadiers and destroyed "Josef Stalin" tanks, summer 1944

SS-Stubaf. *Walter Plöw*

An antitank squad with a *Panzerschreck*

Operation Aster

On September 10, 1944, SS-Obergruppenführer Felix Steiner had to report to Hitler's headquarters at Rastenburg: Hitler communicated his intention of wishing to abandon Estonia but at the same time ordered III.SS-Pz.Korps to hold a bridgehead at Reval, in order to allow evacuation of all German forces by sea. Returning to the Estonian front, Steiner met with Generaloberst Schöner, commander of Army Group North, to discuss the plans to evacuate Estonia, code-named Operation Aster. On September 16, Soviet vanguards of the 3rd Baltic Front began to break into the Dorpat isthmus, establishing favorable positions for successive attacks between Dorpat and Lake Peipus. Two days later, Soviet forces reached Mustvee, near the northwest corner of Lake Peipus. The men of SS-Pz. Aufkl.Abt.11 had to take action to cover the withdrawal of III. (germ.)SS-Pz.Korps from the Tannenbergstellung. The SS units began to withdraw to Latvia in the night between September 18 and 19, heading toward Pernau (Pärnu), on the northern coast of the Gulf of Riga, under the protection of II.Armee-

SS-Pz.Aufkl.Abt.11 half-tracks on the move

Korps. Everything went according to plan: the "Norge" and "Danmark" regiments withdrew without problem, and the next day the motor convoys reached Wesenberg, where there was a large warehouse full of supplies. The SS soldiers took whatever they could before blowing it up. The Germanic volunteers were engaged in defense of the capital of Latvia, Reval, and the port of Pernau. Thanks to the sacrifices of the European volunteers, German ships were able to evacuate more than 80,000 men from Reval in a few days, before the city fell into Soviet hands. The following day, Pernau also fell after having been defended for three days by Kampfgruppe Bunse, consisting of I./"de

Ruyter" and other elements of the Nederland. Soon after, the "Nordland" recon battalion and Kampfgruppe Bunse withdrew to the south, with "Nordland" blocking the road to the Bay of Pärnu east of Moiseküll, and the *Kampfgruppe* engaged in the Wolmar area. On September 24, Kampfgruppe Petersen (II./"de Ruyter") assumed positions along the river Lemmer south of Pärnu, blocking the coast road to the south. On the morning of September 25, the Dutch volunteers of Kampfgruppe Petersen were strung out along the coastal road on the border between Estonia and Latvia. Once Reval had fallen, other German units also retreated to the south along the coast.

While units of III.(germ.)SS-Pz.Korps were withdrawing to the south, those of XXVIII and L.Armee-Korps continued to defend the Walk-Wolmar line, suffering heavy losses during bitter fighting. In particular, 21. Infanterie-Division was overrun and reduced to a small *Kampfgruppe*. SS-Flak-Abteilung 11 was attached to the *Kampfgruppe* of 21.Infanterie-Division, being engaged in tough defensive fighting. When the fighting was over, the division commander, Generalmajor Heinrich Goetz, recommended the German Cross in Gold for SS-Ostubaf. Plöw, commander of SS-Flak-Abteilung 11, and SS-Ostuf. Rolf Holzboog,[3] commander of 4./SS-Flak-Abt.11.

Clashes in the Baldone Area

Stalled along the road to Riga, the Soviets shifted their attacks more to the west, toward the city of Doblen (Dobele), about 60 kilometers southwest of Riga. The units of III.SS-Pz.Korps were to reach the Tukums area, the next fulcrum of defense on the Latvian front. Since September 22, the bulk of the "Nordland" units had entrenched in the great pine forests north of Kekava, southeast of Riga. The "Norge" regiment in particular had been grouped in the area between Dekmeri and Katlapji, while the division's few armored vehicles had been concentrated in the Senbegi area. I./SS-Art.Rgt.11 took up positions north of Tici. The "Danmark" regiment was subordinated to 14.Panzer-Division, commanded by Generalmajor Oskar Munzel, who had been ordered to eject the Soviets from the city of Baldone, on the river Kekava. The "Danmark" commander, SS-Ostubaf. Krügel, moved his command post to the village of Celmini, from where he could better follow the development of operations. The attack was made the next day, employing the II./24 (under SS-Hstuf. Ternedde) and the III./24 (under SS-Hstuf. Bergfeld).[4] The Soviets were initially forced back,

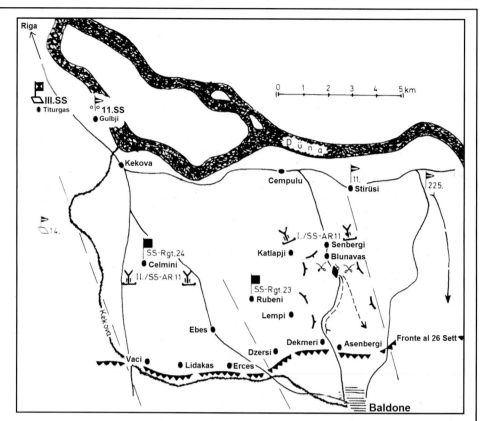
Combat in the area north of Baldone, September 23–26, 1944

Waffen-SS defensive position on the Latvian front, 1944

German grenadiers and Soviet tanks destroyed at close range, 1944

German defensive position with an MG42 machine gun on the Latvian front, 1944

SS grenadier and a destroyed tank

Column of German army PzKpfw.IV Ausf.H tanks, 1944

Crew of a Waffen-SS 75 mm antitank gun loading their gun to face a Soviet tank attack

and cut off from other friendly forces. The officers requested artillery support via radio, and soon thereafter the German guns began to hit enemy positions on the southern bank of the Kekava. The Soviets responded quickly with their own artillery, mortars, and Katyusha rocket launchers.

Losses began to mount horrifically for both sides. Around 1330, the enemy counterattack was somehow stemmed. The order was then given to resume the attack, sending tanks from 14.Panzer-Division forward, followed by the "Danmark" grenadiers. But once again, the momentum of the German units was stalled near the Kekava River by massive enemy barrage fire. Soon after, the Soviets counterattacked, setting off new and furious fighting that did not decrease in intensity until the afternoon, when both parties settled down to a tacit truce to catch their breath and gather the many wounded. The "Danmark" had taken heavy losses; the regiment's two battalions had lost around three hundred men killed, wounded, or missing. SS-Ostubaf. Krügel ordered his men to return to their earlier positions and to assume a defensive posture against any further enemy attacks between Vaci and Erkes. In the afternoon of September 23, the "Norge" regiment was involved in an attack against Baldone, moving from the Dekmeri-Katlapji line, while the division's armored units attacked from the north. The village of Blunavas fell quickly into the hands of the SS grenadiers, but their progress was halted soon after by a counterattack made by strong Soviet tank forces with infantry following them. For the first time, "Nordland" grenadiers faced Sherman tanks, furnished to the Soviets by the Western Allies. The 75 mm antitank guns had to be brought into play to stop the enemy steel monsters. Furious fighting ensued that involved the SS units; among the first to fall to enemy fire was Norwegian SS-Ostuf. Thomas Peter Sandborg, commander of 11./"Norge," hit by a burst of enemy fire while he was leading his men in an attack. The attack continued on September 24, with the SS grenadiers able to gain some ground. SS-Uscha. Petrat of 10./"Norge" was able to destroy a Stalin tank with a *Panzerfaust* at close range. Other Soviet tanks were knocked out the same way. SS-Ostuf. Dirks,[5] commander of 10./"Norge," was badly wounded, while one of his platoon leaders, SS-Hscha. Stolz, was killed. Soviet resistance intensified, and the SS grenadiers were again forced to assume defensive positions. On September 25, after having reorganized and still under constant Soviet artillery and mortar fire, the "Norge" regiment grenadiers resumed their attack and around evening were deployed along the Dekmeri-Asenbergi line, localities situated 2 kilometers north of Baldone.

thanks in part to supporting fire by German artillery and attacks by dive-bombers, which eliminated most of the enemy firing positions. Soon after, Likidas fell into SS hands. However, when those same units approached the Kekava River, they came under massive barrage fire from the Soviets, who had set up numerous antitank positions and many machine gun nests. The grenadiers of 6. and 11./"Danmark" were forced to take shelter in the woods. The arrival of tanks and assault guns from 14.Panzer-Division served little; because of the difficult terrain, the vehicles could not maneuver properly. The Soviets counterattacked soon after with infantry and tanks; hundreds and hundreds of Soviet infantrymen popped up from everywhere, forcing the Danish grenadiers to fall back. The groups that stayed behind to fight were soon surrounded

A soldier armed with a *Panzerschreck*

An MG42 preparing to fire

The Knight's Cross for Martin Gürz

On September 26, the front was stable along the Vaci-Erkes line (SS-Pz.Gren.Rgt.24 "Danmark") and the Dekmeri-Asenbergi line (SS-Pz.Gren.Rgt.23 "Norge"). To the east, contact had been made with 225.Infanterie-Division and elements of 11.Infanterie-Division. During the day, the Soviets had been able to break through in the III./"Norge" sector. The battalion commander, SS-Hstuf. Gürz, counterattacked with all available men, falling at their head. The counterattack by Gürz was supported by 12./"Norge," led by SS-Ostuf. Ahlf.[6] On the basis of a proposal by SS-Ostubaf. Fritz Knöchlein, SS-Hstuf. Gürz was recommended to be posthumously awarded the Knight's Cross, which was officially conferred on October 23, 1944. Following is the text of the proposal: "During the offensive battles southeast of Riga between September 23 and 27, 1944, the regiment was ordered to eliminate the Soviet vanguards (consisting of infantry and tank formations) that had broken into the German lines, cutting them off from the rear area, and to close the gap that they had created in the front line. SS-Hauptsturmführer Gürz and his battalion had to bear the brunt of that offensive action. Because the attack had been interrupted by a strong enemy armored counterattack, Gürz moved forward to personally lead his men in the attack. Thanks to his example, the attack resumed, the breach was eliminated, and the front line was restored. The action and exemplary courage of SS-Hauptsturmführer Gürz were determining in obtaining this victory, thanks to which the threat to Riga was finally eliminated. SS-Hauptsturmführer Gürz died as a hero the day after the attack (on 09.26.1944)."

New Clashes in the Tukums Area

During the night of September 26, the "Danmark" regiment was relieved by an army unit. The Norge abandoned its positions the following day. Due to the pressure of the German counterattack, the Soviets were forced to suspend their attack against Riga and shifted their efforts farther to the west. Because of this, the withdrawal of the Heeresgruppe Nord forces through Riga and Tukums was able to be carried out safely. But in the meantime, the Soviets had assembled numerous forces to make new attacks

SS-Stubaf. Martin Gürz

against the area north of Doblen. SS-Brigadeführer Joachim Ziegler, the "Nordland" commander, was ordered to carry out the withdrawal to the south to intercept the farthest point of the Soviet forces that had advanced toward the sea. On September 28, 1944, both the "Norge" and "Danmark" regiments, along with reconstituted elements of the "Nederland" brigade (after the return of elements of Kampfgruppe Wagner), went on to occupy defensive positions prepared by the Latvian and German

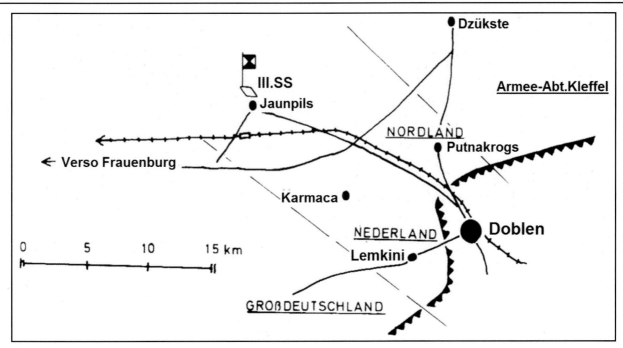

The new front at Doblen, September 28–October 12, 1944

labor companies, north of Doblen. The Soviets began to hit the positions held by the Germanic volunteers with artillery beginning on September 30; this was followed by infantry attacks that were repulsed by the Germanic units. Between October 5 and 6, the III.SS-Pz.Korps units were ordered to move to the Autz sector. The "Nordland" headquarters was ordered to form a *Kampfgruppe* to send as soon as possible to the north of Moscheiken, where numerous Soviet forces had concentrated; the combat group, designated as Sperrgruppe (blocking group) Schäfer, named after its commander, SS-Ostubaf. Max Schäfer,[7] consisted of both of the engineer battalions of the "Nordland" and "Nederland,"

the "Nordland" recon group, the III.SS-Pz.Korps security company, and a group of three artillery batteries from "Nederland." These forces assumed positions in the Moscheiken area, between two Wehrmacht infantry divisions; the defensive line ran along the Vadakalis River, south of the hamlet of Roubas. On October 10, the Soviets attacked on the flanks in the sectors held by Wehrmacht units, overrunning them. The Soviet armored vanguards rapidly got behind the units of Kampfgruppe Schäfer; the grenadiers fell back to escape the enemy's grasp, covered by Dutch supporting artillery fire (I./SS-Art.Rgt.54) and by the armored vehicles of the "Nordland" reconnaissance group.

Waffen-SS artillery on the Baltic Front, 1944. *Michael Cremin*

CHAPTER IX
THE KURLAND FRONT

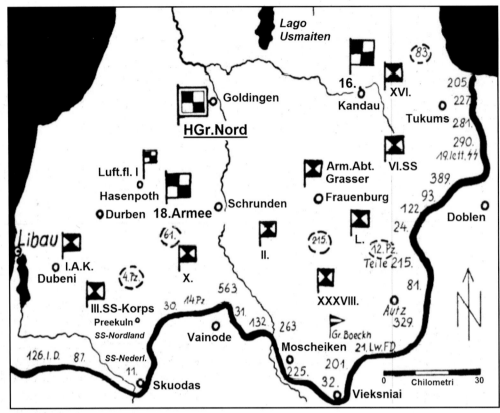

Deployment of German forces in Kurland, October 1944

Waffen-SS grenadiers

In early October 1944, the German forces of Army Group North flowed back from Estonia to the Kurland Peninsula, the last German stronghold in the Baltic region. Felix Steiner's III.SS-Pz. Korps followed the general retreat, leaving the Riga area and deploying along a new defensive line between the villages of Skoudas to the south and Preekuln to the north. During the withdrawal, the Germanic volunteers acted as rearguards, continuing to fight against enemy formations. The VI.SS-Freiwilligen-Armee-Korps (lettisches), led by SS-Ogruf. Walter Krüger, had retired to the Kurland Peninsula. VI.SS-Freiwilligen-Armee-Korps consisted of 15.Waffen-Grenadier-Division der SS (lettische Nr.1) and the 19.Waffen-Grenadier-Division der SS (lettische Nr.2). In reality, the 15.SS had been detached from the corps in late August 1944, having been decimated in earlier fighting, and its complete reorganization was begun in East Prussia. The corps thus had only one division and several attached army units. Krüger and his men fought in the eastern Kurland area. Around mid-October, German forces in Kurland had their backs to the sea, closed in on the peninsula and surrounded by the Soviets; the only way to safety lay in evacuation by sea. In order to prevent that, the Soviets unleashed their attacks toward Libau, the last port still usable by the Kriegsmarine in Kurland. Generaloberst Schörner, commander of Army Group North, had proposed evacuation of all the troops in the pocket toward East Prussia, but Hitler ordered resistance to the last man—Kurland was to be defended at all costs.

A Soviet tank knocked out in front of German positions

The units of the "Nordland" division and the "Nederland" brigade assumed positions in the southern sector of the Kurland front. The "Nederland" and "Nordland" units took positions in the 18.Armee sector, between 11.Infanterie-Division (I.Armee-Korps) and 30.Infanterie-Division (X.Armee-Korps). On October 15, 1944, the units of III.SS-Pz.Korps were deployed as follows, from north to south: II. and III./"Norge" were deployed on two small hills along the Preekuln-Vainode railway line, and II. and III./"Danmark" were east and west of the village of Trekni. The two remaining battalions of the "Nederland" brigade were at the far end of this defensive line, which terminated to the north

A Waffen-SS position in Kurland; note the hulks of several destroyed Soviet tanks in the background.

SS-Hstuf. Richard Spörle

SS-Hscha. Siegfried Lüngen

with units of 30.Inf.Div. and, to the south, with those of 11.Inf.Div. The II./"de Ruyter" was deployed east of Annenhof along the railway line, and I./"de Ruyter" along the Preekuln-Skudas railway line as far as Ozoli. Kampfgruppe Aigner, led by SS-Hstuf. Anton Aigner,[1] consisting of the rest of the units of the "Nederland" plus other German units, took up positions between Ozoli and Flossen. The corps headquarters installed itself in Goldnieki, that of the "Nordland" at Maki and that of the "Nederland" in a group of houses southeast of Susten.

Early Battles

On October 16, the Soviets launched their first attack at the juncture point between the 30.Inf.Div. and "Nordland" positions; in order to plug the breach, the II./"Norge" grenadiers, under SS-Hstuf. Spörle,[2] along with elements of 4.Pz.Div., had to be brought into action and were able to intercept and drive back a Soviet tank attack at Audari. The next day, Soviet artillery took those positions under fire, causing all contact between the SS grenadiers and the army infantrymen to be cut. SS-Hstuf. Spörle had his command post on a hill north of the railway line. Farther north, where the SS units were to maintain contact with the 30.Inf.Div. infantrymen, 7.Kp./"Norge" came under attack from three sides and risked being wiped out. Farther south, 5.Kp./"Norge" was also on the verge of being overrun; after having lost their commander in the fighting, the grenadiers were continuing to fight like furious devils, led by their NCOs. Along the entire front the Soviet vanguards had managed to make several breakthroughs; the outposts and first-line trenches had been lost, and only a few survivors, all more or less badly wounded, were able to make it back to friendly lines. The division headquarters ordered a counterattack to retake the lost ground. One of these was led by SS-Hscha. Siegfried Lüngen, temporarily in command of 6.Kp./"Norge." With only eight grenadiers but with the support of two assault guns, Lüngen was able to reach the positions held by 7.Kp./"Norge," and after fierce hand-to-hand fighting the Soviets were driven back. A few hours later the enemy returned and threw fresh troops against the "Nordland" positions, and, after having made a new breakthrough, the enemy vanguard got as far as the II./"Norge" command post. SS-Hstuf. Spörle called together all the available men, including the signals and administrative personnel of his staff. They scraped up some machine guns and a pair of assault guns, with the aim of retaking the lost positions and restoring contact with the other units on the left with army units and on the right with their comrades of III./"Norge," under SS-Hstuf. Hoffmann, who were deployed on the other side of the railway line to the south and who were also engaged in tough defensive fighting, especially in the area around a hill called Pferdekopf (horse head), held by the grenadiers of 10.Kompanie.

Spörle's counterattack achieved an unexpected success: the Soviets were forced to withdraw, and contact was restored between the two battalions of the "Norge." For that action, Spörle was recommended for the Knight's Cross, which was officially awarded him on November 16, 1944. SS-Hscha. Siegfried Lüngen was awarded the Knight's Cross on the same date.

Two assault guns in combat in Kurland, autumn 1944

SS-Hstuf. Hoffmann

The Soviets renewed their attack against the same positions, first hitting them with artillery fire. New fighting ensued, still against the Pferdekopf, whose northern edge was captured by the Soviets. Leading the last survivors of 10./"Norge" was a simple sergeant, SS-Uscha. Diedrichs. In sheer desperation, these survivors made a final counterattack against the advancing enemy, and after furious hand-to-hand fighting the summit of the hill was again in the hands of the SS grenadiers. The "Nederland" units were, for their part, involved in reinforcing the III./Pz.Korps southern front: I./"de Ruyter" marched to the area northeast of the Tirs-Purvs swamps, then headed east. II./"de Ruyter," starting from the east, was able to make contact with the other Dutch battalion, trapping several enemy units and capturing many heavy weapons. With the help of elements from 11. and 87.Inf.Div., the Soviet forces were pushed back after two days of incessant combat. Farther south, the sector held by the "Danmark" grenadiers was under enemy attack; along the road that led from Gramsden to Purmsati and marked the boundary between II.Bataillon (under SS-Hstuf. Bergfeld) to the north and SS-Hstuf. Rudolf Ternedde's III.Bataillon to the south, the Soviets had gotten as far as the village of Trekni, where heavy fighting was going on. The 11. Kp./"Danmark" grenadiers were falling back, leaving a dangerous open gap, and to close it the regimental assault rifle platoon, led by SS-Uscha. Schwabenberg, was sent in as reinforcement. Once they had reached their positions but before encountering any enemy infantry, Schwabenberg's men came under heavy Soviet artillery bombardment and took numerous casualties in just a few minutes. The surviving group, consisting of three NCOs and twenty-five other ranks, was able to join up with the 11. Kp./"Danmark" grenadiers, led by SS-Hscha. Albrecht. The sight of the reinforcements raised the morale of Albrecht's grenadiers, who had been completely worn out by the fighting of the preceding days. Ammunition and rations were short, but Albrecht somehow found the strength to incite his men to hold out. The Soviets attacked again, putting the resistance of the Germanic volunteers to the test; with no radio communications, red flares were fired into the air, hoping that someone in the rear might understand this as a request for help. SS-Hstuf. Ternedde brought the II./SS-Art.Rgt. artillery into play to halt the enemy attack, and division headquarters sent a few armored vehicles from 3./SS-Aufkl.Abt.11, under SS-Ostuf. Gösta Pehrsson,[3] as reinforcements.

SS-Rottenfüher armed with a Soviet PPSh-41

A German artillery position with a 150 mm howitzer, autumn 1944

SS-Hstuf. Rudolf Ternedde

The First Battle of Kurland

On October 27, 1944, which began with heavy artillery fire, the first battle of Kurland began. The III./Pz.Korps positions were shelled by thousands of Soviet guns, followed a few hours later by an infantry attack supported by tanks, first investing the positions of the "Norge" volunteers and then those of the "Danmark"; tough fighting flared up everywhere, with heavy losses on both sides. In the sector held by the "Norge" grenadiers, the Soviets were able to infiltrate and cut contact between the regiment's two battalions. SS-Hstuf. Hoffmann's III./"Norge" pulled back to the north, while II./"Norge," under SS-Hstuf. Spörle, withdrew to the west. The Soviets continued to advance along the railway line toward Preekuln. Farther north, contact between "Nordland" units and those of 30.Inf.Div. was lost. The breach opened by the Soviets was expanding as one watched, threatening to overrun all the III./Pz.Korps' southern flank. SS-Ostubaf. Knöchlein had moved his command post to a position fairly far away from the line of fire, southeast of Preekuln, from where it was impossible to follow the withdrawal of his units. When he realized the gravity of the situation, he asked for reinforcements, and division headquarters sent 4./SS-Aufkl.Abt.11, under SS-Ostuf. Schirmer. "Find what is left of the 'Norge' regiment and help the grenadiers restore a defensive front," Knöchlein ordered Schirmer. Accordingly, the "Nordland" half-tracks moved out to find the Norge grenadiers in the Adami area and, after having clashed with several enemy formations, made contact with the remnants of III./"Norge" and began to form a new defensive line. At the same time, 3./SS-Aufkl. Abt.11, under the Swede Pehrsson, was sent to the aid of the II./Norge grenadiers. Between October 28 and 30, the Soviets continued to attack, achieving some local successes; the two "Nordland" recon companies continued to be engaged in the hotspots of the front, inflicting very heavy casualties on the enemy.

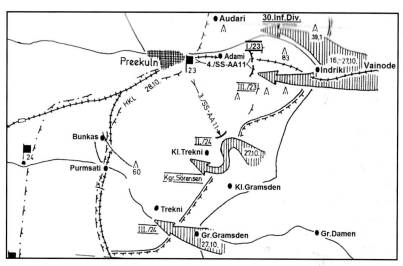

Area involved in fighting in October 1944

German soldiers in a trench, warding off the enemy

Left, soldiers manning a mortar on board an SS-Pz.Aufkl.Abt.11 half-track and, *right*, SS-Hstuf. Hans-Gösta Pehrsson next to a 3./SS-Aufkl.Abt.11 Schwimmwagen

During the final days of October, the "Danmark" companies also continued to be severely stressed in fending off continuous enemy attacks in the Purmsati area. Of the regiment's two battalions, the more hard pressed was certainly the II./"Danmark," led by SS-Hstuf. Bergfeld; his 6.Kompanie had been almost completely wiped out, while 5. and 8.Kp. were short of men. The companies of III./"Danmark," under SS-Hstuf. Ternedde, were also in difficulty, with the grenadiers of 9. and 10.Kp. withdrawing along the road that ran from Gramsden to Purmsati. Only 11./"Danmark," still led by SS-Hscha. Albrecht, remained in place near Trekni, reinforced by the assault riflemen of SS-Uscha. Schwabenberg. Not far from them, the regimental antitank platoon under SS-Uscha. Illum had taken up positions, engaged in halting the Soviet tank columns. The "Danmark" commander, SS-Ostubaf. Krügel, had set up his command post on a hill indicated on military maps as Hill 38.3. Via radio, the commander continued to repeat to his unit commanders, "We have to hold out. Reinforcements are on the way." One of the most fortified points on the "Danmark" defensive line was on another hill, designated as Hill 28.3, where a combat group under Danish SS-Hstuf. Per Sörensen had taken up positions. 5.Kompanie had taken up positions northwest of the hill; 8.Kompanie, with its guns and mortars, to the north; and 6. and 7.Kp. were between Trusi and Ergli. The new Soviet attack was concentrated against Hill 28.3: the regimental headquarters sent a radio message: "Hill 28.3 must be held at all costs." The II.Abteilung batteries of the "Nordland" artillery regiment were right behind that position. Commander Krügel sent two Sturmgeschütz as reinforcements.

Due to their numerical superiority, the Soviets forced the "Danmark" grenadiers to abandon the hill, but then, thanks to fire support furnished by the two German assault guns, it was possible to make a counterattack and push back the enemy.

On October 28, the Soviets resumed their attacks against the hills with larger forces, and this time the two assault guns could cover the retreat only of the "Danmark" grenadiers, who set up a new defensive line along the Preekuln-Skoudas railway line. Among the numerous losses that day was SS-Stubaf. Witten,[4] the

Waffen-SS mortar squad in Kurland, 1944

divisions-adjutant. Shortly after that, the Soviets occupied the Purmsati railway station, but the village remained in the hands of the Germanic volunteers, thanks to support by divisional artillery; for their excellent action during this fighting, both the commander of SS-Artillerie Regiment 11, SS-Ostubaf. Friedrich Karl, and the III.Abteilung commander, SS-Stubaf. Hermann Potschka,[5] were recommended for the Knight's Cross. Both officers were officially awarded the decoration on December 26, 1944.

Following is an extract from the proposal for the award of the Ritterkreuz for SS-Ostubaf. Karl: "On October 16, 1944, while the left flank of 14.Panzer-Division was overwhelmed by the weight of the Soviet attack, SS-Ostubaf. Karl made the decision to go personally to the battlefield and to establish a blocking fire with the artillery of 14.Panzer-Division that were still in position. Demonstrating cold-bloodedness and exceptional courage, he was able to inflict heavy losses on the attackers, thus allowing the armored grenadiers to counterattack and to retake their previous positions."

SS-Ostubaf. Friedrich Karl

SS-Ostuf. Per Sörensen

In the following days, the defensive line held by "Nordland" units was pulled back again, south and southeast of Preekuln. On October 30, stalled at Purmsati, the Soviets attacked farther north, managing to open a gap in the division's thin defensive line. The few panzers available were thrown into a counterattack and were able to stop the enemy advance. On October 31, the Soviets made a final attack, this time aimed at the school at Purmsati, but were once again driven back. Several days of quiet followed. The divisional command took advantage of it to use the lightly wounded and convalescents to try to flesh out the frontline units. A group of seventy-five members of medical personnel from the III.SS-Pz. Korps field hospital were incorporated into 3.Kp. / SS-Btl. Z.b.V. "Nordland," the division's special-task battalion.

In early November, the personnel of the "Nordland's" armored battalion left the front lines and embarked without their tanks at the port of Liepaja (Libau) for Gotenhafen. The unit later assembled in the Landeck area south of Danzig. Then, in January 1945, the members of the unit were sent to the Grafenwöhr training area to be reequipped, and where the unit was to be transformed into a new armored regiment. In the end, only the first battalion was formed, commanded by SS-Hstuf. Grathwohl.

The Second Battle

With the onset of the autumn season and the first heavy rains, the whole front was transformed into an immense bog, slowing down the movement of the units. Nonetheless, after a number of days of calm, on November 12 the second battle of Kurland began, and this time the Soviets attacked in the Purmasti area, in the center of the positions held by "Nordland" units, with numerous infantry forces supported by tanks. In their trenches,

A German defensive position, 1944

the European volunteers replied with weapons of all calibers, inflicting heavy losses on the enemy. The Soviets, not at all impressed by that immense slaughter, continued to mount attack after attack, without sparing either men or machines. On November 24, 1944, another Soviet attack developed south of Purmasti against the positions held by the grenadiers of III./"Danmark," who managed to fend off the enemy forces thanks in part to fire support provided by SS-Vielfachwerfer-Bttr.521. With the worsening of weather conditions, the front stabilized for some weeks, during which the Waffen-SS Germanic volunteers were kept busy mainly in reinforcing their defensive positions.

In early December 1944, with the onset of cold weather, the mud began to harden, allowing the Soviets to resume their attacks. The enemy tanks thus supported the attacks by their infantry, putting to the test the German tank killers, who were armed mainly with *Panzerfäuste* and *Panzerschrecken*. Wherever the actions of the Panzerjäger became impossible, German artillery saw to it to repel the Soviet tank attacks. Despite their great superiority in men and vehicles, the Soviets continued to register only minor successes and remained stalled along the main line of resistance.

The Third Battle

On December 21, 1944, the day of the winter solstice, the Soviets launched a massive new offensive, which passed into history as the third battle of Kurland. The Soviet objective continued to be the port of Libau. Four armies totaling twenty Soviet divisions attacked the German positions on both banks of the river Venta, toward Skundra and Saldus, in an attempt to split the 18.Armee from the 16.Armee. Despite the enormous forces and numbers of vehicles employed, the Soviets were repulsed and their conquests were minimal. During the third battle of Kurland, the III.SS-Pz.Korps sector was relatively calm. The unit commanders took advantage of that to reorganize their units.

Each company was in turn retired from the front line so that the men could rest in the Paplaken forest. The one "Nordland" unit that was most engaged was the recon battalion, involved in making offensive thrusts in the Purmsati area. Fighting did not resume until January 8, 1945, in the Purmsati area. The next day, several "Nordland" recon patrols spotted enemy troop concentrations in Trekni, and the men of 8./"Danmark," now commanded by SS-Hstuf. Birkedahl-Hansen, were committed to eliminate them. The "Danmark" regiment's heavy companies also provided fire support with mortars, machine guns, infantry, and flak guns, as did the divisional artillery's batteries. The Soviets quickly responded with fire from their artillery, after which a strange calm settled over the entire front. Patrols were sent out to try to determine the enemy's intentions but were unable to capture any prisoners to obtain any intelligence. Soviet artillery once again shelled the Purmsati sector on January 20. SS-Brigdf. Ziegler put all units on alert in anticipation of a massive new Soviet offensive.

The Fourth Battle

The fourth battle of Kurland began on January 23, 1945, with massive Soviet artillery fire against the German positions. Then, eleven Red Army divisions attacked on both sides of Preekuln, with the aim of reaching Libau. This time the weight of the attack fell upon positions held by 30.Inf.Div. and III.(germ.) SS-Pz.Korps. Naturally, the positions of the "Nederland" brigade were also subjected to heavy bombardment. 18.Armee headquarters sent all available reserves, including 14.Panzer-Division. The "Nordland" positions in the area north of Purmsati were particularly hard hit, held by the "Danmark" grenadiers, where an enemy armored formation numbering about forty tanks attacked the German positions between Pauseri, Waldhof, and Klabji, pulverizing everything that lay in its path. The infantry followed in trucks, eliminating the last pockets of resistance. Those "Danmark" grenadiers who had miraculously survived

A SS-Vielfachwerfer-Bttr.521 half-track, 1944

A grenadier armed with a *Panzerfaust*, autumn 1944

German defensive position with an MG34, December 1944

Crew of a 20 mm Flak 38 preparing to fight

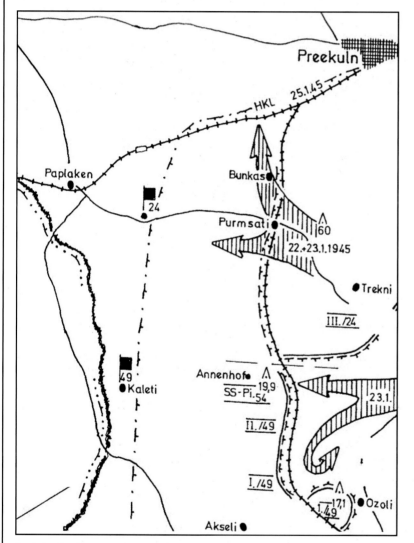

Soviet attacks, January 1945

A group of German soldiers in a defensive position

the deluge of enemy artillery fire courageously faced off against the enemy, and about ten enemy tanks were destroyed in front of the 6./"Danmark" positions at Bunkas, north of Purmsati. Farther north, 7.Kp. and 11. Kp./"Danmark" were busy stopping Soviet tanks and infantry that were trying to reach the Purmsati-Paplaken road, but strong enemy pressure finally forced the SS grenadiers to fall back to avoid being completely wiped out. Among those killed during the latest fighting was the 9.Kp./"Danmark" commander, SS-Ostuf. Knud Maagaard-Hansen, originally from Odense. The main line of resistance was shifted to the north of Purmsati; the "Nordland" artillery batteries fired as fast and as heavily as they could in an attempt to slow down the Soviet advance as much as possible. Other enemy attacks were blocked in the forest west of Bumeistari by fire from the heavy weapons of 13./"Danmark." SS-Hstuf. Sörensen and SS-Hstuf. Lärum rapidly formed a new line of resistance with the survivors of their battalions, while II./"Norge" made an immediate counterattack in the "Danmark" defense sector. The Soviets were repulsed, but losses were heavy: of 6./"Norge," under SS-Ustuf. Spahn,[6] only three men returned; of 7./"Norge," only SS-Ustuf. Madsen and fourteen men were left. 8./"Norge" had four killed and thirty wounded.

In the night between January 23 and 24, some elements of 14.Pz.Div. reached the Purmsati area as reinforcements and at dawn on January 4 were hastily thrown into an attack, wresting the ruins of Purmsati from the Soviets. The reinforcement battalion, SS-Bataillon z.b.V. "Nordland," led by SS-Stubaf. Franz Lang, was assigned to defend it.

On January 25, the Soviets resumed their attack in an attempt to regain the lost ground, but without success. The fighting shifted mainly to the "Nederland's" defensive sector, against two points that had to be defended at all costs: the Gross Gramsden-Kaleti road with the Annenhof heights and south of Ozoli Hill, which were obligatory points for any progress toward the coast and Libau. The fourth battle of Kurland ended on January 27, 1945, with a new defensive success on the part of the Germans.

During the battle on the Kurland front, SS-Flak-Abteilung 11 was attached to VI.SS-Armee-Korps, alongside 19.Waffen-Grenadier-Division der SS (lett. Nr.2), particularly distinguishing itself against Soviet tanks north of Frauenberg. The battalion returned to the "Nordland" during its transfer to Pomerania.

Retreat from Kurland

At the end of January, the German general staff decided to withdraw the German divisions from the Preekuln sector to "Wartaga-Stellung" to establish a new defensive line. Meanwhile, it had been decided to transfer III.SS-Pz. Korps to Pomerania to be attached to the new Army Group Vistula (Heeresgruppe Weichsel), under command of Heinrich Himmler. Felix Steiner was to assume command of 11.SS-Panzerarmee, while Generalleutnant Martin Unrein, former commander of 14.Pz.Div., was assigned to command III.SS-Pz.Korps. The retreat of the SS corps to Pomerania was followed by 32.Inf.Div., by 215.Inf.

Div., and by elements of 11.Inf.Div. and 14.Pz.Div. During the night of January 28, the last elements of III.SS-Pz. Korps. were relieved from their positions to be moved to the Sutas sector, where they found the units of their logistics train. From there, the units of the "Nordland" reached Liepaja, from where they embarked to Stettin, on board the following ships:

Traute Faulbaum: II./"Danmark"
Hernid Visor VII: III./"Danmark"
Malgache: SS-Pz.Gren.Rgt.23 "Norge"
Fährschiff Deutschland: SS-NA 11, SS-Pi.Btl.11
Karin von Bornhofen: Div.-Stab, SS-Pz.AA 11

The final convoys left Liepaja on January 30. SS-Stubaf. Bergfeld and SS-Ostuf. Sporn (Ib/III.SS-Pz.Korps) had left Kurland a few days earlier to organize the rebuilding of the units under OKH responsibility.

Waffen-SS 80 mm mortar ready to fire

A group of German grenadiers on the Kurland front, 1945

Generalleutnant Martin Unrein

Members of 2./SS-Pz.Aufkl.Abt.11 on board a ship during the move to Pomerania, 1945

CHAPTER X
THE POMERANIAN FRONT

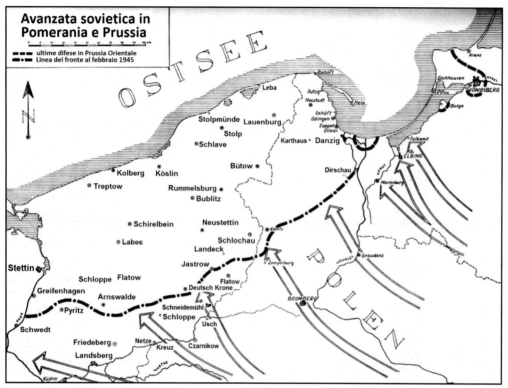

The Soviet offensive in Pomerania and Prussia, January–February 1945

Heinrich Himmler

In late January 1945, III.SS-Pz.Korps was transferred to Pomerania, where the military situation had become extremely critical for the German armed forces. The 1st and 2nd Byelorussian Fronts had overrun the German forces on Poland and had made it as far as the Oder, directly threatening Berlin. In their rapid advance, the Soviets had left all of the northern part of East Prussia and a large part of Pomerania in the hands of 3.Panzer-Armee and 2.Armee. This offered the OKH the ability to threaten their right flank, which was completely open. With a general counteroffensive, the Germans could try to push the Soviet armies from the sacred territory of the Reich. To that end, on January 23, 1945, by Hitler's order a new Army Group was formed under Heinrich Himmler, who surely had no great experience of competence as a military commander. The Reichsführer-SS was thus ordered to regroup all German forces between the Vistula and the Oder to form a new defensive front along the Warthe-Netze line. On January 24, Himmler established his headquarters at Deutsch-Krone. Gradually, all available German units in Pomerania were attached to Heeresgruppe Weichsel.

Employment of III.SS-Pz.Korps Units

Major Karl Schulz-Streek

In late January, while the sea convoys were sailing toward Pomerania, the III.SS-Pz.Korps depot units were grouped together at Hammerstein: these units included the SS-Offizier-Ausbildungs-Gruppe "Scheibe," the SS-Unterführer-Lehr-Bataillon "Hämel," and SS-Frw. Pz.Gren.Rgt.48. All these units together formed Kampfgruppe Scheibe, which was attached to the Korps Tettau, commanded by Generalleutnant Hans von Tettau. At the end of January, SS-Pz.Jäg.Abt.11 was also added. Commanded by SS-Stubaf. Karl Schulz-Streek, the unit had been reconstituted and reequipped with new assault guns at Neuhammer and had been engaged against the northern flank of the 1st Byelorussian Front in the Aranswalde-Pyritz area and, on February 3, 1945, had been able to stall the enemy advance at Hassendorf. Between the river Oder and Lake Madü was Korps Hörnlein (General de Infanterie Walter Hörnlein), to which 4.SS-Polizei-Panzergrenadier-Division was attached. This division,

General der Panzertruppen Decker

Generalmajor Hans Voigt

German grenadiers and assault gun on the Pomeranian front, 1945

An assault gun attacking an enemy position, 1945

being transferred from the Balkans, soon joined the 10.SS-Panzer-Division "Frundsberg" and with it formed XXXIX.Panzer-Korps, under General der Panzertruppen Karl Decker at Stargard. In the same area were the Panzer-Brigade-Munzel and elements of 28.SS-Freiwilligen-Panzergrenadier-Division "Wallonien," engaged in facing the Soviets who were advancing on Stettin.

In the Arnswalde sector, around three thousand men of the Nebelwerfer battery reserve units had been surrounded in the city, under Generalmajor Hans Voigt. To the north, III. SS-Pz.Korps units were moving toward it. Fallschirmjäger-Regiment 25 was at Neuwedell, led by Major Gerhard Schacht, defending the city. East of Neuwedell was the 402.Inf.Div., of Generalmajor Schleinitz.

On February 4, Soviet forces reached the river Ihna in the area southwest of Zachan. That same day, schwere SS-Pz.Abt.503,[1] led by SS-Stubaf. Fritz Herzig, reequipped with the new King Tiger tanks (PzKpfw VI Ausf. B Königstiger), arrived at Arnswalde, going to Generalmajor Hans Voigt's defensive front. Also arriving as reinforcement was the SS-Begleitbataillon, the Reichsführer-SS escort battalion, under SS-Stubaf. Heinz-Dieter Gross. The Soviets continued to advance on both sides of Arnswalde. Panzer Abteilung "Hermann von Salza" finally arrived, which thanks to its new tanks had been transformed into a regiment, still led by SS-Ostubaf. Kausch. The "Hermann von Salza" had originally been equipped with Panther tanks, and after having lost all of its tanks in combat during the summer of 1944, it was reequipped with StuG III Ausf G assault guns and some Panthers. The tanks were loaded aboard trains and moved eastward. Offloading the vehicles at Stettin went rapidly and without incident on February 5. At Stettin, the unit mustered thirty assault guns and thirty Panzer Vs, which moved off toward the area north of Arnswalde. On February 6, fifteen assault guns of SS-Pz.Rgt.11 "HvS," under SS-Ostubaf. Kausch, advanced toward Arnswalde from the north, supporting SS-Begleit-Bataillon "Gross" in the recapture of Schönwerder. In the evening, Gruppe Kausch moved toward Reetz.

In the meantime, the Soviets had already taken Petrznick, Schlagenthin, Pammin, and Stolzenfelde. SS-Begleit-Bataillon "Gross" was recalled to Arnswalde, around its defensive ring. At Nantikow, elements of Kampfgruppe Schulz-Streek were surrounded by Soviet forces, while the bulk of the combat group was engaged south of Reetz. Farther east, Fallschirmjäger-Regiment Schacht and elements of 402.Inf.Div. were trying to hold their positions in the Neuwedell area. During the day of February 6, elements of 28.SS-Frw.Pz.Gren.Div. "Wallonien" reached Stargard and assumed positions along the Scheidersfelde-Kremzow-Repplin line. Still farther east were two battalions of 27.SS-Frw. Gren.Div. "Langemarck." The German main line of resistance was established along the course of the river Ihna. On February 7, elements of SS-Pz.Jg.Abt.11 who had been surrounded at Nantikow managed to open an escape route and rejoin the rest of the unit on the new defensive line.

Meanwhile, the first III.SS-Pz.Korps units had begun to arrive from Pomerania; as they reached Stettin piecemeal, the SS units were quickly moved farther south. The "Nederland" units were sent to Gollnow, while the bulk of the "Nordland" headed for Massow, where SS-Brigdf. Ziegler set up his headquarters. While it had been decided to upgrade the "Nederland" brigade into a new SS division, the 23.SS-Frw. Pz.Gr.Rgt. "Nederland," surviving elements of the "de Ruyter" regiment, veterans of Kurland, were transferred to Ravenstein, where a *Kampfgruppe* was formed under the leadership of SS-Ostubaf. Hanns Heinrich Lohmann, consisting of the "de Ruyter" headquarters, the I./"de Ruyter," the II./"Norge," a motorcycle company, an army antitank unit, and a police detachment. At the same time, a Dutch artillery battery was transferred to the SS-Polizei division, while the rest of the batteries were displaced to positions at Fürstensee, Draumburg, and Neu Weden. Kampfgruppe Lohmann was attached to the Führer-Begleit-Division (under Generalmajor Otto Ernst Remer). The engineers and some of the artillery of the "Nederland" division were immediately committed to the front line.

The Battle for Reetz

Between February 6 and 7, hard fighting flared up northeast of the city of Reetz (now Recz), following the appearance of several strong Soviet vanguards. Gross Silber was recaptured by units of the Führer-Begleit-Division. However, the Soviets counterattacked in force soon after, retaking the position. On February 7, the Soviets broke into Reetz, an important road hub for all the surrounding area, whose defense had been entrusted to Kampfgruppe Lohmann. In that same sector, because of operational exigencies dictated by the deteriorating military situation, a new combat group was formed, Kampfgruppe Schäfer, commanded by the commander of the III.SS-Pz.Korps engineers, consisting of the "Nordland" engineer battalion and other surviving units of the "Nederland." The next day, the battalions of the "de Ruyter" were sent to reinforce the defenses around Reetz. Meanwhile, east of the city a breach had been

Walloon volunteers just arriving in Stargard, picking up individual weapons and some Panzerfäuste, before going to the front line, February 1945

Other Waffen-SS troops just arriving in a Pomeranian village aboard trucks, early February 1945

Waffen-SS grenadiers in a defensive position, February 1945

SS-Stubaf. Hanns Heinrich Lohmann

SS-Staf. Max Schäfer

opened through which enemy forces were moving to the north. SS-Pz.Jäg.Abt.11 was sent in an attempt to block them; on the outskirts of Reetz, the "Nordland" assault guns were thus able to temporarily stall the enemy columns who had been caught by surprise along the road to the city. The Soviets threw in fresh tank formations, setting off ferocious clashes; SS-Stubaf. Schulz-Streek's own StuG was hit, and he was wounded seriously in the face. Despite his wounds and his damaged assault gun, Schulz-Streek led a new attack against the enemy tanks, knocking out a number of them. In the fury of the fighting, his assault gun was hit again by a round fired by a T-34 at close range. His men managed to pull him from the smoking wreck in time and to transport him to the hospital in Stargard. Meanwhile, other units were arriving from Kurland: SS-Flak-Abteilung 11 reached Jakobshagen. The II./"Norge" was transferred to Altenwedell. On February 8, SS-Ostubaf. Kausch ordered a counterattack in the area between Ziegenhagen and Klein Silber to eliminate some Soviet armored vanguards; engaged in the action were a Tiger II of 1./s.SS-Pz.Abt.503, two from 2./s.SS-Pz.Abt.503, a dozen assault guns from SS-Pz.Rgt.11, and about ten from SS-Panzerjäger-Abteilung 11, along with a Fallschirmjäger company as accompanying infantry. During the clashes that ensued, the Soviets lost three JS-2 tanks and numerous antitank guns. The German armored units took up defensive positions south of Klein Silber, toward Reetz. On February 9, new fighting flared up in the area northeast of Reetz. Gross Silber was retaken by the Führer-Begleit-Division around 1500. But in the evening, the Soviets counterattacked and reoccupied it. The Soviets continued to attack the next day as well, making new penetrations in the area between Arnswalde and Reetz.

The ring around Arswalde continued to tighten, and the positions at Hohenwalde, Schulzendorf, and Kähnsfelde were lost. On February 12, the Soviets called upon Generalmajor Voigt to surrender, but he refused to give up. Reinforcement of the garrison was made by air. That same day, in Zieganhagen, SS-Hstuf. Rudolf Rott, commander of 1./SS-Pz.Abt.11, was killed in combat. In the days that followed, the Soviets reached the city's suburbs and seized the Arnswalde railway station.

An assault gun, February 1945

SS-Stubaf. Herzig

Arnswalde. King Tiger of SS-Ustuf. Karl Bromann, damaged during the clashes around the city, in front of the cathedral.

One of the first models of the Tiger II during field trials

A Waffen-SS grenadier launching a grenade with his Mauser rifle, using an adapter

CHAPTER XI
OPERATION SONNENWENDE

Pyritz, February 11, 1945. Elements of 4.SS-Polilziei-Panzergrenadier-Division arrive in Pomerania.

With the restoration of contact between Stettin and East Prussia around mid-February, German headquarters was able to have substantial reinforcements sent to the Pomeranian front. A new large offensive was planned to try to free the encircled city of Arnswalde, in the context of Operation Sonnenwende (Operation Solstice). The general objective was, however, to try to hold back the Soviets as far as possible from the borders of the Reich with a counteroffensive all along the northern flank of the enemy's attack front. In the beginning, this counteroffensive was to be made in concert with 6.Panzerarmee, which, from the Guben-Crossen area, was to advance northward and make contact with the troops under SS-Ogruf. Steiner on the Warta at Landsberg and thus eliminate the vanguard of the 1st Byelorussian Front. It was an overly ambitious plan for the Germans at this point in the war. Hitler finally sent 6.Panzerarmee to Hungary, and Operation Sonnenwende was able to be launched with only the scant forces available to Steiner. These consisted of the units that had been withdrawn from Kurland (III. SS-Pz.Korps), some from the Western Front (10.SS-Panzerdivision "Frundsberg"), and some from the Balkan front (4.SS-Polizei-Panzergrenadier-Division).

A group of army grenadiers, 1945

SS-Obergruppenführer Felix Steiner

A group of grenadiers from an army unit

Grenadiers aboard a StuG.III during an attack

The rest was completed with divisions constituted at the last minute, badly trained, badly equipped, and incomplete, such as the "Bärwalde" and "Köslin" divisions. The 11.SS-Panzerarmee was in reality a reinforced army corps. The goal of the offensive was thus revised: after having freed the Arnswalde garrison, it would be necessary to advance to Landsberg and the river Warta, then move against the advancing Soviet forces under Marshal Zhukov while at the same time establishing a defensive front in Pomerania to impede a direct assault on Berlin. The offensive was to be led by SS-Ogruf. Felix Steiner, now commanding 11.SS-Panzerarmee;[1] its start date was fixed as February 16. 11.SS-Panzerarmee was subordinated to Heeresgruppe Weichsel, commanded by Heinrich Himmler.

The Forces in the Field

Around mid-February, 11.SS-Panzerarmee deployed its three corps (XXXIX.Pz.Korps, III.SS-Pz.Korps, and X.SS-AK) along the line Fiddichow (on the Oder)–Pyritz–Lake Mädu–Zachan area north of Reetz–Mark Frieland forest–area south of Neustettin. From west to east were the following units:

4.SS-Polizei-Panzergrenadierdivision
10.SS-Panzerdivision "Frundsberg"

11.SS-Panzerdivision "Nordland"
23.SS-Panzerdivision "Nederland"
SS-Kampfgruppe "Langemarck"
281.Infanterie-Division
Führer-Begleit-Division
Führer-Grenadier-Division
402.Infanterie-Division
5.Jäger-Division
Infanterie-Division "Bärwalde"
Infanterie-Division "Köslin"

Three *Schwerpunkt* (focal points) were organized for the attack, which was to extend over a front of about 100 kilometers:

- a *Westgruppe* between Lake Mädu and Stargard under the command of XXXIX.Panzer-Korps, which consisted of the Pz.Div. "Holstein," the 10.SS. "Frundsberg," the 4.SS-Polizei-Gr.Div., and the 28.SS "Wallonien"
- a *Mittlergruppe* in the Zachan-Jakobshagen area under the command of III.SS-Pz.Korps, which consisted of the Führer-Begleit-Division, the 11.SS "Nordland," the 23.SS "Nederland," and the 27.SS "Langemarck"
- an *Ostgruppe* from Nörenberg under Generalmajor Munzel, with Panzer-Jäger-Brigade 104, the Führer-Grenadier-Division, the 281.Inf.Div., and the 163.Inf.Div.

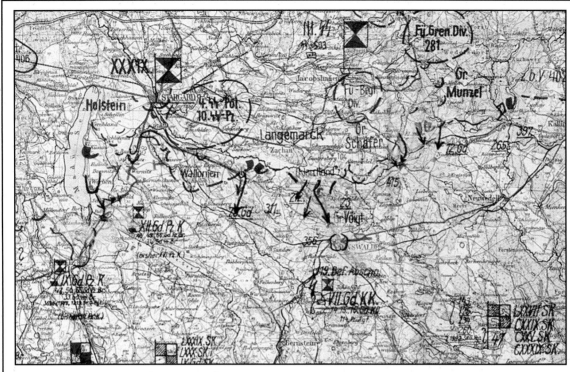

Deployment of opposing forces on February 15, 1945

SS-Hstuf. Per Sörensen

Preliminary Actions

Before the offensive kicked off, the "Nordland" units were involved in the capture of positions that would be more favorable for the advance, and to that end, II./"Danmark" under SS-Stubaf. Sörensen, after having passed through the "Langemarck" positions at Zachan, crossed the river Ihna near Fährzoll, establishing an early solid bridgehead on the eastern bank. The engineers quickly went to work reinforcing a wooden bridge in order to allow motor vehicles to cross. At the same time, elements of the "Nordland" panzer regiment, the divisional SPW battalion, the 3Kp./SS-Pz.Jäg.Abt.11, and the "Klösel" platoon of 1.Kp./SS-Pz.Jäg.Abt.11 crossed through Reichenbach and headed toward Marienberg, making contact with the units that had contact with the besieged garrison at Arnswalde.

II./"Danmark" and III./"Norge" were also sent to Reichenbach. As soon as SS-Stubaf. Sörensen reached the area, he prepared his grenadiers for an attack: on the left he deployed the 6.Kp., and on the right the 7.Kp., while 5.Kp. was kept in reserve. 8.Kp. was to support the attack with fire from its heavy machine guns and mortars. Divisional artillery was also to support the attack by the grenadiers. Several tanks, armored cars from the recon group, and assault guns from 3Kp./SS-Pz.Jäg.Abt.11 also arrived shortly thereafter, along with an antitank platoon.

The Danish Stubaf. placed himself at the head of his men, leading the attack, and right behind him were Ustuf. Rasmussen, Ustuf. Stipeprnitz, and Uscha. Scholles. The SS grenadiers rapidly reached the eastern outskirts of the village, preceded by artillery fire and the passage of the panzers. The attack continued in order to give the enemy no respite: 7.Kp., on the right, was to capture Hochberg; 6.Kp., in the center, was to seize Hohenfriedberg; and 5.Kp., on the right, was to

Waffen-SS troops moving to attack Arnswalde

Hetzer tank destroyers in combat in the Kallies area

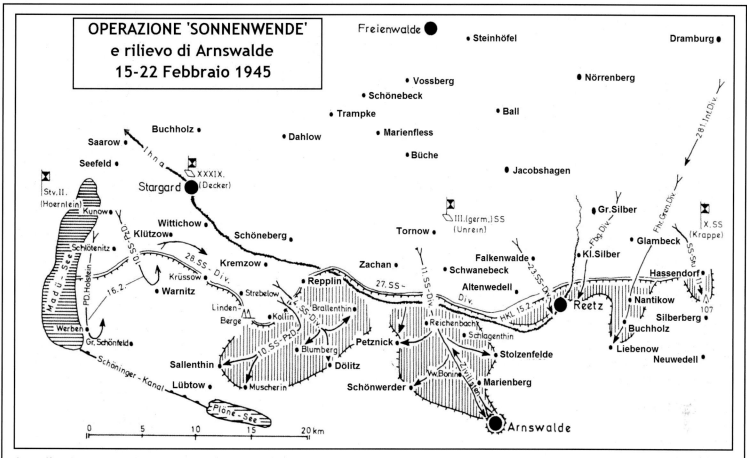

Operation Sonnenwende
and the relief of Arnswalde
February 15–22, 1945

Waffen-SS grenadiers and half-tracks in an attack, 1945

aim at Bonin. The companies moved out at 1300 and after about an hour reported via radio: "Objective reached. Little enemy resistance." On February 15, units of the "Nordland" division were able to create a narrow corridor to Arnswalde, allowing the evacuation of the mass of refugees still present within the city.

The Offensive Begins

On February 16, the offensive itself began, and Himmler personally made a thunderous proclamation to the troops, which ended with the words "Forward! Forward through the mud. Forward through the snow. Forward during the day. Forward during the night. Forward to free the ground of the Reich." The German units had to advance under a freezing rain and, in the mud, to reach their departure positions. Due to a lack of ammunition, the preparatory artillery fire was practically nonexistent. The three army corps advanced along the Stargard-Reetz-Kallies line. General Decker's XXXIX.Pz.Korps, with the "Polizei" and "Frundsberg," was able to make rapid progress to the south: those units were still solid and very determined. At the center of the deployment, the "Nordland" and the other III.SS-Pz.Korps forces ran into serious difficulty against a well-organized Soviet defense.

Pomerania, February 1945: Waffen-SS soldiers and a "Nordland" division StuG.III seeking to halt the Soviet offensive against the northern territory of the Reich. *Cremin*

SS-Hstuf. Spörle's II./"Norge" had not been able to occupy the village of Schlagenthin, just as the "Danmark" units had not been able to advance past Reichenbach. The Flemish volunteers of "Langemarck" had also been stalled in front of the Soviet positions at Petznick; Kampfgruppe "Langemarck," with its two battalions, faced an entire Soviet division along the Petznick-Schlagenthin line. After having been able to capture Gut Marienfelde, north of Arnswalde, after furious and bitter fighting, the Flemish volunteers were unable to make any further progress against strong enemy resistance. The "Nederland" units had been repulsed in front of Reetz: the 1./"de Ruyter" attacked along the Ravenstein-Reetz road, supported by SS-Pz.Jäg.Abt.54 under SS-Hstuf. Aigner, but the attack was stopped by massive Soviet barrage fire north of the city. The II./"de Ruyter" arrived as reinforcement to support the I./"de Ruyter" attempt to capture the city from the Altenwedell area and thus to break into the Soviet defenses. While the Dutch units were crossing the Ihna, the Soviets attacked with tanks, blocking the II./"de Ruyter" attack at the outset.

The major counteroffensive had thus been transformed into a new defensive battle. In an attempt to at least seize Reetz, the tanks of Pz.Rgt. "Hermann von Salza" were thrown into the battle, but when the panzers got close to the city, they also came under enemy fire and were forced to withdraw.

German grenadiers fighting on the outskirts of a village in Pomerania where several Soviet tanks have been destroyed

SS grenadiers advancing through the ruins of a destroyed farm during fighting in Pomerania. *MNZS*

A Stug.III loaded with grenadiers moving in Pomerania

Attack against Arnswalde

Throughout the day of February 17, the "Nordland" grenadiers sought to expand the gap that had been opened toward Arnswalde: after fierce hand-to-hand combat, the "Norge" volunteers were able to capture Schlagenthin but by now did not have enough forces to advance any farther. SS-Hstuf. Ternedde's III./"Danmark," supported by three assault guns and several armored cars from the Führer-Begleit-Division, was to advance to Bonin, while the recon group's other assault guns and armored cars were to support the attack by Sörensen's II./"Danmark" against Schönwerder. Ternedde's grenadiers managed to take Bonin, but the Flemish volunteers who were supposed to cover their flank were themselves pushed back in front of Marienfeld. Ternedde then decided to attack the village with his men, while at the same time, SS-Stubaf. Sörensen and II./"Danmark" attacked the village of Schönwerder; as soon as they reached the outskirts of the village, they came under enemy fire that forced them to withdraw, and it was thanks only to the intervention of the three supporting assault guns that it was possible to continue the attack. However, when the StuGs tried to enter the village, they ran into enemy mines. Having lost the armored support, the "Danmark" grenadiers lost all hope of dislodging the Soviets from their positions. SS-Ostubaf. Krügel reached the position to order Sörensen to make yet another effort: Ustuf. Leo Madsen[2] and his 7.Kompanie threw themselves into a furious assault against the center of the village, followed by other grenadiers of 5. and 6.Kp. on trucks.

A group of assault guns fighting on the Pomeranian front, February 1945

The house-to-house fighting lasted late into the night, when the Soviets finally abandoned the village. Farther east, the comrades of Ternedde's battalion had been able to reach the railway line that led to Arnswalde, where they had dug into defensive positions. At the same time, contact had been made with the German units that were surrounded in Marienberg, and despite the enemy encirclement, six "Nordland" panzers were able to break into Arnswalde, joining the besieged troops and opening a corridor about 2 miles long into the city. Farther west, the Flemish volunteers of "Langemarck" continued to fight tenaciously in an attempt to reclaim Petznick. At Schwanbeck, Ustuf. Fernand Laporte's Flemish company (7./SS-Frw.Rgt. 66) was engaged in a desperate counterattack to recapture the village. On February 18, while the evacuation of Arnswalde was put into motion under the protection of SS-Pz. Rgt.11 tanks, SS-Stubaf. Schulz-Streek's assault guns managed to push as far as the hills south of Hassendorf, setting off one of the most furious tank battles on the Pomeranian front, during which seventeen Soviet T-34s were knocked out on Hill 107 at Hassendorf and another three were captured intact. But meanwhile, the Soviets continued to attack and amass troops behind the Arnswalde-Stargard railway line and were able to break through the German lines at Gut Marienfelde. On February 19, Operation Solstice could be considered to have failed. The Reetz-Hassendorf sector had to be evacuated even though the "Danmark" regiment had almost managed to capture Schönwerder.

The same day, a Soviets were driven back at Friedrichsruh, 3 kilometers northeast of Arnswalde. The 3rd Platoon of 1.Kp./SS-Pz.Jäg.Abt.11 destroyed two KV-Is, one T-34, and one Josef Stalin tank. Between February 19 and 20, enemy pressure against the "Norge" and "Danmark" regiments intensified, with massive Soviet artillery fire. Enemy attacks on both sides of Schönwerder were repulsed by fire from the "Danmark's" heavy weapons. On February 21, III.SS-Pz.Korps and "Nordland" withdrew across the river Ihna. The last elements of the Arnswalde garrison left the city around 1900 under protection of PanzerKampfgruppe "Gross." The southern flank of the retreat was covered by II. and III./"Danmark."

Dead Soviet soldiers and destroyed tanks after the hard fighting on the Pomeranian front, February 1945

A Hetzer tank destroyer followed by a Panzer II in Pomerania, 1945

A German defensive position on the Pomeranian front, February 1945

Waffen-SS grenadiers on the march in Pomerania. *MNZS*

Several King Tigers in combat, March 1945

The Soviet Counteroffensive

After having withdrawn to the north, III.SS-Pz.Korps had to regroup its remaining forces to defend Stargard and Stettin. Accordingly, on February 24, the "Danmark" regiment was sent to the south of Stargard; III./"Danmark" assumed positions on the western flank, between Streesen and Langen Bergen, and II./"Danmark" of Streesen, along the Faule Ihna (an affluent of the Ihna), where the right wing of the Wallonien division was deployed. The "Norge" regiment took positions on the Ihna at Altenwedell, west of Reetz, while SS-Stubaf. Schulz-Streek's *Kampfgruppe* remained dug in on the Hassendorf hills. The SS troops were able to take advantage of a few days' rest to catch their breath before the Soviets kicked off their grand counteroffensive on February 28, with the goal of securing their northern flank before making a final assault on Berlin.

From the early-morning hours, the III./"Danmark" positions were heavily shelled by Soviet artillery between the Ihna and Lake Mädu. II./SS-Art.Rgt.11, emplaced in the Warnitz-Krüssow sector, attempted to respond to enemy fire. On March 1, Soviet artillery fire intensified against all the III.SS-Pz.Korps positions. Soon after, Soviet infantry and tanks attacked en masse: Kampfgruppe "Langemarck," the Walloon units, and those of the "Nederland" were forced to withdraw to avoid being wiped out. German defenses concentrated around Stargard to avoid the collapse of the entire front. Withdrawal of the various units took place in a climate of great confusion, with the Soviets appearing to be everywhere. During the night between March 1 and 2, the "Danmark" units were grouped together at Klützow, thence to proceed to Stargard. From there, SS-Stubaf. Sörensen's II./"Danmark" was ordered to reach Freienwalde to support the Nederland, while III./"Danmark" was sent to Dahlow. At dawn on

March 2, Soviet advanced tank elements reached the Stargard-Freienwalde road but were stopped by a hasty counterattack made by the "Nordland" tanks and assault guns along with the remaining Tigers of SS-Pz.Abt. 503. Sörensen's II./"Danmark" grenadiers at Freienwalde had to face several enemy attacks supported by tanks, managing to hold the position at great sacrifice; the SS grenadiers had initially taken up positions in the northwest corner of the city. 6./"Danmark" was south of and 7./"Danmark" was north of the road that led to Steinhöfel-Noblin. Before the companies were able to get into position, Soviet tanks attacked. SS-Stubaf. Sörensen ordered a withdrawal toward the city's outskirts, where the companies were able to fend off the enemy. The 1st Platoon of 6./"Danmark" was unable to withdraw in time; with Lake Gross Starlitz at his back, SS-Oscha. Pösch and his platoon fought desperately with machine pistols and hand grenades against Soviet tanks, opening a gap near the lake's southern shore. In the end, only SS-Oscha. Pösch and four grenadiers reached the southern part of Freienwalde: five of his men had been captured, and all the rest were killed in the fighting. In their new positions on the outskirts of Freienwalde, the II./"Danmark" grenadiers continued to repel Soviet attacks on February 3. Other hard fighting developed east of Stargard, where the remnants of the Wallonien were entrenched south of the city in the villages of Klützow and Wittichow.

A New Defensive Front

Strong Soviet pressure convinced III.SS-Pz.Korps headquarters to order Stargard to be abandoned, ordering the formation of a new defensive line that ran from Lake Mädu to Massow (now Maszewo). On March 4, the II./"Danmark" grenadiers abandoned Freienwalde and fell back to Massow. SS-Pz.Rgt.11 and SS-Pz. Aufkl.Abt. 11 mounted counterattacks while small groups of grenadiers from the "Danmark" and "Norge" regiments sought to stop the Soviet advance. The Soviets bypassed the German defenses from the north: stalled by a *Kampfgruppe* from the "Frundsberg" at Neuendorf, they shifted their attacks toward Speck, on the road to Gollnow, nearing the coast of the Baltic Sea. Meanwhile, the III./"Danmark" grenadiers had been able

Grenadiers and assault guns in a defensive position

to establish new defensive positions around the village of Mülkenthin, but in the face of continuous Soviet attacks and with reduced manning, SS-Stubaf. Ternedde's grenadiers finally had to fall back. During March 6, after having driven off several enemy attacks, the two battalions of the "Norge," led by their commander, SS-Ostubaf. Knöchlein, pulled back to the village of Wachlin, in the same area in which the Soviets were amassing large tank forces. The SS soldiers soon came under massive Soviet barrage fire, then coming under tank and infantry attack. The "Nordland" engineers came in as reinforcements, and thanks also to fire from heavy machine guns and mortars, it was possible to stem the enemy attacks. On March 7, Massow was abandoned and the new withdrawal was covered by II./"Danmark" and Pz.Aufkl.Abt.115, under Major Wolf.[3] That same day, Gollnow also fell into Soviet hands. The "Norge" grenadiers were engaged in fighting on both sides of the Stettin highway; a new defensive line was established between Lüttenhagen (in cooperation with the Frundsberg), Hinzendorf (where the remnants of SS-Flak-Abt.11 had regrouped), and Bruchhausen.

Waffen-SS grenadiers on a recon patrol in a Pomeranian city. *MNZS*

CHAPTER XII

THE ALTDAMM BRIDGEHEAD

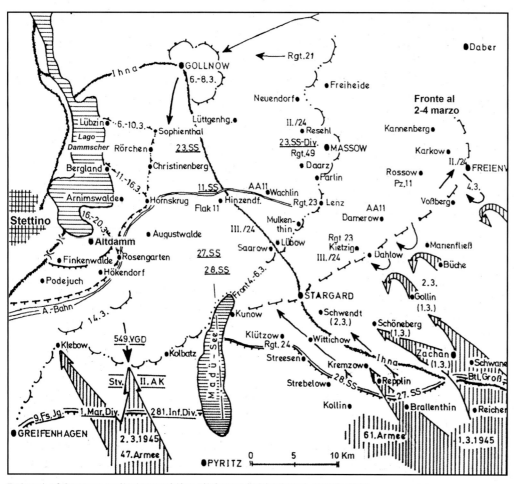

Retreat of German units toward the Altdamm bridgehead, March 1945

"Nordland" grenadiers

Between March 7 and 8, 1945, the remaining units of III. SS-PzKorps were once again forced to retreat, occupying the Altdamm bridgehead, southeast of Stettin. Defending the northern part of the bridgehead, from Lübzin to Hornskrug, were a Kriegsmarine infantry company, the II./SS-Pz.Gr.Rgt.21 of the "Frundsberg," the II./"Danmark," the Falsch.Rgt. Schacht, the remnants of Pz.Aufkl.Abt.115, and the remnants of the "Nederland." The central sector, between Hornskrug and the German autobahn, was held by the "Nordland" recon battalion and by the remnants of the "Norge" regiment. Farther south were the III./"Danmark" and elements of SS-Pi.Btl.11 and SS-Flak.Abt.11. The "Langemarck" and Wallonien units took up positions between Höckendorf and Finkenwalde. Soviet attacks against the Altdamm area began around noontime on March 8, mainly involving the positions held by II./"Danmark" and Pz.Aufkl.Abt.115, which were forced to abandon Sophintal and Rörchen. While SS-Stubaf. Sörensen had his men pull back to Friedrichsdorf, Major Schacht launched a counterattack, using his paratroopers and 5./SS-Pz.Gr. Rgt.21, managing to reoccupy the two positions that had been lost.

A 75 mm antitank gun in position

Waffen-SS grenadiers sheltering in a trench, facing an enemy attack

SS-Ustuf. Rasmussen

SS-Ustuf. Willi Hund

While the II./"Danmark" grenadiers regrouped at Friedrichsdorf, two panzers secured the road to Christinenberg and the northern part of the city. The SS companies had by now been reduced to only a few dozen men able to fight. 5./"Danmark," under SS-Hstuf. Seyb,[1] could muster thirty-one men.

The Battle for Friedrichsdorf

In the night between March 10 and 11, the units holding the Altdamm bridgehead began to withdraw to the west; the artillery regiment's batteries remained in place to provide fire support to the "Frundsberg" units that were in bloody combat north of Altdamm. The batteries of the "Nederland" artillery regiment shifted to the area south of Arnimswalde. Elements of the "Frundsberg" that were still in Lübzin and Ibenhorst followed those batteries. A new defensive line was set up between Bergland and Friedrichsdorf. The entire sector was under the command of the "Nederland" commander, SS-Brigdf. Wagner. The Soviets awaited reinforcements before attacking the new German positions; on March 11, around 0700, the Soviets broke through north and south of Friedrichsdorf. Despite everything, the II./"Danmark" grenadiers held on. However, when the Soviets reached the Friedrichsdorf-Oberhof road, their situation became particularly critical, risking being surrounded. Around 1300, the German defenses between Lake Dammscher and Arnimswalde collapsed, increasing the threat to Friedrichsdorf. Kampfgruppe Sörensen was thus forced to pull back toward Oberhof.

Of the entire battalion, there were only about twenty survivors, led by the commander of 7./"Danmark," SS-Ustuf. Josef Stippernitz, while all the other company commanders had been badly wounded in combat. The battalion adjutant, SS-Ustuf. Rasmussen,[2] assumed command of what was left of 8./"Danmark," the heavy-weapons company, which took up positions at Arnimswlde. At Hornskrug, the front continued to be held successfully by the "Nordland" recon battalion, reinforced by elements of the "Frundsberg." The remaining men of the "Norge" regiment were dug in south of Hornskrug; in particular, SS-Ostuf. Hund[3] and the remnants of 6. and 7./"Norge" were busy

A German soldier armed with a Mauser rifle

holding positions along the highway south of Hornskrug. III./"Danmark" and elements of SS-Flak-Abt.11 were engaged in blocking the Reichsstrasse 104 from Altdamm to Hohenkrug. Soon after, the main line of resistance had to be shifted farther west because of massive Soviet attacks. While SS-Flak-Abt.11 assumed positions east of Rosengarten to continue to watch over Reichsstrasse 104 and the highway with its weapons, the "Danmark" regiment assumed positions at Hammermühle and Plänebach. The regimental command post was moved to Stutthof. These new positions came under Soviet artillery fire and soon thereafter were attacked by tanks and infantry units. The 10. and 11./"Danmark" were forced to abandon their positions, which were then reoccupied after a quick counterattack. At the same time, enemy penetrations at Rosengarten forced SS-Flak-Abt.11 to pull back to Altdamm. During the night between March 14 and 15, III./"Danmark" was forced to abandon its positions and withdraw to the outskirts of Altdamm.

The situation remained fairly stable in the Bergland-Oberof-Hornskrug sector between March 12 and 15. SS-Oberscharführer Vandborg changed the positions of his mortars of 8./"Danmark" several times from Arnimswalde to Oberhof in order to provide fire support to the other companies.

New Attacks against the Bridgehead

On March 15, the Soviets renewed their attacks against the Altdamm bridgehead: III./"Danmark" found itself defending the railway station, under attack from the previous day. The Soviet infantry attacks were temporarily stalled by SS-Uscha. Kruse, platoon leader of the 11./"Danmark" headquarters platoon, who was able to create a barrier of flames by setting fire to several barrels of gasoline in an antitank ditch. In the afternoon the Soviets attacked along the Stargard-Altdamm railway line, capturing the railway station and forcing the German units to pull back toward the center of the city. A counterattack was promptly made, but without success.

On March 16, SS-Ostubaf. Krügel ordered another counterattack to try to recapture the station, leading it personally.

SS-Ostubaf. Albrecht Krügel

After having gotten about twenty men together, about a dozen 11./"Danmark" grenadiers and some engineers, the little *Kampfgruppe* threw itself against the position, immediately coming under massive enemy blocking fire just a few meters from the station; all the leading soldiers were killed, including the "Danmark" commander himself, who was hit by a splinter. SS-Ostubaf. Krügel's death was a hard blow to the morale of all the soldiers of all the German units that were fighting amid the ruins of Altdamm.[4]

The battle for Altdamm reached its apex on March 17, when a massive Soviet artillery bombardment hit the entire German defensive front. The remnants of the "Norge" regiment were forced to withdraw along the Altdamm-Gollnow railway line. SS-Ostubaf. Paetsch, commander of SS-Pz.Rgt.10, was killed after having provided support with his last panzers to units in difficulty. Because of strong enemy pressure, the "Danmark" survivors were forced to dig in in the Altdamm cemetery, where SS-Stubaf. Ternedde with around fifty men managed to hold out until March 19, when the northern part of the bridgehead began to be evacuated by German forces. The SS units began to pull back to the west in the area between Schwedt and Bad Freienwalde toward Stettin; the Walloons remained as rearguards to cover the retreat. The battle for Pomerania had come to an end.

Waffen-SS grenadiers marching after having been in tough fighting, March 1945

Chapter XIII
THE ODER FRONT

Left, Rudolf Klotz with *SS-Untersturmführer* insignia. *Center*, Wilhelm Körbel, with *SS-Obersturmführer* insignia. *Right*, two members of the Britische Freikorps, Kenneth Berry and Alfred Minchin, with the SS uniform.

In late March, the remaining III.SS-Pz.Korps units were subordinated to General Manteuffel's 3.Pz.Armee and were deployed in defensive positions along the western bank of the Oder, near Schwedt, later to be regrouped in the area between Wussow, Sommersdorf, and Wattin, southwest of Stettin. Thanks to the influx of personnel that had been found in the rear area, old Kriegsmarine and Luftwaffe personnel and stragglers from other disbanded units, the "Nordland," like other SS units, was able to be reorganized. Within "Nordland," command of the "Danmark" regiment was assumed by SS-Ostubaf Klotz,[1] and the "Norge" by SS-Ostubaf. Körbel.[2] A group of British volunteers of the Britische Freikorps[3] were also transferred to III.SS-Pz.Korps, were assigned to the "Nordland" recon group, and were engaged in building fortifications rather than serving on the front line. The "Nordland" units were sent to the area west of the Schwedt-Freienwalde line, continuing their reorganization and at the same time engaged in building defensive works. The division headquarters was set up in Alt-Künkendorf, the "Danmark" headquarters at Hohenlandin, and that of the "Norge" at Liepe. I./SS-Pz.Rgt.11, led by SS-Hstuf. Grathwol,[4] deployed near Albrechtshöhe, and II.Abteilung, under SS-Hstuf. Falke,[5] at Frauenhagen. Because of a lack of tanks, two hundred men of the tank regiment were transferred as simple infantrymen to II/SS-Pz.Gren.Rgt.24 "Danmark."

The remnants of SS-Art.Rgt.11 took up positions at Dobberizin, while the batteries of SS-Art.Rgt.54 emplaced farther northwest. The other elements of the "Nederland" also were deployed in the area northwest of Schwedt. Each of the "Nordland" grenadier companies received fifty MP44 assault rifles, twenty MG42 machine guns, four sniper rifles with scopes

Waffen-SS troops retreating, April 1945

(Gewehr 43), and eight grenade launcher rifles. The heavy companies had three 75 mm Pak 40s, three 75 mm infantry guns, eight 81 mm mortars, and twelve MG42 on tripods. It should be remembered that the reconstituted I./"Norge" and I./"Danmark" did not return to the division but, since December 1944, had been transferred to the "Wiking" division, so the two regiments of "Norge" and "Danmark" continued to consist of only two battalions each. On April 7, the "Nordland" units were moved to prepared positions in a vast area west of Schwedt. The transfer to these new positions did not end until April 9.

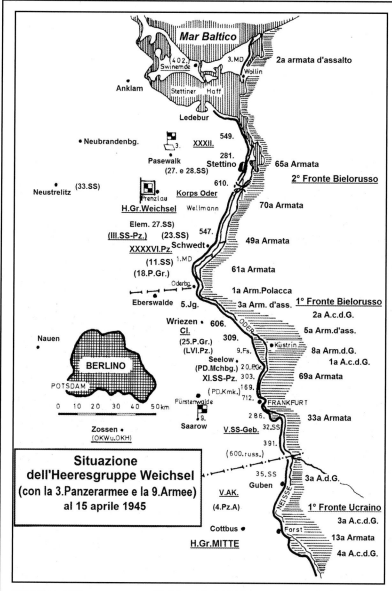

Situation of Heeresgruppe Weichsel (with 3.Panzerarmee and 9.Armee) on April 15, 1945

German soldiers in a defensive position on the Oder front

At that moment, the positions held by Heeresgruppe Weichsel, under the command of Generaloberst Heinrici, ran from the sea to the confluence of the Oder with the Neisse. 3.Panzerarmee was deployed in the Stettin area, while Busse's 9.Armee occupied the area between Küstrin and Frankfurt-am-Oder. 9.Armee was to defend Berlin with fourteen incomplete and very exhausted divisions: the other side fielded the 1st Byelorussian Front, with eighteen armies totaling seventy-seven rifle divisions, seven tank and mechanized corps, and eight artillery divisions. The Germans could field 512 tanks and 344 artillery pieces, while the Soviets had 3,155 armored vehicles (tanks and assault guns), and 16,934 artillery pieces.

The Soviets Cross the Oder

Despite Manteuffel's proclamation that was read to the German troops that were strung out along the river that "the Oder is the front, not a stop along the retreat," on April 15, 1945, the Soviets crossed the Oder, breaking into the German defenses in at least twenty places, overrunning the 9.Armee positions. The III.-SS-Pz.Korps units were placed on alarm and sent to close the gaps that had been opened in the defensive line. On April 16 the "Nordland," held as 3.Panzerarmee reserve, was also placed on alert: SS-Stubaf. Saalbach's SS-Aufkl.Abt.11 was thrown into the battle toward the south, in the Küstrin sector, along with a parachute unit and some army infantry, managing to stall the advance of a Soviet column. Following the shifting of the Soviet axis of advance, the "Nordland" units were shifted to the Seelow area west of Küstrin, where the enemy attacks were concentrating; the "Danmark" set up its headquarters at Hohenlandin along with elements of II.Bataillon, while the rest of the battalion assumed positions at Niederlandin, and III./"Danmark" at Flemsdorf. The "Nederland" units were engaged in different areas: while General Seyffardt moved to the south, the "de Ruyter," attached to 547.Volks-Gr.Div., remained in its positions in Garow and Garz, along with I./SS-Art.Rgt. 54. During the night of April 16–17, orders were received by III.SS-Pz.Korps to urgently regroup in the area between Strausberg and Eberswalde, because the Soviets were attacking with superior forces between Küstrin and Frankfurt-am-Oder. The "Danmark" regiment in particular was ordered to regroup in the forests east of Strausberg; SS-Stubaf. Ternedde displaced the III./"Danmark" companies into some woods west of Hermesdorf, while farther south, the two battalions of the Norge deployed west of Dahmsdorf. Farther north, holding the sector, was a battalion of about five hundred youngsters of the Hitler Youth. SS-Pz.Aufkl. Abt.11 was involved in supporting the companies of 9. Fallschirmjäger-Division during their retreat to the west.

The SS scouts occupied new blocking positions northwest of Seelow; elements of 3./SS-Pz.Aufkl.Abt.11, along with army personnel, repulsed a Soviet infantry attack. Soon after, the Soviets attacked with tanks; the SS recon troopers were ordered to withdraw to a forest farther west. The mortars of 3./SS-Pz.Aufkl.Abt.11 also followed the withdrawal. Three men, however, remained in position, armed with *Panzerfäuste*. When Soviet tanks got to within about 30 meters, they popped up from their shelters and faced the

German grenadiers digging a trench on the Oder front

1.Marine-Inf.Div. position

enemy: the three tanks were hit and knocked out. Soon after, another two tanks were destroyed. Thus, three unknown Waffen-SS soldiers destroyed five enemy tanks within a few minutes, temporarily halting the Soviet advance.

On April 18, after having overrun the first defensive line, the Soviets invested the "Nordland" positions, preceded by a heavy-artillery bombardment, followed by a tank and infantry attack. The position held by the "Hitlerjugend" youngsters was quickly overrun, as was that of the "Norge" grenadiers, which wavered under the blows of the enemy armored masses, pulling back as far as the village of Strausberg. During the fighting, SS-Hstuf. Richard Spörle, the III./"Norge" commander, was killed. The III./"Danmark" grenadiers were able to hold their positions until nighttime, when, under the protection of Oscha. Illum's 16.Kp. engineers, they withdrew to Garzau. The "Danmark" units were then regrouped in the village of Hohenstein, but not all the companies were able to reach their assigned positions in time, especially those of Sörensen's II./"Danmark."

SS-Brigdf. Ziegler, the "Nordland" commander, set up his command post near the Strausberg airfield. A few hundred meters farther east was the "Danmark" command post, which at dawn on April 20 was attacked by an enemy armored formation: SS-Ostubaf. Klotz and SS-Stubaf. Ternedde decided to join their men, who were entrenched about 100 meters farther east. They hopped aboard a vehicle and advanced to a depression; as soon as they left it, they were hit by a round from an enemy tank. SS-Ostubaf. Klotz and three radiomen were killed; SS-Stubaf. Ternedde was wounded and SS-Ustuf. Gräf lost a leg. Only the driver came out unharmed. With Klotz dead, SS-Stubaf. Per Sörensen took command of "Danmark." Throughout the day of the twentieth, the Soviets incessantly attacked the Nordland positions, putting the SS grenadiers severely to the test. The fighting was centered mainly between Gielsdorf, held by Kampfgruppe Sörensen, and Strausberg, where the Soviet attacks were concentrating. At the same time, Saalbach's recon battalion continued to support the 9.Fallsch.Div. paratroopers, who were slowly falling back toward the area northwest of Seelow. While the "Nordland" grenadiers continued to doggedly hold their positions, the Soviets were able to pass south and north of Strausberg, once again

A Waffen-SS grenadier with a *Panzerfaust*

A German antitank squad armed with Panzerfäuste, April 1945

German grenadiers in a village supported by a Hetzer tank destroyer

A *Flakvierling* on the Oder, 1945

A German grenadier with a *Panzerfaust*

SS-Stubaf. Rudolf Ternedde

forcing the SS troops to withdraw in order to avoid being surrounded. The "Norge" was ordered to move to Alt-Landsberg, while "Danmark" had to pull back to Bucholz. The division headquarters moved to Mahlsdorf, where SS-Stubaf. Ternedde also went after having recovered from his wounds. Some Soviet tanks broke into Mahlsdorf soon after; after having scraped together some men and a few *Panzerfäuste*, Ternedde went on the hunt for the Soviet tanks. After having spotted them, two were knocked out and another two put to flight. Before any more enemy tanks arrived, the "Nordland" command post was moved again, to the suburbs of Friedrichshagen, a few kilometers from the autobahn that encircled Berlin.

Toward Berlin

During the night of April 20–21, 1945, SS-Brigdf. Ziegler became aware that the Soviets had managed to penetrate the area east of Neuhagen, and he was requested to quickly send forces to close the breach. To that end, 16.(Pi.)./"Danmark" was sent along with the regiment's assault platoon, some half-tracks, and two assault guns. Along the way, the German column was intercepted by an enemy armored force consisting of four T-34 tanks: the enemy tanks were engaged by the assault guns, and at the end of the engagement, two T-34s had been knocked out. Meanwhile, Soviet forces were drawing ever closer to the capital of the Reich, and after Zhukov's offensive, Busse's 9.Armee was by now in chaos. General Weidling's LVI.Pz.Korps was sent to support XI.SS-Armeekorps, which, after having held its positions for a few days, withdrew to the west, ending its flight in the Halbe pocket. On April 21, Armeegruppe Steiner,[6] north of the Finow Canal, was ordered by Hitler himself to make contact with the LVI.Pz.Korps forces, to which the "Nordland" was officially subordinate. On the morning of April 22, the "Nordland" units were still in the hamlet of Mahlsdorf, west of Berlin. The Soviet columns continued to flow north and south of the capital, overwhelming the last German pockets of resistance. The "Nordland" units were completely cut off and had no contact with each other. SS-Brigdf. Ziegler, knowing that Berlin would be the last stop for his division, decided on his own initiative to move the division's service personnel in the capital to the Tiergarten, the Berlin zoo. Meanwhile, the units continued to be involved in defensive fighting around Mahlssdorf and along Reichstrasse 1, the highway that led to Berlin. Before withdrawing to the capital, the "Nordland" units were regrouped at Karlshorst, including the II. and III./"Norge," the III./"Danmark," the 8./"Danmark," the recon battalion with a few half-tracks, the flak group, and the engineer battalion. Missing were the surviving elements of the artillery regiment and the antitank battalion, and the remaining tanks of the panzer regiment. The other elements of the II./"Danmark" were not able to return to the regiment, and it is supposed that from Hohenlandin they moved to Berlin or to the west, joining Armeegruppe Steiner. Most of the men who reached Karlshorst were on foot and without any heavy weapons. Only the flak crews had managed to drag their 88 mm guns behind them and in fact were quickly sent to Adlershof to intercept an enemy armored column. Meanwhile, LVI.Panzer-Korps gave the order to move to Berlin: "The 'Nordland,' as corps rearguard, has to hold the bridges over the Spree from Treptower Prk to Adlershof." Ziegler then moved his command post to Neukölln, a Berlin neighborhood, south of the city center.

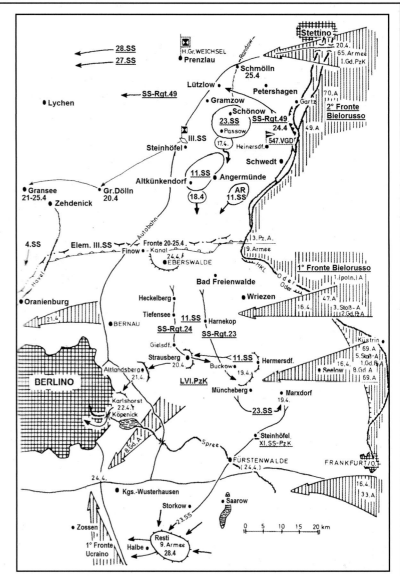

Employment of 11.SS and 23.SS with 9.Armee (April 16–28, 1945)

An assault gun in combat on the Oder front

Chapter XIV
BERLIN, THE FINAL BATTLE

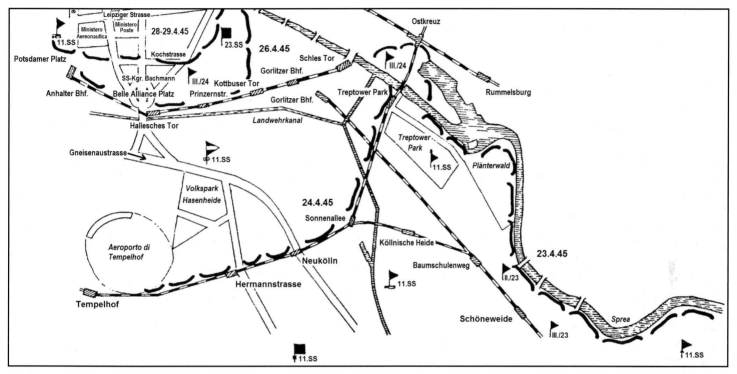

Employment of "Nordland" units in Berlin between April 23 and 29, 1945

A trench on the outskirts of Berlin, April 1945

At dawn on April 23, the "Nordland" division commander, SS-Brigdf. Ziegler, moved his command post to Neukölln, in the southeast part of Berlin, not far from Tempelhof airfield. The "Nordland" grenadiers had been ordered to hold the bridges over the river Spree, from Treptower to the Adlershof neighborhood; the Waffen-SS soldiers took up positions on the western bank of the river, awaiting the arrival of the Soviet vanguards, who were completing their encircling movement around the city from the south. One after another, the bridges over the river fell into enemy hands, despite strenuous resistance by the defenders. Some positions were held to the last man. The last pieces of the "Nordland" artillery, emplaced in the Britz quarter, in the southern part of Berlin, continued to fire until they had used all their ammunition.

SS-Stubaf. Sörensen had taken positions along the Spree with the remnants of "Danmark" in the Niederschönweide area, and a little farther away was SS-Ostubaf. Körbel with the remnants of the "Norge." Contact between the various units had broken down, and the units fought isolated from each other and abandoned to their fates, no longer receiving ammunition, resupply, and, above all, orders. In the Treptower Park area, the Soviets had been able to drive a wedge, breaking through between the "Norge" and "Danmark" positions; the "Nordland" engineers then drove the enemy back and restored contact between the two regiments. A counterattack was attempted, but when it reached close to the first trees of Treptower Park, SS-Stubaf. Voss's engineers were greeted by heavy Soviet artillery fire. At the same time, some Soviet self-propelled guns crossed the Spree, nipping any further progress by the SS units in the bud.

Contact between the two regiments was again broken, forcing them to fight separately for the rest of the battle. Meanwhile, SS-Stubaf. Sörensen reported back to Neukölln to confer with Ziegler to be updated on the military situation.

The analysis by the "Nordland" commander was very clear: "The only certain thing is that the Soviets are trying to completely encircle Berlin from the north and from the south, overrunning everything and everyone in their way. I have no precise orders to give you; you are now the judges of the situation. Do your best."

The Soviets had in the meantime reached Neukölln, and in the sector held by the "Danmark," the Spree had been crossed in several places. After an hour of furious fighting, Sörensen's grenadiers had to fall back, establishing a new semicircular defensive line in front of the Köllnische Heide station, in the Neukölln district. Ziegler used the last tanks of his panzer regiment and the last armored cars of SS-Aufkl.Abt.11 to make a desperate counterattack and to stall the Soviet advance. Soviet artillery continued to hammer the center of the city, limiting any vehicle movement, not only directly by its fire but also because of the subsequent rubble that clogged all the streets. The Soviets finally reached the Schöneweide station, where Sörensen had set up his new command post. Suddenly, the noise of battle lowered in intensity; Sörensen went outside to take stock of the situation. A moment later, a Soviet sniper hidden in the ruins shot him. The "Danmark" commander swayed brusquely and fell dead without saying a word. Two of his men hastened to him and brought him lifeless to the entrance. They could only verify his death in the field. Command of the "Danmark" passed to SS-Ostuf. Petersen, formerly the commander of 14.(Flak)Kp., a simple lieutenant, since there were no longer any higher-ranking officers. In the Britz area, the gunners of III./SS-Art.Rgt.11, after having fired all their ammunition, led by their commander, SS-Stubaf. Potschka, continued to fight as grenadiers, scavenging for automatic weapons and a few heavy machine guns, reaching Neukölln and joining the rest of the "Nordland." The "Norge" grenadiers were also giving their all, fighting against the advancing Soviet forces, and their commander, SS-Ostubaf. Körbel, was badly wounded during the fighting. Other officers were also killed or wounded by Soviet snipers, among them SS-Hstuf. Hermann Hinrich Lührs, the "Danmark" adjutant, who died of wounds sustained while he was in the radio tower that had been transformed into a field hospital. In the night of April 24–25, SS-Uscha. Christensen, with the engineers from 16./"Danmark" and SS-Oscha. Illum, with the regimental assault platoon, reached the Jungfernheide park. In expectation of the arrival of the Soviets, the two NCOs had set up their command post in an old restaurant. At dawn on April 25, SS-Ustuf. Hans Dircksen arrived at the position, having taken over command of the remnants of III./"Danmark," bringing fresh orders: Christensen's engineers and Illum's grenadiers were to follow him to Neukölln to take part in a counterattack. They were to be relieved by a Volkssturm unit.

SS-Hstuf. Per Sörensen. *Lars Larsen*

German soldiers fighting in the street in Berlin, April 1945. The soldier in the foreground is armed with a Sturmgewehr 44 assault rifle.

A group of young soldiers in the streets of Berlin

Joachim Ziegler

April 1945: Hitler passing out awards

SS-Staf. Gustav Krukenberg

That same day of April 25, resistance of German units along the Spree and on the Teltow Canal continued; strong enemy pressure was pushing the defenders bit by bit toward the center of the city. For that reason, SS-Brigdf. Ziegler was accused of negligence because his units had not been able to hold their assigned positions. A few days earlier, Hitler had issued the following order: "Officers who ignore and do not carry out their orders will be shot. They are personally responsible." SS-Brigdf. Ziegler was moved to the Reichs Chancellery and placed under arrest, but at least he had escaped the death sentence.

The "Charlemagne" Assault Battalion

In Berlin, the "Nordland" received a battalion of French volunteers as reinforcement, detached from the remnants of 33.Waffen-Grenadier-Division der SS "Charlemagne." After the fighting in Pomerania, all the surviving elements of "Charlemagne" had been regrouped at Jargelin, northwest of Ankam. Then, around the end of March 1945, they were moved to the Neustrelitz camp, in Mecklenburg. On March 25, the SS-FHA ordered that "Charlemagne" be restructured as a new grenadier regiment, with two grenadier battalions and a heavy battalion. SS-Brigdf. Krukenberg[1] nominated SS-Staf. Zimmermann as regimental commander, while SS-Bataillon 57 was led by W-Hstuf. Fenet;[2] SS-Bataillon 58, under W-Ostuf. Géromini; and the Schwere Bataillon, by W.Stubaf. Boudet-Gheusi. In early April, the strength of the "Charlemagne" was around a thousand men, but not all of them were disposed toward continuing to fight, in view of the way the military situation on the various war fronts was unfolding. After having spoken with Himmler, SS-Brigdf. Krukenberg decided to reorganize the French unit with only those men who were firmly decided to continue the fight, in order to eliminate the demoralized elements, who would be transferred to a Bau-Bataillon, or labor battalion. Firm in his decision, Krukenberg assembled

W-Ostuf. Pierre Michel

all the men and made a speech: "I want only volunteers with me. Whoever does not feel up to it won't fight anymore. You will still be in the Waffen-SS, but as laborers. Only those who still want to continue to fight will remain with me." Two-thirds of Fenet's battalion and about half of Géromini's battalion responded to Krukenberg's appeal. The other four hundred men opted for the labor battalion.

Departure for Berlin

During the night of April 23–24, with the Soviets now only a few kilometers from Berlin, Krukenberg was ordered to report immediately to the capital of the Reich to assume command of the "Nordland," and at the same time he was authorized to bring the French volunteers with him. Meanwhile, the Soviets had overrun the German defenses along the Oder and were advancing toward Berlin in two columns. General Weidling's LVI.Pz.Korps, east of the city, had been pushed into the suburbs of the capital and was engaged in desperate defensive combat. That same night Krukenberg also received a telegram that ordered him to form an assault battalion (*Sturmbataillon*) with the remnants of "Charlemagne" and to reach Berlin as soon as possible. Because there were not enough weapons for all the French volunteers, Krukenberg asked his unit commanders to select the best men for the battalion and to leave those who were undecided in place. In the end, the *Sturmbataillon* was composed of Fenet's entire SS-Bataillon 57, the 6th Company of Pierre Rostaing's SS-Bataillon 58, and the *Kampfschule* of SS-Ostuf. Weber.[3] Almost all the grenadiers of SS-Bataillon 57 were equipped with the new Sturmgewehr assault rifle. Heavy weapons consisted of machine guns and *Panzerfäuste*.

On April 24, the French SS troopers set off to Berlin in eight trucks, while Soviet artillery had been shelling the outskirts of the city and enemy armored vanguards were already in Potsdam and Oranienburg. South of Fürstenburg, two trucks lost their way; when they got back on the right road, they were low on gas and had to return to Carpin. The other trucks, having gotten to within about 20 kilometers from Berlin, were halted by a destroyed bridge and unloaded the Frenchmen, who had to then proceed on foot; about three hundred were left. After an exhausting march of many hours, around 2200 the French volunteers reached the area of the Berlin Olympic stadium (the Reichssportsfelde), finding shelter for the night in the Grunewald woods along the banks

Henri Fenet, *at left with glasses*, with other French volunteers, January 1944

SS-Ustuf. Wilhelm Weber

Army soldiers and Volkssturm members in Berlin, April 1945

German soldiers in Berlin, April 1945

Helmuth Weidling

Wilhelm Mohnke

Volkssturm members erecting a road block

of the river Havel. Leaving his men to rest, SS-Brigdf. Krukenberg, in a civilian car, headed to the Chancellery to receive orders. After having met with Generals Krebs and Burgsdorf, Krebs ordered Krukenberg to report to General Helmuth Weidling, who a few hours earlier had been nominated by Hitler as the first military commandant of Berlin. At dawn on April 25, the Soviet encirclement of Berlin had in the meantime been completed. W-Hstuf. Fenet had reorganized the companies of the *Sturmbataillon*: 1.Kompanie was led by Ustuf. Jean Clement Labourdette, 2. Kompanie was under Ostuf. Pierre Michel, 3.Kompanie was under Hscha. Pierre Rostaing, and 4.Kompanie was led by Oscha. Jean Ollivier. The *Kampfschule* and the former honor company were still led by SS-Ostuf. Wilhelm Weber.

The Defense of Berlin

After having rested for a few hours, on the morning of April 25, Krukenberg reported to Weidling's headquarters. The LVI Panzer-Korps commander had few troops available to effectively defend the German capital; in addition to the remnants of his corps, which had suffered heavy losses in the earlier fighting, there were some Volkssturm units, some administrative service units, Luftwaffe personnel, and "Hitlerjugend" youths. In addition to what was left of "Nordland," there were also some Waffen-SS units commanded by SS-Brigdf. Wilhelm Monke, about 1,200 men from the following units: LSSAH Wach Regiment, LSSAH

BERLINO, APRILE 1945

Aus.u.Ers.Btl., Führer-Begleit-Kompanie, and the Reichstührer SS Begleit Bataillon. Also present were the remnants of s.SS-Pz.Abt.503, which was left with six King Tigers that had joined with the last of the assault guns and Panthers of the "Nordland." Weidling informed Krukenberg that the sector southeast of the city, designated as defense sector C, had been assigned to the "Nordland" division, whose command he was to assume, replacing Ziegler. With respect to the French volunteers, Weidling authorized them to be assigned to the "Nordland" as an independent battalion.

Because phone contact with "Nordland" had been cut off for some time, Weidling told Krukenberg that its last position had been reported in the Hasenheide park between the suburbs of Neukölln and Kreuzberg. A system of outer perimeter defense had been planned to defend the capital of the Reich, inside of which the city had been subdivided into eight defensive sectors, each assigned to the various forces available:

- **A** and **B** (eastern area of Berlin): Volkssturm and "Hitlerjugend" units, led by Generalmajor Erich Bärefänger
- **C** (Neukölln): 11.SS-Frw.Pz.Gr.Div. "Nordland" (under SS-Brigdf. Gustav Krukenberg)
- **D** (Tempelhof and Steglitz): Panzer Division Munchenberg (under Generalmajor Mummert)
- **E** (area southwest of Berlin and Grune forest): 20.Pz.Gr.Div. (under General Scholz)
- **F** (Spandau and Charlottenburg): "Hitlerjugend" and Volkssturm units and mixed formations led by Oberleutnant Eder

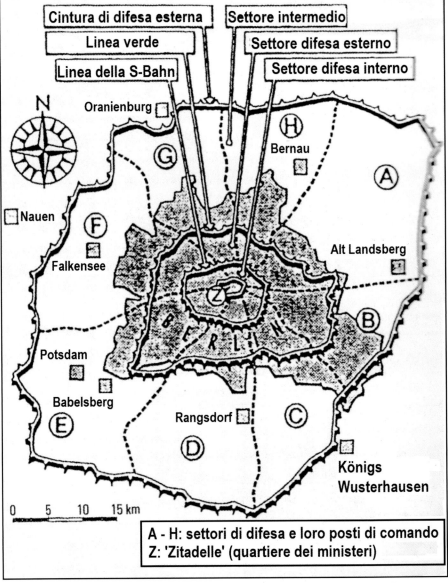

A–H: Defense sectors and their command posts
Z: "Zitadelle" (ministry district)

TCHAPTER XIV: BERLIN, THE FINAL BATTLE

"Hitlerjugend" bicycle tank-hunter companies headed toward the outer defensive perimeter to defend the main approach routes

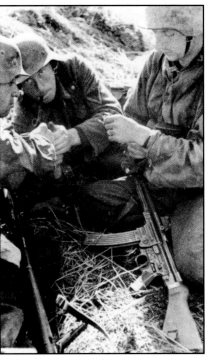

German soldiers during a lull in the fighting

SS-Brigdf. Krukenberg

G and **H** (north Berlin): mixed formations and the remnants of 9.Fallsch.Div. (under Oberst Hermann)

Z (city center): Kampfguppe Mohnke and Luftwaffe forces

Inside the external perimeter defense line, another perimeter was formed that ran along the ring of the surface trolley system (the S-Bahn). This inner defensive ring bordered on the Landwehr Canal to the south, with the Spree to the north. To protect the skies over Berlin from Soviet air incursions were three flak towers in reinforced concrete that were located in the zoo, in Humboldt Park, and in Friedrich Park. They were armed with 128 mm guns and 20 mm guns. Weidling had under his command a total of about 45,000 men in military formations (Wehrmacht and Waffen-SS) and about 40,000 men of the Volkssturm militia. For the capture of Berlin, the Soviets fielded about 1,500,000 soldiers. During a conference in the Chancellery bunker the previous night, between April 25 and 26, Weidling had outlined a pessimistic report on the defense of Berlin. In order to report a bit of optimism, General Krebs noted that Steiner's army and Wenck's 12.Armee were trying to break through. But Steiner's army, which was to move from the north, existed only on paper and with respect to Wenck's 12.Armee, which was to move from the south, which was blocked by the Soviets.

In Command of the "Nordland"

When Krukenberg took over command of the "Nordland," after having delivered Weidling's written order to Ziegler that designated him as the new commander of the unit, he quickly became informed of the status of the units: the two regiments of the "Nordland," the "Norge" and the "Danmark," were down to the strength of a company or at most of a scant battalion. Arriving as reinforcements were groups of army soldiers, sailors, "Hitlerjugend" youths, and old men of the Volkssturm. Most of the division's unit commanders had been killed in combat, and SS-Stubaf. Rudolf Ternedde found himself, in practice, in command of both regiments. Ziegler was accompanied to the Chancellery in a car, where he was placed under arrest for having failed in the defense along the Spree and the Teltow Canal. Having assumed command of "Nordland," Krukenberg decided to make a quick trip to the forward positions to take stock of the situation personally. At that moment, all of the Hasenheide park was under Soviet artillery fire. Defending the park and the nearby area were a few isolated groups of soldiers from his new division, as well as elements of the Volkssturm, armed with assorted weapons that could not be relied upon. He then met with the officer responsible for the sector and found out that the Soviets were advancing from the east and that the Treptow district had already fallen into

Soviet tanks in the streets of Berlin, April 1945

A Volkssturm soldier with a *Panzerfaust*

their hands the day prior. The situation on his left and on his right was no better: violent battle was raging in the Tempelhof airfield area at that time. Meanwhile, the French volunteers had been moved to the "Nordland" sector, and while they drove through the streets of Berlin in their trucks, some civilians mistook them for the vanguard of Wenck's army, which had been long awaited, as described by Henri Fenet: "The Berliners greeted us from their windows, from the sidewalks, in front of their houses . . . it was a great emotion; tears came to our eyes. Groups of people formed in the streets, at crossroads, despite the bombardments that were underway, clapping, to which we responded warmly." In the afternoon, the French battalion reached the Neukölln area, assuming positions in the neighborhood north of the Hasenheide, between the Hermannplatz and the church on the Gardenpionierplatz. Rostaing's company found a spot in the cellar of a brewery, Weber's *Kampfschule* in a restaurant, and the men of Michel's company on the ground floor of a store. Soon thereafter, all the companies were ordered to send out recon patrols to intercept the enemy advance, and clashes with Soviet tanks began almost immediately, putting the experience of the French volunteers with the *Panzerfäuste* to the test. Grenadier Ronzier of 2.Kompanie was the first to knock out a Soviet tank in Berlin, soon followed by Uscha. Fodot and grenadier Jean-Francois Lapland from the same company, who was just eighteen years old. Both of them destroyed a Soviet tank with a *Panzerfaust*.

That same day, Krukenberg was ordered to move the "Nordland" units to sector Z (Zentrum) of Berlin, practically in the center of the city, where the Chancellery and other buildings of German power were located. SS-Brigdf. Krukenberg set up his command post in the basement of the Opera Theater (Opernhaus), while his units began to shift to the new sector. The commandant of sector Z was Oberstleutnant Seifert of the Luftwaffe, whose command post was in the Air Ministry building (LuftMinisterium). Seifert was very cold toward Krukenberg, having a profound aversion to the Waffen-SS. He categorically refused to collaborate with the SS units, arguing that the defenses had already been planned and that there was no need for any reinforcements.

The "Nordland" defensive sector began at the Jannowitz bridge over the Spree and ran along the Neanderstrasse and Prinzenstrasse as far as the Landwehr Canal and along the Belle-Alliance Platz. A divisional *Kampfgruppe* held the Anhalter railway station. The last of the heavy weapons of the "Nordland," infantry guns and light howitzers, were emplaced in the area of the zoo, where what was left of the logistics train was also located. The last remaining tanks were sent to the center of the city. While the "Nordland" and "Charlemagne" troops began their battle to defend Berlin, on April 25, 1945, Soviet and American troops had already linked up on the Mulde, a tributary of the Elbe, thus cutting Germany in half.

German soldiers in the ruins of Berlin

German soldiers with an MG42, April 1945

UL: SS-Oscha. Erik Wallin

An SdKzf.250 of SS-Pz.Aufkl.-Abt.11

A Soviet tank in Berlin

Memoirs of SS-Oberscharführer Wallin

Relating to the move of the "Nordland" to Berlin, following are the memoirs of the Swedish SS-Oscha. Erik Wallin,[4] a member of 3.Kp./ SS-Pz.Aufkl.-Abt.11: "Around noontime of April 25, 1945, we could no longer hold the position and had to abandon Britz to the Bolsheviks. In order to reach Neukölln, there was only one road open that crossed the canal at Teltow over a very narrow bridge. The noise of combat continued to grow louder as the division got closer to the canal. The units that were supposed to provide cover for the withdrawal continued to be subject to increasing pressure. Everything got more nervous while we were on the road to get to the trucks. There were men from all of the division, surely around a thousand. It was all that was left of the glorious 'Norge' and 'Danmark' regiments and of the other units of the division. They were waiting, still waiting, with impatience. For the vehicles, it wasn't easy to make a way through the ruins. They finally made it to the canal, and the loading began. At the same time, a desperate cry was heard behind us: 'The tanks have crossed.' The fear of tanks got hold of everyone. Hundreds of men, who for years had looked death in the face without losing their sense of calm, were suddenly overcome by a savage panic, running without thinking and seeking to take shelter under the vehicles. The companies to the rear were pushing those in front of them, and all these men ended up forming a huge, compact mass. The shells and bursts of fire from the two Soviet tanks that had appeared on the street along the canal and fired down it opened gaps in the human mass that was milling there. In front of me, behind me, to the right, to the left, bloody men fell to the ground screaming. The anguish of death cried out in a savage yell. I pointed what remained of my platoon to our vehicles, which fortunately were a little farther away in front of us. When we put our trucks in gear, hundreds of men approached and tried desperately to grab on. The fire of machine guns and shells mowed down many of them, and our vehicles were covered with blood.

"When we got close to the bridge, I became aware that the fuses for explosive charges under the bridge were already burning. In the general panic, someone had lit them too early. The fuse set off sparks attached to the four charges, which were to blow the bridge before the Soviets could cross it with their tanks. How could we get out of this? A Stalin organ salvo landed behind us, right in the midst of a mass of panicked men who were following us. The effect was terrifying. In the vehicle the men ignored the fact that the fuse was burning. My knees were shaking. The vehicle advanced slowly, with an exasperating slowness, opening a way through the fugitives in order to reach the other end of the bridge. A cold sweat broke out on my forehead; I was going crazy. Finally, we reached the other bank. Our vehicle had barely left the bridge when it exploded with a frightening blast. Human body parts were thrown above our heads and then fell with a deafening thud on the asphalt of the street and on the walls of houses. Toward the Hermannstrasse, the crew of an 88 mm gun were trying desperately to get their gun in battery to fire against the Soviet tanks. Before they could do that, a new Stalin organ salvo hit the western bank and blew them to pieces.

"What had happened to the platoon's other vehicles? It was impossible to know what the situation was on the other bank of the canal. The bridge's superstructure had collapsed sideways and obstructed the crossing. Clouds of dust and pieces of rubble obscured the view. Was one of our vehicles on the bridge when it blew up? Had the men been blown into the air or had they been able to jump into the canal? I could still see that behind us, the men had begun to jump in order to cross by swimming. Uneasy because of the fate of our comrades, we continued to march northward along the Hermannstrasse. The rallying point was the Stadtmitte metro station, where the new division command post was set up. For about an hour we advanced in a zigzag fashion through the almost unusable streets. For the first time we saw a sign hastily scrawled on the wall of a building that read: 'SS traitors! They are prolonging the war.' The German Communists had entered into action. They had begun to raise their heads. Was the morale of the civilian population, which until then had held up magnificently under terror bombings, beginning to slacken? They still greeted us with 'Heil Hitler' when we stopped to ask some civilians who were looking for water how to get to the Stadtmitte. But it was only due to fear of soldiers wearing the skull that they still greeted us that way. Did we have to worry about fighting an internal enemy as well? I didn't have the time to think of anything else when, crossing the Hermannplatz, a rain of bullets, fired from a rooftop, hit our vehicles. They were German Communists, who had joined the Soviets, who were firing on us with machine guns stolen from the Volkssturm depots. SS soldiers from another unit came on the run and jumped into a building on the other side of the square in order to fire toward the roof from which the fire was coming. Others ran as far as the Bolshevik nest to set fire to the upper floors. Then they stopped at the entrance of the building and waited. Did the Reds up there prefer to burn in the fire or come down and be hanged? We saw other signs of a general straggling along the way, while we continued on toward the Stadtmitte. Many unarmed soldiers stood in building entrances. When they saw our vehicles, they took care to blend into the shadows. Some soldiers, completely drunk, wandered through the streets without any heed of bullets and bombs. In the entrance to another building, a woman gave herself completely to a soldier. In front of us, we could see an old man along with several women around the cadaver of a horse that was already bloated, intent on cutting it to pieces. An artillery shell landed, and they threw themselves behind the carcass for a brief instant but then quickly resumed their scavenging, with their hands full of blood. Civilization was only a veneer that was starting to fall apart and could be seen in signs of moral collapse. We finally reached the Stadtmitte. There wasn't an intact house on the Leipzigstrasse, one of the best-known avenues in the world. In other times, there were multicolored luminous signs; in the windows of shops, luxury items caught the eye of people, of financiers and businessmen who passed by with quick steps. Now, everything was gray on gray, with the remains of stones and bubble and metal frames that were twisted and scorched.

Soldiers scavenging material from an SS vehicle in flames

Soviet soldiers fighting in the ruins of Berlin, April 1945

"Soldiers and generals were amassed in the underground metro station. I was able to contact an *Untersturmführer* from the division who ordered me to continue on to Grünewald, where the division's logistics units were located, and to await new orders. We didn't lose any time and marched to the west, passing through Potsdamer Platz, which was completely destroyed, the heart torn out of Berlin; the Tiergartenstrasse, along the Tiergarten, looked like a petrified forest, with its oaks that were burnt, naked, and fallen, then we went up the Kurfürstendamm. The cafés along the avenue, with their clientele from all over the world, the elegant luxury stores, the dance halls with their beautiful girls—all of this had been swept away by the fist of

An aerial photo taken in April 1945 of the Pariser Platz and the Brandenburg Gate. In the upper right is the Tiergarten. The devastating effects of Allied bombing of the city are clearly visible.

Long columns of military units and groups of civilians in the streets of Berlin trying to escape the advancing Soviet units, April 1945

A defensive position on the outskirts of Berlin occupied by aged Volkssturm members armed with *Panzerfäuste*, April 1945.

war. We continued on the Halensee toward the Hundekehle, in the Grünewald woods. It was there in the woods that circled the lake that we found elements of the logistics train.

"We got there as night was falling. It wasn't until the next day that we resumed our march to rejoin our comrades who were fighting in Neukölln. In fact, I had been ordered to assemble the mortar crews of the other regiments, which existed only on paper. With four vehicles and about forty men, we managed to return to the city. Among them, my veterans, boys I could count on: Kraus, Leisegang, and Lindnau. At dawn, they had been able to cross the Teltow Canal by swimming. That night, they were able to reach the logistics train. Old wolves!"[5]

The Noose Tightens

The following day, April 26, the Soviet forces made their final decisive attack against the capital's defensive perimeter: from the north, Zhukov's tank forces, and from the south, those under Konev. Faced with a deteriorating situation, General Weidling asked Hitler to leave the city and to reach Wenck's army, in a last-minute attempt to avoid a battle within the interior of the capital. But Hitler categorically refused to flee from Berlin, in order to continue the fight to the last. General Keitel also tried to convince the führer, but Hitler interrupted him, saying, "The decision has already been made. I will not leave Berlin. I will defend the city to the last. Either I win this battle for the capital of the Reich or I will fall as a symbol of the Reich." At dawn on that day of April 26, the companies of SS Sturmbataillon "Charlemagne" left their shelters north of the Hasenheide and silently made it toward the Neukölln town hall to be committed to a counterattack that had been scheduled for five in the morning, along the Berlinerstrasse. The men of the "Nordland" were to advance at the same time to their left along the Landwehr Canal and provide armored support. As soon as they reached their assigned departure points, the Frenchmen saw the "Nordland" tanks come upon the scene: a King Tiger of s.SS-Pz. Abt.503 and two Panthers at the Donaustrasse and Fuldastrasse crossroads, while several assault guns were stationed near the town hall.

Fernet decided to use Rostaing's 3.Kompanie and Michel's 2.Kompanie for the counterattack, while Ollivier's 4.Kompanie would be held in reserve. Labourdette's 1.Kompanie had been temporarily detached from the battalion to be used in the Tempelhof sector. Battalion headquarters had been set up in the town hall. Soviet artillery quickly began to shell the positions occupied by the French volunteers, claiming some victims. Just before 6:00, the final attack order came: the French volunteers began to advance, followed closely by the "Nordland" panzers. The Soviets opened fire with their Maxims and their antitank guns. Rostaing's company advanced along Brunauerstrasse, supported by a King Tiger, which soon was forced to stop because it had run out of gas. It did continue to provide fire

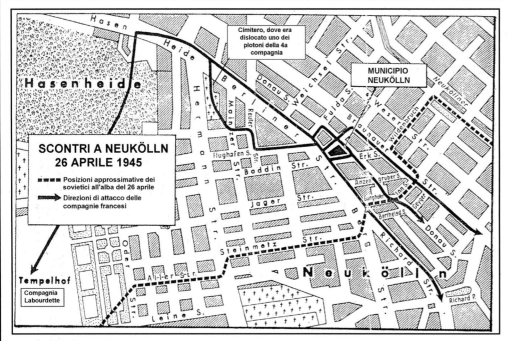

Map relating to the Neukölln fighting of April 26, 1945

A Soviet tank and antitank gun

support with its lethal 88 mm gun. To the left was Oberjunker Baumgartner's platoon; to Rostaing's right, along with his adjutant, Oberjunker Dumoulin and Oberjunker Ginot's 1st Platoon. After having gone a few dozen meters, they came under enemy fire: Oberjunker Dumoulin, who was behind Rostaing, fell to the ground, mortally wounded.

Rostaing then ordered the 1st Platoon to continue to advance, but he was forced to replace Ginot, who was seized by panic and completely paralyzed by fear. There was an antitank barrier right in the middle of the street that had been occupied by the Soviets; in order to try to get past it, Rostaing went down a side street, where, however, there was a T-34 parked with its crew outside the tank. Without a second thought, he opened fire with his Sturmgewehr, killing two of the tankers and chasing off the other three. Then, after taking a *Panzerfaust* from one of his grenadiers, the *Hauptscharführer* fired against the tank, hitting it right below the turret at close range and making it explode. The explosion was so violent, perhaps because Rostaing's rocket had hit the ammunition compartment, that a hail of splinters was spewed out toward the French grenadiers; one of them was decapitated by a piece of flying steel, and Rostaing himself was hit in his right temple by a metal fragment and lost consciousness. When he woke up shortly afterward, he saw the corpses of at least a dozen of his men on the pavement. Other victims were caused by fire from Soviet snipers, who were everywhere in the ruins of Berlin.

The advance of Michel's 2nd Company, which was supposed to cover Rostaing's attack, was stalled by enemy fire and had cost the unit numerous losses; the 2nd Company, which was attacking along the Berlinerstrasse, parallel to the Braunauerestrasse, with Oscha. Mongourd's platoon in the lead, soon came under Soviet fire, and one of the first to be hit was Ostuf. Michel, seriously wounded in the face. After he had been brought to shelter in a basement to be medicated, nothing else was known of him. He probably did not survive his serious wounds. The immobilized King Tiger had managed to knock out two T-34 tanks. Rostaing then decided to break off the action and to pull the survivors

One of the last photos of Hitler, outside his bunker, along with his aide Julius Schaub, observing the effects of Allied bombing around the Chancellery, April 1945

A King Tiger in the Berlin streets, 1945

A King Tiger in Berlin, April 1945

A Soviet tank knocked out in Berlin

Soviet riflemen in combat

T-34 tanks advancing amid the Berlin ruins

Resist or Die

After the failed counterattack, the French units at Neukölln were subjected to Soviet moves and were on the verge of being surrounded. The "Nordland" units had not taken part in the action because of a lack of personnel, since in the meantime the Soviets had intensified their pressure against the city center, forcing the SS troops to remain in their defensive positions. Without any contact with other units, Fenet had no choice but to order his companies to hold their positions and avoid being flanked by the enemy. Around noon, Ostuf. Weber's *Kampfschule*, which until then had been kept in reserve near the Hermannplatz, was engaged in attacking toward Tempelhof airfield, supported by a "Nordland" assault gun and by other groups of German soldiers. This action was also nipped in the bud by strong enemy fire that forced the French and German troops to withdraw after having taken heavy losses. In short order, the French positions around the Neukölln town hall became the main center of German resistance in the southeast sector of Berlin. Thanks to the arrival of fresh reinforcements consisting of several hundred men, mainly "Hitlerjugend" youngsters and old men of the Volkssturm, armed with Mauser rifles and *Panzerfäuste*, the French *Sturmbataillon* continued to hold its positions.

In the afternoon the situation seemed to deteriorate suddenly, with the Soviets only a few hundred yards from the French command post; returning from an inspection tour, Fenet came under enemy fire and was wounded in the foot. In order to avoid being completely surrounded by the enemy, Fenet ordered Oberjunker Douroux to clear the enemy out of the area around the command post. Having scraped together some grenadiers,

back; nevertheless, after having managed to gather together his company's survivors as best he could, he was forced to send them back into the attack in order to fend off a fresh Soviet attack. The French counterattack continued under enemy mortar fire until the barricade in the street was freed, and it was possible to get as far as the Richard Platz and from there to continue the advance toward the Tempelhof-Treptow S-Bahn line. Even though it had been kept in reserve, Jean Ollivier's 4th Company was also taken under Soviet artillery fire, but mainly by fire from a "Nordland" tank that had fallen into Soviet hands.

The men of Bellier's platoon had been able to silence the tank with *Panzerfaust* rounds after having lost many soldiers. Olivier himself, wounded, was forced to turn command of the company over to Oberkunker Protopopoff. After having been treated in one of the many aid stations in Berlin at the Tiergarten, he ended up in command of a German artillery battery crewed by soldiers of the SS "Das Reich" division, who had no experience as gunners and were acting in an antitank role near a crossroads. After having destroyed at least a dozen enemy tanks and running out of ammunition, he took a patrol toward the Chancellery sector in an attempt to rejoin his own countrymen.

Jean Ollivier

Oberjunker Protopopoff

A Soviet artillery piece in Berlin

Douroux headed for the buildings where enemy soldiers had been spotted, dislodging them with grenades and bayonets. It was a small local victory, insignificant if looked at in terms of the inexorable march of enemy units toward the center of the city. When a Soviet column came down the Berlinerstrasse, the French grenadiers picked up their *Panzerfäuste* and set off against them.

Stationed on the Jägerstrasse, a street that ran perpendicular to the Berlinerstrasse, was a Tiger that waited patiently for enemy tanks to show up so that it could hit them from the side. W-Hstuf. Fenet and Douroux waited there for the beginning of the deadly fight: when the first T-34 was in its sights, the Tiger opened fire and hit it. In a few minutes, other Soviet tanks met the same fate, forcing others to turn around. But the situation at Neukölln continued to become ever more critical; the French held out, but the defensive front on the flanks had completely collapsed. Even though Fenet was immobilized by the wound to his foot, he had himself placed on a chair and continued stoically to direct his men, while his *Sturmbataillon*, completely isolated, had been cut off from the main line of resistance. When the Soviets were on top of his position, only at that point did he decide to order the most-forward grenadiers to pull back; the groups of French grenadiers began to withdraw along the Donaustrasse, the Bruanauerstrasse, and the Berlinerstrasse, reinforcing the defenses around the "Charlemagne" command post. From the "Nordland" headquarters, Krukenberg was attentively and apprehensively following the actions of the French units, who had particularly distinguished themselves in knocking out enemy tanks. On April 26 alone, the Frenchmen of the "Charlemagne" were credited with destroying fourteen enemy tanks. Meanwhile, the Soviets were getting closer to the Hermannplatz, about a kilometer northwest of the French command post. At that point, Fenet decided to have his men withdraw toward the Hermannplatz before the enemy got there.

After having quickly pulled together his grenadiers and the "Hitlerjugend" boys, Fenet ordered Rostaing's 3.Kompanie to cover the disengagement, with the support of the last of the Nordland's panzers still on the scene. After about a quarter of an hour, the square was reached without any problems, and defensive positions and barricades were hastily set up, since the Soviet tanks were only 100 meters away. All the streets east of the Hermannplatz had fallen into enemy hands, and at any

A German antitank gun fighting in Berlin

A Soviet self-propelled gun on a Berlin street, 1945

"Hitlerjugend" youths and Volkssturm members in Berlin

"Hitlerjugend" youths defending a position

A German soldier with a *Panzerfaust* in an ambush position

moment enemy tanks would show up from the Bruanauerstrasse and the Weserstrasse. The "Nordland" assault guns were engaged in dealing with the approaching enemy tanks, while other tanks would be dealt with by the French tank hunters/killers at close range with *Panzerfäuste* or with bundles of hand grenades. In the space of an hour, at least four Soviet tanks were knocked out in the area around the Hermannplatz. The follow-on attack by Soviet infantry against the barricades on the Weserstrasse was stopped by fire from the French grenadiers, as well as those of the "Nordland," while the "Hitlerjugend" youths, along with the oldsters from the Volkssturm and the Kriegsmarine sailors, threw themselves like wild beasts against the enemy. Frightened by that sudden attack, the Soviets withdrew in all haste, leaving many of their comrades lying in the street. On the night of April 26, some elements of Ustuf. Labourdette's 1.Kompanie finally linked up with the rest of the French battalion on the Hermannplatz, after having been engaged with the rest of the company in defensive fighting in the Tempelhof sector.

In the central sector, after having prepared the demolition charges for the bridges near the Hallesches Tor, the German troops withdrew toward Hallescher Platz. The Hallesches Tor and the Belle-Alliance Platz guarded the access to the two great arteries of central Berlin, the Wilhelmstrasse and the Friedrichstrasse. Barricades had been hastily thrown up in order to stop the enemy. The bridges were blown sky high as soon as the Soviets approached them. Nonetheless, the Red Army soldiers continued to advance. SS-Ustuf. Bachmann, leading a *Kampfgruppe* of about a hundred men, including personnel of the "Danmark" logistics train, and although being lightly wounded, had been deployed to defend the Hallesches Tor and, despite being subjected to massive Soviet artillery and mortar fire, continued to hold their positions. The situation began to be critical when the Soviets managed to cross the Landwehr Canal in several points. SS-Ustuf. Dircksen's platoon showed up as reinforcement, which helped repulse the enemy attacks.

A German soldier during the fighting in Berlin

Soviet soldiers advancing along a Berlin street

At the same time, the remnants of SS-Pz.Aufkl.-Abt.11 were busy defending the Anhalter station, supported by two 8./"Danmark" infantry cannons. Then, toward evening, the SS scouts were forced to fall back to the north, in Oberstleutnant Seifert's sector. In the night between April 26 and 27, the "Nordland" received a naval infantry battalion as reinforcement, with reduced manning, which had just landed at Gatow airfield with one of the last available planes.

New Defensive Positions

During the night between April 26 and 27, W-Hstuf. Fenet was ordered by "Nordland" headquarters to carry out a new withdrawal to the northwest, toward the center of the city. While the maneuver was being carried out, Labourdette's company was again detached from the battalion to be used to plug a new breach in the defensive front. The other men of the French *Sturmbataillon* took shelter for the night in the Thomas Keller brewery, on the other side of the Anhalter Bahnhof station. Other French volunteers followed Weber's *Kampfschule* to the Opernhaus. At that moment, the battalion numbered little more than 150 men. On the morning of April 27, Fenet and Douroux decided to go to the "Nordland" HQ to get new orders, but because Fenet could not walk due to his wounded foot, any mode of transport was sought in vain. Marching on foot, the two men somehow managed to reach the "Danmark" command post, in the cellars of the Reichsbank, where they were warmly greeted by their Scandinavian and German comrades. That same day, command of sector Z passed to SS-Brigdf. Mohnke, who subdivided it into two subsectors, one led by Oberstleutnant Seifert, consisting of the western area, and another under Krukenberg, consisting of the eastern sector, with the Wilhelmstrasse as the demarcation line between the two zones. That way, the "Nordland" elements still subordinate to Seifert would return as soon as possible to the division's subordination. The new "Nordland" headquarters was thus moved to the central metro station (Stadtmitte).

German soldiers in a defensive position, armed with rifles and a *Panzerfaust*

The Soviets continued their attacks, ever tightening the noose around the city center, overwhelming everything and everyone. The defenders of Belle-Alliance Platz ended up under Soviet tank fire. Around 1430, a Soviet tank took up position on the damaged bridge and thus provided fire support to the infantry that was attacking along the canal. SS-Ustuf. Dircksen and his men counterattacked, temporarily easing the pressure. An enemy tank was destroyed with a *Panzerfaust*. But soon after, Soviet infantry was able to infiltrate in the ruins and destroyed houses, forcing Dircksen's men to pull back south of Kochstrasse.

A Soviet soldier during an attack

Hidden in the ruins of a destroyed house, an MG42 opens fire against Soviet infantry.

Soviet soldiers advance under enemy fire.

A Josef Stalin 2 tank in Berlin, April 1945

During the morning of April 28, Krukenberg held a meeting with the "Nordland" officers and with Fenet, during which he ordered everyone to prepare for a new counterattack for the following night. Meanwhile the SS troops occupied a new defensive sector, after having been split into three groups with specific tasks: one group was assigned to the front line and deployed between the ruins south of the Hollmanstrasse, with the mission of limiting themselves to observe enemy movements and to deal with any recon patrols. In case of an enemy attack in force, it was to withdraw to the main defensive line along the Besselstrasse and the Ritterstrasse. A second group, consisting of the assault troops, was to remain close to the command post, ready to act and block any enemy penetrations. The last group, consisting of men who needed to rest and also including the lightly wounded, stayed in the buildings along the Leipzigerstrasse. Throughout April 28, the "Nordland" front was relatively quiet, except for the continuous bombardment by Soviet artillery and aviation. In the afternoon, the "Nordland" HQ was moved to the Stadtmitte underground station, in several abandoned cars that had no electricity and no phones. The rest of the *Sturmbataillon* had reached the station about that time, led by Ostuf. Joachim von Wallenrodt,[6] which along the way had also picked up Oscha. Ollivier. The rest of the men of Labourdette's 1.Kompanie were still missing, since they continued to be engaged in other sectors, and only a few volunteers finally were able to join up with the rest of the battalion. A few hours later, SS-Brigdf. Krukenberg, by candlelight in his new command post, awarded several Iron Crosses to the French volunteers who had distinguished themselves in the battle for Neukölln.

The Battle Continues

That same day, "Nordland" headquarters reported that Wenck's army had finally reached the area around Potsdam, but at the same time the Soviets had launched a great offensive over the Oder River south of Stettin and had already reached Prenzlau. In the Berlin area, since dawn on April 28, the Soviets had begun to build bridges over the Landwehr Canal near the Hallisches Tor, allowing their tanks to cross. The Belle-Alliance Platz was also in their hands, and from it emanated the three main streets that led to the Reichs Chancellery. During the night, the *Sturmbataillon* sent two tank-killer teams to Belle-Alliance Platz, one led by Wallenrodt and the other by Oscha. Lucien Hennecart. Shortly thereafter, Weber's *Kampfschule* was also sent there to try to bar the road to the Chancellery. The French grenadiers, armed with *Panzerfäuste*, continued to take a frightful toll on enemy tanks, while in the Stadtmitte underground station, Fenet and Krukenberg continued to follow the course of the battle north of Belle-Alliance Platz, thanks to runners who risked their lives to go back and forth from the front line. Even though he was wounded, Fenet wanted to go back up to the surface to personally follow the evolving battle. At that moment, the French units were in position between the Hedemanstrasse and Mockernstrasse. Passing through the metro tunnel as far as the Kochstrasse station, Fenet and Douroux were finally able to get aboveground, where they found Weber, who greeted them and then led them to shelter in a destroyed house. SS-Ostuf. Weber reported to Fenet that during the day, between five and six more tanks had been knocked out with *Panzerfäuste* and that numerous infantry attacks had been driven back with heavy enemy losses.

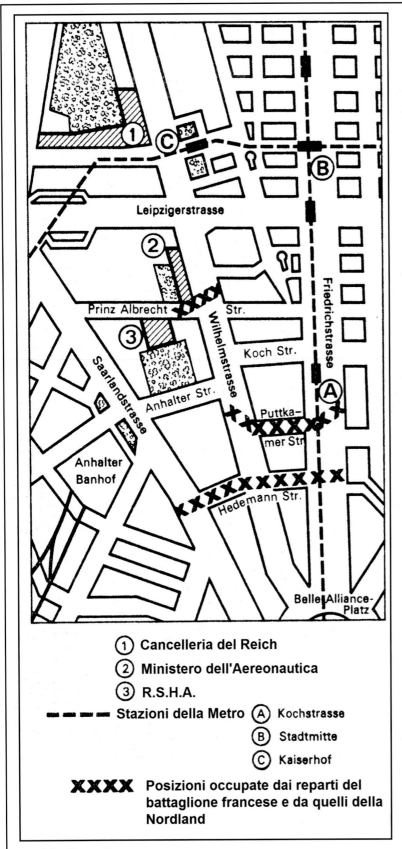

① Cancelleria del Reich

② Ministero dell'Aereonautica

③ R.S.H.A.

▬ ▬ ▬ ▬ Stazioni della Metro Ⓐ Kochstrasse

Ⓑ Stadtmitte

Ⓒ Kaiserhof

XXXX Posizioni occupate dai reparti del battaglione francese e da quelli della Nordland

1. Reichs Chancellery
2. Air Ministry
3. RSHA

Metro stations   A. Kochstrasse
                  B. Stadtmitte
                  C. Kaiserhof

XXXX: Positions occupied by units of the French SS battalion and by those of the "Nordland"

Positions occupied by units of the French SS battalion and of the "Nordland" from April 28 to May 2, 1945, in Berlin

Saturday, April 29, a new massive Soviet tank attack hit the positions held by the SS grenadiers along the Wilhelmstrasse; well hidden in the ruins, the French volunteers with their *Panzerfäuste* were able to knock out the leading tanks and thus stall the entire enemy armored column. Distinguishing themselves in this horrific battle against the tanks were Uscha. Eugene Vaulot,[7] who could claim the destruction of at least four tanks, and Uscha. Albert Brunet.[8] The Soviets replied with a massive artillery bombardment, in the hopes of eliminating the centers of enemy resistance. Then they came on again with tanks, unleashing a hurricane of fire and flames. Fenet could order his men only to pull back along the Puttkamerstrasse, and at the same time he sent grenadier Louis Levast of the *Kampfschule* to the CP under the Stadtmitte to ask Krukenberg for reinforcements and ammunition. Levast returned soon thereafter with several dozen "Nordland" grenadiers and with several cases of ammunition and *Panzerfäuste*. With these reinforcements it was possible to set up a new defensive front along the Puttkamerstrasse and to fend off the enemy infantry attacks. When the Soviets came back to attack with tanks, Weber's Panzerjägers swung into action again with their *Panzerfäuste*.

Stalled in that sector, the Soviets mounted a new attack along the Friedrichstrasse, where, however, the tanks could not pass through due to the many bomb craters. The men of Kampfgruppe "Danmark" were then called in to face off against the Soviet infantry. Meanwhile, Kampfgruppe Bachmann had been relieved by men of 13./"Danmark." Kampfgruppe Bachmann was soon thereafter involved in an attack to the south, moving from the Kochstrasse metro station. Although sustaining some losses, Bachmann was able to get to the corner of Friedrichstrasse and Puttkamerstrasse, taking up positions in the Herold Insurance building. SS-Ustuf. Bachmann had been wounded, and two of his men brought him to the aid station that had been set up in the Hotel Adlon. SS-Uscha. Scholle assumed command of the remnants of the *Kampfgruppe*. During the morning, a battalion from the Soviet 79th Rifle Corps had been able to cross the Moltke Bridge over the Spree, thus preparing to assault the Reichstag. The remnants of the "Nordland" continued to fight in the Spittelmarkt quarter. Following is a report of a *Kampfgruppe* of SS-Pz. Gren.Rgt.23 "Norge":[9] "The Soviets crossed the metro line and then tried to get past the mountain of rubble on the Seydlerstrasse but were not able to. They then replied to their failure with a furious barrage fire with artillery and mortars. It fell amid the ruins. More walls fell; wood and beams flew into the air. Then the firing stopped. The sound of the squeaking of tracks announced the arrival of tanks. The men of SS-Panzer-Grenadier-Regiment 23 'Norge' took up positions with *Panzerfäuste* in the rubble on the corner of the Wallstrasse. The tanks fired in all directions. The *Panzerfäuste* answered. Two tanks were hit in the Wallstrasse, thus blocking the street to the Spittelmarkt. The tanks that were followed backed up and turned around the corner where the post office was on the square. Three tanks continued to advance, firing against everything. When they had run out of ammunition, they turned back. While they were turning, the *Panzerfäuste* found other targets. Half an hour passed. The 'Norwegians' regrouped

Photo of a young Henri Fenet

Eugène Vaulot in an LVF uniform

in a house near the Gertraude Bridge, from where they could keep an eye on the square. Then they moved toward the metro. A head raised up cautiously and looked around. The *Kampfgruppe* commander ordered: 'Silence; we'll let them get close. Open fire only on my command.' Eight Soviets were advancing in the Spittelmarkt. Then the German guns entered into action. Only one of the Soviets managed to get back toward the metro. Once again, a hail of steel fell upon the Germans. The light of day was replaced by the opaque red light of fire. The ruins and the rest of the walls had a spectral effect in the light of the fires. A squad of 'Norwegians' disappeared into a cellar. They had just gotten there when their refuge was invaded by flames. They fled the cellar and moved into a nearby room. There, the Spiess of the headquarters company of SS-Panzer-Grendiaer-Regiment 23 'Norge,' SS-Hauptscharführer Danner, found his men."

After having been engaged in destroying Soviet tanks with its antiaircraft guns at Strausberg, at Neukölln, and near the Tempelhof airfield, SS-Flak-Abteilung 11 was forced to sabotage its guns and heavy equipment after having run out of ammunition. The gun crews, around sixty men, continued to fight as ordinary infantrymen under SS-Hstuf. Rolf Holzboog.

German soldiers in combat

A column of JS-2 tanks in Berlin

A twin flak gun abandoned in Berlin

A column of Josef Stalin 2 heavy tanks moving in Berlin, April 1945

François Appolot

Karl-Heinz Gieseler

SS-Ustuf. Oskar Schäfer

The Last Knight's Crosses

When SS.Brigdf. Krukenberg found out that Uscha. Vaulot of the *Kampfschule* had destroyed his eighth tank in a single day, he recommended him for the Ritterkreuz. The awards ceremony was held early in the afternoon on April 29, in the presence of some officers from "Nordland" and "Charlemagne," by candlelight in the Stadtmitte underground. That same day, as reported by Krukenberg, other Knights Crosses were conferred: to the commander of s.SS-Pz.Abt.503, SS-Stubaf. Fritz Herzig, and to three other members of the French *Sturmbataillon*: Hstuf. Fenet, SS-Ostuf. Weber, and Oscha. François Appolot, the latter for having knocked out six enemy tanks in one day Weber had been wounded in combat on April 29 and moved to an aid station in the Reich Chancellery. SS-Brigdf. Mohnke questioned him about the situation in the sector held by the French, and after having heard his report, Mohnke went to General Burgdorf to propose the award of several Ritterkreuz to members of the *Sturmbataillon*. Mohnke personally presented the award to Weber, announcing that Fenet and Apollot would also be receiving the Knight's Cross. The documents were to have arrived at "Nordland" HQ the next day, but they never made it, probably destroyed during the course of the battle. Fenet, for example, learned that he had received the Knight's Cross only many years after the end of the war. In addition to Herzig, two other members of s.SS-Panzer-Abteilung 503 had been awarded the Knight's Cross that same day: SS-Ustuf. Oskar Schäfer and SS-Hscha. Karl Körner. On April 19, Körner had destroyed seventeen Soviet tanks coming from Strausberg, east of Berlin, bringing his tally to 101 tanks destroyed. Another awardee of the Knight's Cross on April 29 was SS-Hstuf. Karl-Heinz Gieseler,[10] a young officer barely nineteen years old, head of an assault group attached to the "Nordland," who distinguished himself for having personally knocked out eleven Soviet tanks.

CHAPTER XV
ESCAPE PLANS

The entrance to the Chancellery bunker in Berlin, April 1945

A German soldier armed with a *Panzerfaust*

On the night of April 29, 1945, General Weidling proposed a breakout move to the west, using the few remaining operational tanks, along the Heerstrasse, crossing over the bridges at Pichelsberg, still held by "Hitlerjugend" units. Hitler rejected the plan. His hopes still lay in outside action by Steiner's and Wenck's forces. These were forlorn hopes because their action had been blocked by the quick response of the battle-hardened Soviet forces that had surrounded the capital of the Reich. During the same day, Hitler had consulted SS-Brigdf. Wilhelm Mohnke, and a discussion followed that was at the same time contentious and dramatic.

"Where are the Soviets?" asked Hitler.

"To the north, at the Weidenammer Bridge. To the east, at Lustgarten. To the south, at Potsdamer Platz and near the Air Ministry. To the west, in the zoo, 300–400 meters from the Chancellery," responded Mohnke.

"How much longer can we hold out?" asked Hitler again.

"Twenty-four hours at the most" was Mohnke's stony reply.

During the last conference in the Chancellery bunker with Hitler present, held at 2200, in response to requests made to the OKW via radio, it was communicated that the relief attacks by Steiner and Wenck were blocked and that 9.Armee had been surrounded in the Halbe pocket. Berlin and its defenders were left to their fates. Between April 29 and 30, the Soviets unleashed their final assault against the center of Berlin but, before attacking with their infantry and tanks, dumped more than 25,000 tons of shells on the German capital. For their part, the Waffen-SS and French units in particular, even knowing that they were fighting a lost battle, continued to oppose the enemy attacks with all their strength. The NCOs continued to remain on the front line, paying for their example with their lives. Hstuf. Fenet

Soviet heavy artillery in Berlin, April 1945

Left, Soviet tanks and infantry attacking along a Berlin street, April 1945. *Right*, a German grenadier armed with a StG44 assault rifle and a *Panzerfaust* in a defensive position.

General Hans Krebs

had in the meantime moved his command post to the basement of a library, and at dawn's first light the Soviets came back to attack his sector with tanks; by now the French grenadiers had become masters in antitank action and, *Panzerfäuste* in hand, destroyed three enemy tanks. The Soviets then sought to root out the French tank hunters with flamethrowers, moving amid the ruins. That same day a Soviet soldier was captured who told Fenet that the Red Army had issued a bulletin that announced the imminent capture of Berlin for May 1, the feast of the worker. In witness of that, the Soviets had intensified their attacks against the center of Berlin to reach the Chancellery as quickly as possible. But they still had to deal with the fierce resistance of the European combatants, who were decided to sell their lives as dearly as possible.

That day of April 30, after Hitler had rejected an escape plan from Berlin, General Weidling held a meeting with his unit commanders to discuss the situation and possible measures to be taken. In the end, it was decided to try to flee the city in small groups. At 1345, Hitler authorized Weidling's new plan with a written message: "To the commandant of the Berlin defensive area, General der Artillerie Helmut Weidling. Because of the lack of ammunition and rations for the defenders of the capital of the German Reich, I authorize a breakout maneuver." It was a decision taken perhaps too late, when by then the ring around the capital was closed and escape seemed almost impossible. Throughout the day, the fighting carried on around the Reichstag with greater intensity. Having lost all hope of victory, Hitler committed suicide. The news was kept secret until the following day. With Hitler dead, General Hans Krebs ordered Weidling to make contact with the Soviets to agree upon a ceasefire. The Soviets naturally requested an unconditional surrender.

Also on May 1, the French tank hunters covered themselves with glory, continuing to slaughter enemy tanks. During the evening, Krukenberg reported to the Führerbunker for instructions, bringing with him SS-Stubaf. Wienczek,[1] the "Nordland" chief of staff, and SSHstuf. Paul Pachur. There he met first with SS-Brigdf. Ziegler, still officially under arrest, whom he updated on the latest developments: Hitler had committed suicide the day before, and before dying he had married Eva Braun, SS-Ogruf. Fegelein's sister-in-law.

Fegelein had been condemned to death by Hitler's order, supposedly for treason. Meanwhile, Wenck's army had definitively ceased any further effort to reach Berlin, and negotiations with the Western Allies had broken down. When he met with Mohnke, he confirmed to Krukernberg all that he had learned from Ziegler, and also reported that Krebs's attempt to get an immediate ceasefire had failed, because the Soviets requested an unconditional surrender. Finally, the "Nordland" commander was ordered to assume command of the defense of the center of the city with all the forces still available to him, a fictitious command because at the same time Mohnke told him that General Weidling had authorized all soldiers to try to find a way to escape the city, to the northwest. In order to avoid panic and disbandment, the news of Hitler's death had been pushed back to 2100.

The Last Battle

For those who hoped to flee Berlin and avoid being captured by the Soviets, there were two directions to go: the first was to the north toward the Weidendammer Bridge, toward Oranienburg and Armeegruppe Steiner. The other ran through Spandau-Staaken to the west and southwest, where it was hoped that there were still the troops of Wenck's 12.Armee. On the morning of May 1, SS-Stubaf. Ternedde, commanding the last combat groups formed with the survivors of the "Norge" and "Danmark" regiments, was called by SS-Brigdf. Krukenberg to get his last orders. "The city is surrounded. The führer is dead. We have to try to get out of Berlin. It's our last chance," said Krukenberg. He then continued: "Today, at eleven at night, all the 'Nordland' combat groups should regroup near the Weidendammer Bridge to try to break out to the north. We have to make contact with elements of Armeegruppe Steiner that are advancing from the north and have reached the northern suburbs of Berlin. But we have no contact with them and don't know exactly where they are." "Will there be any reinforcing units for this breakout attempt, Brigadeführer?" asked Ternedde. "Yes, a few Tigers from s.SS-Pz.Abt.503 and some half-tracks

A wounded soldier on the shoulders of other German soldiers, Berlin 1945

Soviet tanks and soldiers in the streets of Berlin, April 1945

A King Tiger abandoned near the Potsdamerplatz

Soldiers moving in Berlin in the shadows

Soldiers and Volkssturm members during a lull, before returning to fight the Soviets

A long column of German soldiers on a Berlin street

from the recon group of our 'Nordland' division. It will be necessary to try to reach the Finow Canal. On the other side, I think that we can find our comrades of Armeegruppe Steiner," Krukenberg concluded. Having received his orders, Ternedde quickly saw to getting all his men together, not an easy task, since they were scattered and hidden in the ruins in the center of Berlin and still engaged in dealing with enemy attacks. Runners were sent out in all directions to scrape together as many men as possible, even though in effect there were only a few hundred combatants left of the "Nordland." Most of them were gathered under the Reichsbank's vaults. Along with them were also civilians, women, and children. Initially, they did not know that the führer was dead, and thought that they were to take part in a counterattack to free the Chancellery. Their uniforms were filthy and in tatters after days of exhaustive fighting. Many were wounded, medicated as best as possible. SS-Stubaf. Ternedde briefed them on the breakout move to the north. No one asked for explanations. Orders were orders. The checked their weapons and their ammunition, as they always had before. At the given hour, one after another, the last grenadiers of the "Nordland" left the ruins of the Reichsbank and went out into the street, headed to the Hausvogteilplatz, and then got onto the Unter den Linden. Dark figures that moved in the shadows, hauling their weapons and ammunition, amid the columns of smoke that obscured the sky. The march continued toward the Friedrichstrasse metro station. Fighting had been bitter along this vital Berlin artery, but there were still some positions held by the French volunteers. The men continued to march, stumbling over corpses that littered the ground, and over abandoned ammunition crates and weapons. Shortly thereafter, a new order arrived: rally at the Opera House. Having reached the new rally point, they were informed by SS-Brigdf. Krukenberg of the führer's death and of the breakout move to the north. Not only were Waffen-SS soldiers present, but also soldiers of all branches of the Wehrmacht, including soldiers and airmen. "Nothing has changed. Discipline is the same as always. You will give the example of order to everyone. You will follow your orders until the end. The war is not over." Soon after, SS-Brigdf. Krukenberg sent SS-Ustuf. Valentin Patzak to SS-Hstuf. Fenet, who was defending the Gestapo headquarters on Prinz-Albrechtstrasse to bring his men up to date on the general breakout order, which was planned for 2300. But SS-Ustuf. Patzak never made it to Fenet, and nothing more was ever heard of him; he probably was killed along the way. Thus, Fenet and the forty or so men under him stayed in their positions, totally unaware that their comrades were making a breakthrough.

Breakout Maneuver

Shortly afterward, the soldiers left the Opera House in small groups and headed for the Weidendammer Bridge, going up the Friedrichstrasse toward the Stettin station. It was 2300. There, the "Nordland" survivors, led by SS-Stubaf. Ternedde, found their old commandant, SS-Brigdf. Ziegler, who was no longer under arrest. He took part in the breakout as a simple grenadier, armed with an assault rifle. He waited for the signal to attack, like everyone else. Near him was also SS-Brigdf. Mohnke, who gave the last orders, looked at his watch, and shouted, "Forward, to the Weidendammer Bridge. Forward!" The last of the Tiger tanks and a few assault guns were in the lead, followed by the "Nordland" grenadiers and personnel carriers. The men guarding the bridge were ordered to open the antitank barrier that was blocking it. The tanks then resumed their advance toward the Soviet positions. These movements on the bridge had not escaped the notice of the Soviets, who quickly opened fire with their antitank guns. The Tigers and assault guns answered the fire.

A Tiger was hit in the tracks and was immobilized, and its crew were forced to continue on foot. Behind it, SS-Uscha. Gaul's StuG.III, one of SS-Pz.Rgt.11's last remaining operational vehicles, was also hit and was stopped dead on the bridge; the vehicle commander, badly wounded, and his driver were able to get out of the flaming hulk. The Soviets had guessed that the Germans were trying a desperate maneuver to leave Berlin, and reacted ferociously, bringing more tanks to the area. The German column came under Soviet artillery and tank fire: the mass of soldiers broke up into small groups that took off in different directions. During the fighting at the Weidendammer Bridge, SS-Stubaf. Saalbach, commander of the "Nordland" reconnaissance battalion, was killed. SS-Ostubaf. Kausch, commander of SS-Pz.Rgt.11, who had been badly wounded two days earlier, was also aboard one of the "Nordland" personnel carriers. Coming under enemy fire, the vehicle was buried under the wall of a house, and Kausch sustained further wounds. SS-Hstuf. Johann Hartak, the unit's medical officer who was with him, managed to move him to an aid station at the Hotel Adlon, where Kausch was operated on as best as could be. The following morning, along with all the other wounded present there, SS-Ostubaf. Kausch was captured by the Soviets.[2]

According to the memoirs of SS-Sturmmann Wolfgang Venghaus,[3] first secretary of the "Nordland" staff, there were five attempts at breaking through on the Weidendammer Bridge. Venghaus remained in the Chancellery bunker until the last moment and was among the first to abandon it on the evening of May 1, along with other "Nordland" soldiers. SS-Brigdf. Joachim Ziegler, who had finally been freed from arrest, attached himself to this first group. The group made it near the Weidendammer Bridge to try to cross through the Soviet lines: "The first attempt was made just after midnight. A Tiger tank and two other armored vehicles, along with personnel from the 'Leibstandarte,' approached the antitank barrier on the bridge. The tanks fired and destroyed a second antitank barrier that was approximately 300 meters farther north. The tanks began to advance and

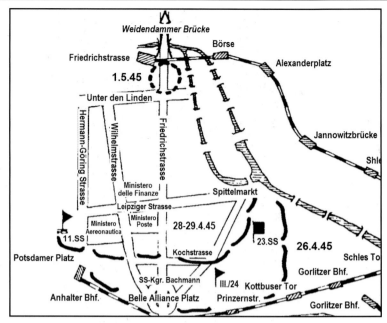

The area in which SS units were engaged in early May 1945

A Soviet antitank gun on a Berlin Street

SS-Stubaf. Saalbach

SS-Ostubaf. Kausch

Wolfgang Venghaus in a 1943 photo, when he was serving in the RAD

SS-Brigdf. Joachim Ziegler

A Soviet antitank gun in action

initially were quite fast. The mass of soldiers followed close behind. Soon after, a tank was knocked out and the infantry following it was stopped by enemy fire. The other tanks continued to move forward and were able to make their way past the second antitank barrier. Suddenly, on the side opposite the second barrier, there were two flare-ups of flames. These led one to believe that those tanks were destroyed by enemy fire.

"The second attempt was made about fifteen minutes later: the remaining troops of the Feldherrnhalle battalion and other units present advanced on both sides of the street. These troops had no heavy weapons but were supported by a 20 mm quad flak gun mounted on a vehicle. This attempt also failed because of the massive fire unleashed by the Soviets.

"The third attempt was made at 0100 on May 2; once again, groups of men formed up on the bridge. Other civilians and soldiers continued to arrive. With the support of half-tracks (probably from 'Nordland'), a new attack was made. During that advance, the vehicles drew a lot of fire around them. They moved forward, passing over dead and wounded. After a number of meters, the first vehicle began to burn, blocking the road to the others. Other vehicles, also coming under enemy fire, began to burn near the second antitank barrier. From inside a building, a Soviet machine gun dominated the street. Other heavy enemy fire came from the eastern side of the street. Thus, even that attempt failed.

"The fourth attempt was around 0200: a new assemblage of civilians and soldiers. There were no organized military units, just a mass of desperate people. For the first time, the Soviets directed artillery and mortar fire against this human mass that was clustered on the bridge. An assault gun and a heavy towed howitzer came in as support, in addition to other transport vehicles. A half-track was burning on the bridge. The heavy howitzer positioned itself on the bridge and fired against a house on the other side. The front wall of the house collapsed into the street; the street was blocked by the rubble. The second antitank barrier was no longer visible, and because of that, this new attempt also failed.

"The fifth attempt was made after 0400. The last vehicles of SS-Pz.Aufkl.-Abt.11 supported this attempt. I turned to the left directly after the bridge, to the west toward Am Schiffbauerdamm street. There, several antitank obstacles were neutralized. Chaos reigned, with civilians and soldiers trying to avoid enemy fire, sheltering behind the few vehicles present. This mass of people continued to the tram bridge near the Charité quarter. There, most of the vehicles were destroyed. So, even that attempt failed. The mass of civilians and soldiers scattered in all directions."

On the left, the metal footbridge over the Spree near the metro station on the Georgen-Strasse for pedestrians, in a prewar photo. *On the right*, a German grenadier. His tired face shows all the tragedy of war.

Diversionary Maneuver

Even though he documented the five attempts at the Weidendammer Bridge, in reality the Venghaus group did not take part in this fighting. Venghaus's small group, consisting of about a dozen "Nordland" personnel, moved from the Chancellery at 2200. It was led by SS-Sturmmann Venghaus, who knew the area perfectly, having been employed as a liaison agent between the "Nordland" headquarters and the Chancellery during the latest round of fighting. He thus acted as a guide, along with his comrade, SS-Oscha. Illner. Around 2215, SS-Brigdf. Ziegler joined the group, who was no longer under arrest. For his part, SS-Brigdf. Krukenberg had left his command post near the Stadtmitte station between 2300 and 2400, accompanied by his staff and other elements of the French battalion. His group was the first to arrive and cross the Weidendammer Bridge without being seen by the Soviets. He then temporarily hid on the Albrechtstrasse, northwest of the bridge.

Moving through a metro tunnel, in complete darkness just before midnight, the group with Ziegler and Venghaus reached the Georgen-Strasse metro station. But it did not go to the Weidendammer Bridge, following another route, as reported by Venghaus himself:[4] "SS-Brigdf. Ziegler pointed out a footbridge over the Spree near the station. We made a slight curve to the right and found ourselves in front of it, but it was blocked by a tangle of barbed wire. We cut the barbed wire and crossed the river on the footbridge, about a meter wide. It allowed us to cross the Spree to the north, to the west of the station. Once we had crossed the footbridge, we climbed a metal ladder and found ourselves on the Schiffbauerdamm. It was around midnight.

"We crossed the street, moving amid the ruins, following an underground passageway built through the cellar walls of the destroyed houses. We thus arrived at the vor dem Neuen Tor Platz near the Invalidenstrasse, where we arrived around 0100. About half an hour later, at 0130, we arrived at the Chaussee-Strasse, resuming our march to the north. But after only a few meters, there was a wall in front of us. A closer look allowed us to establish that it was a stone wall more than 2 meters high,

SS-Brigdf. Gustav Krukenberg

serving as an antitank obstacle that blocked almost the entire street. On the right, this wall led directly to the entrance of a perpendicular street, the Schwarzkopfstrasse. On the left side of the street there was a very narrow passageway about a meter wide. Our fear of having to scale the wall (which in reality some of the group were already doing) was thus lessened. Everything was still calm but was, unfortunately, the calm before the storm. As soon as we got past the antitank wall and we inspected the entrance to the perpendicular street, and having gone a short way to the north, we came under heavy small-arms fire coming from the houses on the right side of the street. Everyone crossed the street,

Destroyed vehicles and dead Germans abandoned on a Berlin street, May 1945

A German soldier with a *Panzerfaust* in Berlin, 1945

seeking shelter in the doorways of houses. It was the end of our rapid advance. Now we could make it only from one doorway to the next, risking being completely stalled. All attempts to make any forward progress failed. Machine guns kept the street under fire from upper windows. We tried getting close to these machine gun nests. As soon as they fired on us, we threw grenades. The street was becoming a dangerous place. In addition to small-arms fire, we began to get hit with mortar fire. At that time, the Soviets held the upper stories, and we held the lower stories. Time passed and we were still stalled. It was around 2:30 in the morning. A great number of soldiers had amassed in the houses and cellars. There were also civilians. Suddenly, we heard the noise of tracks. In front of us we saw a half-track with a 20 mm Flakvierling. It must have been a vehicle of the Nordland recon group. This group was led by SS-Sturmbannführer Rudolf Saalbach. The vehicle advanced in the center of the street, where it took up its position and opened fire with its four barrels against the upper windows . . . calm reigned after the first salvo of our 'Vierling.' Once again, we tried to move under the protection of the balconies of the houses situated on the right, but in vain. Any move on our part led to Soviet machine guns as well as mortars resuming fire. The Vierling itself came under enemy fire. Then there was a sudden cry: 'Free the street for our panzers!' (it was the last tanks of the

'Nordland'). The Flakvierling pulled back, then what I think was a Panzer IV arrived and took up a position on the right where the Flakvierling also was. Under protection of the panzer, some men advanced along the street. I could see them from my shelter. They were protected by the fire from the panzer. The tank aimed its gun at the upper windows, from which bursts kept on coming. Then there was a powerful explosion. When our panzer was ready to fire, it was hit from behind. A huge flame arose. The back of the panzer was burning. The crew abandoned the vehicle; I saw the commander get out of the turret amid the flames before jumping to the ground. The driver got out from the right and disappeared. The men near the panzer threw themselves on the ground. Apparently, there were no losses, because soon after I saw them all get up and take shelter. What had happened? One of our own men had hit the panzer with a *Panzerfaust*, thinking that it was a Soviet tank. Meanwhile, the Soviets continued on without decreasing their intensity. Hoping that the Soviets were distracted by the panzer in flames, we tried again to advance.

"Glued to the wall, we were in a dead space with respect to the machine guns firing from the windows. But once again, the attempt failed. The Soviets were alert and grenades began to fall. A bound to the next door allowed me to take shelter. Soon after, two comrades joined me from a building farther north. One of the two said, 'The general is dead' (I thought it must be General Ziegler). 'When did it happen?' I asked. 'It was when the panzer passed in front of us on the street; he was literally pulverized by a Soviet artillery shell.' Around 0400 in the morning, we got to within sight of a railway line and continued our progress to the northeast."

The Fate of the "Nordland" Combatants

According to other sources and authors, SS-Brigdf. Ziegler was killed during the assault on the Weidendammer Bridge. Venghaus's testimony should be considered reliable, because he knew the officer well and was with him during the last of the fighting. However, according to Krukenberg, Ziegler was killed later and farther away, on the Brunnerstrasse at the Lortzingstrasse, by Soviet artillery fire, along with W-Oscha. François Appolot and W-Uscha. Eugène Vaulot.

Krukenberg himself, after that artillery bombardment, returned to the center of the city, near the Weidendammer Bridge, with his command group and abandoned their uniforms and put on civilian clothes. Dressed as simple Berlin citizens, they were able to get past a number of Soviet patrols. At Pankow, Krukenberg entered the house of a railway worker to change his clothes once again. When he went outside, his men were no longer there. On the other side of the street were two Soviet soldiers who were waiting for him. After having turned over his gold watch, he managed to go toward the Schönholzer Platz, where for more than an hour he sought his men in vain. He finally was convinced that they had been taken prisoner. Alone, he headed toward the Wilhelmstrasse. Around 1230 he was arrested by a Soviet artilleryman.[5]

The Venghaus group was able to continue its journey and reach a rally point, joining other groups of soldiers near the Flakbunker in Humboldthain Park. Many German soldiers had gathered there, and most of them were armed. There were also tanks and trucks. The troops that were gathered there were under the command of General Erich Bärefänger. Some decided to surrender; others wanted to try a new breakout to the north. A first attempt, made with the tanks in the lead, was blocked by Soviet fire. A second attempt also resulted in failure. General Bärefänger preferred to commit suicide along with his wife to avoid being taken prisoner by the Soviets.

Once again, the soldiers tried their luck and split up into small groups. During the night between May 1 and 2, several thousand civilians and military personnel were miraculously able to escape to the west and northwest, getting past the Soviet barriers.

Elements of the "Nordland" division's logistics train located near the zoo followed the breakout attempt by Generalmajor Mummert, commander of Panzer-Division "Müncheberg," to the west in the Spandau sector, where the bridges over the Havel at Pichelsdorf and Spandau were still held by several "Hitlerjugend" *Kampfgruppen*. But even that attempt was prevented by Soviet troops, and in the end only a few men managed to escape to the west. Among them, a small group of soldiers from the "Nordland," led by Danish Hstuf. Svend Birkedahl-Hansen, were able to reach the port of Warnemünde, north of Rostock, from where they embarked on a small sailboat, reaching the island of Falster, in Danish territory, safe and sound.

Another dramatic scene with abandoned vehicles and dead bodies after a failed escape attempt

A "Nordland" vehicle destroyed and abandoned on a Berlin street. The divisional insignia is clearly visible.

In the foreground is one of the last soldiers to have fallen in Berlin.

In the foreground is an SdKfz.250/1 of 3.Kp./SS-Pz.Aufkl.-Abt.11 destroyed in the fighting in Berlin, May 1945.

Another SdKfz.250/1 abandoned on a Berlin street

Soviet tanks and soldiers on a Berlin street, May 1945

The Fate of Kampfgruppe Fenet

Not having received any message about the breakout to the north, W-Hstuf. Fenet with his thirty-odd men of the *Sturmbataillon*, for the entire day of May 1, 1945, remained in the RSHA building cellars on Prinz Albrechtstrasse. With him were two other officers, SS-Ostuf. Von Wallerodt and W-Std. Ob.Ju. Douroux. Among the NCOs present were W-Hscha. Rostaing, W-Uscha. Lacombe, and W-Uscha. Albert-Brunet. When at dawn on May 2, after having sent out several recon patrols, Fenet realized that there was no one left in the sector and that the Soviets were about to reach the Air Ministry buildings at the corner of Wilhelmstrasse and Leipzigstrasse, right behind their position, in order to avoid being cut off he decided to pull back to the ministry buildings. Bringing as many weapons and as much ammunition as possible with them, the Frenchmen fell back and made contact with some Luftwaffe soldiers. There, however, it was discovered that the German soldiers had decided to surrender, so in agreement with his men, Fenet decided to proceed to the Chancellery, in order to learn personally what had happened. An unnerving silence had fallen over the city, and the streets teemed with civilians and disarmed soldiers. In order to avoid the Soviets, they used the metro tunnels, finally reaching the Kaiserhof station, near the Chancellery. Fenet was the first to reach the surface, taking much attention not to be spotted. The Chancellery was completely destroyed, deeply scarred by projectiles of all calibers. All around were enemy soldiers and tanks, a sign that now everything was really over. With his heart in his throat, he went underground

Roger Albert-Brunet

Henri Fenet

Alfred Douroux

again. His men surrounded him, wanting to know what he had seen. "The Soviets are everywhere; the führer certainly is dead," he said somberly. In order to try to evade capture and save their skins, the only solution for Fenet was to try to leave the city toward Potsdam and to make contact with Wenck's army. They would continue to use the metro tunnels to move. They thus moved toward Potsdamer Platz. Having reached there around noontime, they were forced to go aboveground. In view of the impossibility of being able to continue to move in daylight, they decided to wait until night, splitting into small groups. One of the metro tunnels led the Frenchmen to a destroyed bridge, full of rubble and abandoned objects, an ideal place to hide. Some were quickly captured, then the Soviets began to sweep the entire area, discovering other groups of Frenchmen. Only one group managed to keep hidden, that consisting of Fenet, Wallenrodt, and Douroux. Albert-Brunet also managed to join them. But their freedom was short lived because the Soviets returned to sweep the area more carefully, and this time they discovered the six Frenchmen. With their hands in the air, they were soon stripped of all that they had: watches, bracelets, chains, wallets, and finally their weapons. They were forced to march under the threat of weapons: along the way, other Soviet soldiers who were completely drunk approached the prisoner column, insulting them and threatening them with their weapons. Albert-Brunet was behind Fenet. A drunken Soviet soldier came up suddenly, pulled him by the arm, and brought him next to a house. One of the guards intervened and was able to get him back into the column. But the Soviet returned to attack, this time with a pistol in his hand, shooting Albert-Brunet in the head. The poor fellow fell to the ground, dead on the spot, the last French volunteer to fall in Berlin. The others, impotent, were forced to continue their march, with the death of their comrade on their minds. Passing near the Chancellery, they saw hundreds of enemy tanks parade along the Tiergarten to the Brandenburg Gate. It was a devastating spectacle for the European volunteers who had fought so ferociously to defend Berlin. Years after the war, General Krukenberg, with respect to the valor shown by the French during the battle of Berlin, said, "Without the Frenchmen, the Soviets would have conquered Berlin eight days earlier."

On May 2, a deathly silence fell over Berlin, and the last defenders of the capital, above all the European volunteers, surrendered to the Soviets after having tried in vain to escape capture. Those who were not shot on the spot, for being Waffen-SS combatants, were sent to prison camps, from which very few returned.

German soldiers surrendering and turning their weapons over to the Soviets, May 1945

A long column of German prisoners filing under the Brandenburg Gate, May 1945

APPENDIXES

A. UNIT INFORMATION

Divisional Insignia

The Sonnenrad (solar wheel) enclosed in a circle

Division designations

Kampfverbände "Waräger" (February 1943)
Germanische-Freiwilligen-Division (February 1943)
14.(germ.) SS-Panzer-Grenadier-Division (March 1943)
(11).SS-Freiwilligen-Panzer-Grenadier-Division "Nordland" (March 17, 1943–November 12, 1943)
11.SS-Freiwilligen-Panzer-Division "Nordland" (November 12, 1943–May 1945)

Commanders

SS-Gruppenführer Fritz von Scholz	May 1, 1943–July 27, 1944
SS-Brigadeführer Joachim Ziegler	July 27, 1944–April 26, 1945
SS-Brigadeführer Dr. Gustav Krukenberg	April 26, 1945–May 1945

Vehicle insignia

Painted on most of the division's motor vehicles, almost never on armored vehicles, tanks, and assault guns.

Divisional collar tab

A special collar tab with the Sonnenrad was produced for "Nordland"; however, most of its members, especially veterans, preferred to use the classic SS tab with the double runes.

Arm patches

The Danish and Norwegian volunteers of "Nordland" were authorized to wear on the left sleeve, under the Nazi eagle, a patch with the Danish or Norwegian national colors. This patch was also worn by many German officers who served with the "Norge" and "Danmark" regiments.

B. War Diary

1943

Period	Army corps	Army	Heeresgruppe	Operational area
August	*Forming*			Germany
September–November	*Forming*	2.Panzerarmee	F	Croatia
December	*In transfer*		Nord	Leningrad

1944

Period	Army corps	Army	Heeresgruppe	Operational area
January	*III.SS*	*18.Armee*	Nord	Leningrad
February	*LIV*	18.Armee	Nord	Leningrad
March	*LIV*	*AA.Narwa*	Nord	Narva
April–September	*III.SS*	*AA.Narwa*	Nord	Narva
October	*In reserve*	-	Nord	Kurland
November	*III.SS*	*18.Armee*	Nord	Kurland

1945

Period	Army corps	Army	Heeresgruppe	Operational area
January	*III.SS*	*18.Armee*	Nord	Kurland
February	*III.SS*	11.Armee	Weichsel	Pomerania
March	*III.SS*	*3.Panzerarmee*	Weichsel	Pomerania
April	*z. Vfg.*	*3.Panzerarmee*	Weichsel	Oder
May	*LIV*			Berlin

C. ORDER OF BATTLE

Aufstellungsstab: formed in May 1943 to be later transformed into the Divisions-Stab
SS-Divisions-Kartenstelle (mot.)
SS-Divisions-Begleit-Kompanie 11
SS-Feldgendarmerie-Trupp 11
SS-Kriegsberichter-Zug 11
SS-Bewährungs-Kompanie 11

SS-Kradschützen-Regiment: Formed on paper in May 1943, it was finally transformed into a reconnaissance battalion on June 28, 1943.

SS-Grenadier-Regiment "Norge": Formed in May 1943, based on the Den Norske Legion. It was later renamed SS-Grenadier-Regiment 2 "Norge;" then SS-Panzergrenadier-Regiment "Norge"; then SS-Panzergrenadier-Regiment 23 "Norge" on November 12, 1943; then SS-Panzergrenadier-Regiment 23 "Norge" (norwegisches Nr.1) on January 22, 1944. Its I Bataillon was disbanded in spring of 1944 before being reconstituted during the summer and autumn of the same year. In January 1945, it was equipped with half-tracks and transferred to the Hungarian front, where it was assigned to the 5.SS-Panzerdivision "Wiking."

SS-Grenadier-Regiment "Danmark": Formed in May 1943, based on the Freikorps "Danmark." It was renamed as SS-Grenadier-Regiment 1 "Danmark"; then as SS-Panzergrenadier-Regiment 24 "Danmark" on November 12, 1943; and finally as SS-Panzergrenadier-Regiment 24 "Danmark" (dänisches Nr.1) on January 22, 1944. Its I Bataillon followed the same path as did I./SS-Pz.Gren.Rgt.23.

SS-Panzer-Abteilung 11 "Hermann von Salza": Formed in summer 1943. It was upgraded to a regiment (SS-Panzer-Regiment 11 "Hermann von Salza") in late 1944. Probably its second battalion was never equipped with tanks and was employed as an infantry unit during the battle of Berlin in April 1945.

SS-Artillerie-Regiment 11: Formed in spring of 1943. It consisted of three groups: the first two were equipped with 105 mm le.FH18 howitzers, and a third with 150 mm s.FH18 howitzers and a 105 mm s.FK battery.

SS-Panzer-Aufklärungs-Abteilung 11: Formed on June 28, 1944, based on the SS-Kradschützen-Regiment

SS-Pionier-Bataillon (mot.): Formed in spring of 1943. It was renamed SS-(Panzer)-Pionier-Bataillon 11.

SS-Nachrichten-Abteilung (mot.): Formed in spring of 1943. Rebaptized SS-(Panzer) Nachrichten-Abteilung 11.

SS-Sturmgeschütz-Abteilung 11: Rebaptized SS-Panzerjäger-Abteilung 11 in 1944

SS-Flak-Abteilung 11: Formed in summer 1943 at Arys in East Prussia. It did not reach the division until December 1943. It consisted of the following elements:
- Stabs-Batterie: SS-Ostuf. Schneider
- 1.(8.8 cm) Flak-Batterie: SS-Hstuf. Leube, then SS-Hstuf. Wirth
- 2 (8.8 cm) Flak-Batterie: SS-Hstuf. Delfs
- 3 (8.8 cm) Flak-Batterie: SS-Hstuf. Mende
- 4 (3.7 cm, then Zwillig) Flak-Batterie: SS-Hstuf. Rolf Holzboog

SS-Divisions-Nachschubtruppen 11: Consisted of the following elements:
1.–4.SS-Kraftfahr-Kompanie
5–8.grosse SS-Kraftwagen-und-Nachschub-Kompanie

SS-(Panzer) Instandesetzungs Abteilung 11

SS-Wirtschafts-Bataillon 11: Rebaptized SS-Verwaltungstruppen-Abteilung 11 in August 1944

SS-Sanitäts-Abteilung 11
1. and 2. Sanitäts-Kompanie 11
SS-Feldlazarett 11
SS-Krankenkraftwagen-Züge

SS-Feldersatz-Bataillon 11: Also known as SS-Bataillon z.b.V. "Nordland"

D. FELDPOST NUMBERS

The Feldpost (field post office) number served to identify the unit within the German military postal system. This system served mainly to hide the unit affiliation of a soldier to a specific unit, but above all to be able to identify the exact location of the unit itself. That is why, even for families to correspond with their loved ones, they had to use the Feldpost number.

Unit	Feldpost Number
Divisionsstab	33 316
SS-Panzergrenadier-Regiment 23 "Norge"	41 891
I.Bataillon	32 298
II.Bataillon	42 264
III.Bataillon	32 878
14.Kompanie	38 387
15.Kompanie	33 725
16.Kompanie	43 509
SS-Panzergrenadier-Regiment 24 "Danmark"	35 408
I.Bataillon	40 670
II.Bataillon	37 826
III.Bataillon	34 531
14.Kompanie	35 637
15.Kompanie	41 702
16.Kompanie	33 362
SS-Artillerie-Regiment 11	42 973
I.Abteilung	35 179
II.Abteilung	32 895
III.Abteilung	34 885
SS-Panzer-Abteilung 11 "Hermann von Salza"	32 192
SS-Panzer-Aufklärungs-Abteilung 11	33 756
SS-Wirtschafts-Bataillon 11	39 384
SS-Pionier-Bataillon 11	38 749
SS-Flak-Abteilung 11	43 111
SS-Nachrichten-Abteilung 11	48 843
SS-Feldersatz-Bataillon 11	59 858

E. RANK EQUIVALENTS, WAFFEN-SS/HEER

SS Rank	Collar tab	Corresponding Heer rank	until 1941
Oberstgruppenführer		Generaloberst	
Obergruppenführer		General der Infanterie	
Gruppenführer		Generalleutnant	
Brigadeführer		Generalmajor	
Oberführer		—	
Standartenführer		Oberst	
Obersturmbannführer		Oberstleutnant	
Sturmbannführer		Major	
Hauptsturmführer		Hauptmann	
Obersturmführer		Oberleutnant	
Untersturmführer		Leutnant	
Sturmscharführer		Stabfeldwebel	

SS Rank	Collar tab	Heer rank	until 1941
Hauptscharführer		Oberfeldwebel	
Oberscharführer		Feldwebel	
Scharführer		Unterfeldwebel	
Unterscharführer		Unteroffizier	
Rottenführer		Obergefreiter	
Sturmmann		Gefreiter	
Oberschütze, Schütze, SS-Reiter		Oberschütze	

Abbreviations Used for Waffen-SS Staff Officers

Ia   Chief of staff, or principal operations officer for units above division level (army, army corps, etc.)
Ib   Logistics, service and supply officer
Ic   Intelligence officer
IIa   Deputy personnel officer (for officer personnel)
IIb   Deputy personnel officer (for NCO personnel)
III   Legal officer
IVa   Military commissariat officer
IVb   Medical officer
IVc   Veterinary officer
IVd   Dentist
V   Engineer
VI   Political training officer
01   1st orderly officer assigned to Ia
02   2nd orderly officer assigned to Ib
03   3rd orderly officer assigned to Ic
04   4th orderly officer assigned to division headquarters
Arko   Army corps artillery commander
FG   Military police
Harko   Army artillery commander
KB   War correspondent
Stopi   Army corps engineer commander
WaMun   Officer in charge of arms and ammunition (ordnance) until 1943
WuG   Officer in charge of arms and equipment (ordnance) from 1943 onward
TFK   Technischer Führer im Kraftfahrwesen: Technical officer assigned to vehicle maintenance

Ranks for Cadet Officers

When they attended the SS-Junkerschule, officer cadets were given the rank of SS-Junker (equivalent to the rank of SS-Unterscharführer). About halfway through this course, the cadets were given a very hard exam, and those who passed it received the rank of SS-Standartenjunker (equivalent to the rank of SS-Scharführer) and began the second phase of the course. Once the training was completed, the rank of SS-Standartenoberjunker (SS-Hauptscharführer) was awarded. They were then sent to various specialist schools to complete their military training. The cadets (who were not yet officers) then had to complete their training directly at the front, serving in a combat unit, after which they were promoted to the rank of SS-Untersturmführer.

F. "NORDLAND" KNIGHT'S CROSS RECIPIENTS

Ritterkreuz

Mit Eichenlaub

Mit Eichenlaub und
Schwerte

The institution of the Iron Cross (Eisernes Kreuz) hearkens back to the period of the Napoleonic Wars, during Prussia's fight for independence, and in the following years remained as the highest decoration of the German and Prussian armies. The decoration was awarded to soldiers of every branch and rank. There were two classes, 1st Class (EK I Klasse) and 2nd Class (EK II Klasse). For higher ranks there was the Grand Cross (Grosskreuz). With the beginning of the Second World War, Adolf Hitler modified the rules for decoration as well as its appearance. The Iron Cross of 1939 differed from earlier versions because of the presence of the swastika in its center (in place of the Prussian crown) and because of the year of its adoption (1939) displayed in the lower portion. The degrees of the decoration rose to four: in addition to the 1st Class, 2nd Class, and Grand Cross, the Knight's Cross was added (Ritterkreuz des Eisernen Kreuzes), which like the Grand Cross was worn on the neck with a ribbon (which was 45 mm wide) in the colors of the Reich: black, white, and red. For veterans of the First World War who had already been awarded the Iron Cross, a special badge was instituted (Spange 1939) to be attached to the award's ribbon, representing a National Socialist eagle, with the year 1939 indicated at the bottom of the badge. The dimensions of the Iron Cross were 44 × 44 mm, while those of the Grand Cross were 63 × 63 mm. The Grand Cross was awarded only once, to Air Marshal Hermann Göring. Awarding the various decorations was strictly sequential, in the sense that a given degree of the Iron Cross could be awarded only if the preceding degree had already been awarded. This meant that, for example, to receive the Knight's Cross, it was not enough to distinguish oneself in combat, but that the recipient already had to have been awarded the Iron Cross 1st and 2nd Classes. In particular, the Ritterkreuz was awarded for "acts of particularly decisive heroism in combat along with great personal determination." Hitler personally ordered that the population was to show gratitude toward those who were awarded the Ritterkreuz. The Iron Cross and the Knight's Cross were very similar in appearance but were easily distinguished by how they were worn on the uniform. The Iron Cross was "pinned" to the left side of the uniform. When the Iron Cross First Class was awarded, the Second Class was represented by a small ribbon attached to the second uniform button from the top. Because of the lengthening of the war, in 1940, degrees higher than the Knight's Cross were instituted. On July 3, 1940, the "Oak Leaves" (Eichenlaub) was instituted, consisting of three oak leaves in silver to be affixed to the eyelet that held the Knight's Cross. On June 21, 1941, the "Oak Leaves with Swords" (Eichenlaub und Schwerten) was added, which consisted of two crossed swords below the oak leaves. On July 15, 1941, diamonds were added to the oak leaves (Ritterkreuz des Eisernes Kreuzes Mit Eichenlaub, Schwerten und Brillanten).

Ritterkreuz des Eisernes Kreuzes mit Eichenlaub und Schwerten: Knight's Cross with Oak Leaves and Swords

Name	Rank	Unit and position	Date
Fritz von Scholz	SS-Brigadeführer	Divisions-Kommandeur	8.8.1944

Ritterkreuz des Eisernes Kreuzes mit Eichenlaub: Knight's Cross with Oak Leaves

Name	Rank	Unit and position	Date
Fritz von Scholz	SS-Brigadeführer	Divisions-Kommandeur	03.12.1944
Albrecht Krügel	SS-Obersturmbannführer	Kdr. SS-Pz.Gren.Rgt.24 "Danmark"	11.18.1944
Paul-Albert Kausch	SS-Obersturmbannführer	Kdr. SS-Pz.Rgt.11 "Hermann von Salza"	4.23.1945
Fritz Bunse	SS-Sturmbannführer	Kdr. SS-Pi.Btl.11	2.5.1944
Albrecht Krügel	SS-Sturmbannführer	Kdr. II. / SS-Pz.Gren.Rgt.23 "Norge"	3.12.1944
Hanns-Heinrich Lohmann	SS-Sturmbannführer	Kdr. III. / SS-Pz.Gren.Rgt23 "Norge"	3.13.1944
Rudolf Saalbach	SS-Hauptsturmführer	Kdr. SS-Pz.Aufkl.-Abt.11	3.25.1944
Georg Langendorf	SS-Untersturmführer	Chef 5.Kp. / SS-Pz.Aufkl.-Abt.11	3.25.1944
Walter Seebach	SS-Obersturmführer	Chef 5.Kp. / SS-Pz.Gren.Rgt.24 "Danmark"	3.25.1944

Arnold Stoffers	SS-Sturmbannführer	Kdr. SS-Pz.Gren.Rgt.23 "Norge"	3.25.1944
Philip Wild	SS-Oberscharführer	SS-Pz.Abt.11 "Hermann von Salza"	4.5.1945
Heinz Hämel	SS-Hauptsturmführer	Chef 7.Kp. / SS-Pz.Gren.Rgt.24 "Danmark"	6.5.1944
Egon Christophersen	SS-Unterscharführer	Gruf.i.d.7.Kp. / SS-Pz.Gren.Rgt.24 "Danmark"	6.5.1944
Josef Bachmeier	SS-Hauptsturmführer	Fhr. II. / SS-Pz.Gren.Rgt.23 "Norge"	8.27.1944
Paul-Albert Kausch	SS-Sturmbannführer.	Kdr.SS-Pz.Abt.11 "Hermann von Salza"	8.28.1944
Albert Hektor	SS-Oberscharführer	Zugführer 7.Kp. / SS-Pz.Gren. Rgt.24 "Danmark"	8.23.1944
Joachim Ziegler	SS-Brigadeführer	Divisions-Kommandeur	9.15.1944
Hermann Potscha	SS-Sturmbannführer	Kdr. III.SS-Art.Rgt.11	9.15.1944
Friedrich-Wilhelm Karl	SS-Obersturmbannführer	Kdr. SS-Art.Rgt.11	9.27.1944
Martin Gürz	SS-Hauptsturmführer	Fhr. III. / SS-Pz.Gren.Rgt.23 "Norge"	11.6.1944
Kasper Sporck	SS-Unterscharführer	SS-Pz.Aufkl.-Abt.11	11.16.1944
Richard Spörle	SS-Hauptsturmführer	Fhr. II. / SS-Pz.Gren.Rgt.23 "Norge"	11.25.1944
Siegfreid Lüngen	SS-Hauptscharführer	Fhr. 6.Kp,/SS-Pz.Gren.Rgt.23 "Norge"	11.25.1944
Fritz Knöchlein	SS-Obersturmbannführer	Kdr.SS-Pz.Gren.Rgt.23 "Norge"	11.25.1944
Willi Hund	SS-Obersturmführer	Chef 7.Kp. / SS-Pz.Gren.Rgt.23 "Norge"	4.20.1945
Karl-Heinz Gieseler	SS-Untersturmführer	Chef of a Kampfgruppe in Berlin	4.29.1945
Karl-Heinz Schulz-Streek	SS-Untersturmführer	Kdr. SS-Pz.Jg.-abt.11	5.2.1945

G. "Nordland" German Cross in Gold Recipients

The German Cross (Kriegsorden) was instituted on September 28, 1941, by Adolf Hitler (Führer und Oberster Befehlshaber der Wehrmacht), to honor acts of heroism by German units on the Eastern Front. The award existed in two classes, gold and silver, independent of each other, with no hierarchy. The Gold Class was awarded for repeated acts of heroism in the face of the enemy, which, however, did not justify the award of the Knight's Cross. The Silver Class was awarded for single acts of valor in the conduct of military operations.

"Nordland" German Cross in Gold Recipients

Name	Date conferred	Rank	Unit and position
Heinz Fechner	3.12.1944	*SS-Obersturmführer*	Fhr. 3.Kp.SS-Pz.Gren.Rgt. "Norge"
Günther Viercks	3.25.1944	SS-Hauptsturmführer	Chef 7.Bttr. / SS-Art.Rgt.11
Hermann Potschka	3.29.1944	SS-Sturmbannführer	Kdr. III.SS-Art.Rgt.11
Hermenegild von Westphalen	4.23.1944	SS-Obersturmbannführer	Kdr. SS-Pz.Gren.Rgt.24 "Danmark"
Walter Körner	4.28.1944	SS-Obersturmführer	Chef 8.Kp. / SS-Pz.Gren.Rgt.23 "Norge"
Clemens Diedrichs	4.30.1944	SS-Obersturmführer	Chef 7.Kp. / SS-Pz.Gren.Rgt.23 "Norge"
Erhard Göttlich	4.30.1944	SS-Obersturmführer	Chef 6.Kp. / SS-Pz.Gren.Rgt.23 "Norge"
Helmut von Bocklberg	8.19.1944	SS-Obersturmbannführer	Div. Ia
Friedrich-Wilhelm Karl	8.19.1944	SS-Obersturmbannführer	Kdr. SS-Art.Rgt.11
Karl-Heinz Schulz-Streek	8.19.1944	SS-Hauptsturmführer	Kdr. SS-PzJg.-Abt.11
Artur Grathwohl	8.29.1944	SS-Hauptsturmführer	Chef 4.Kp. / SS-Pz.Abt.11 "HvS"
Rolf Holzboog	9.17.1944	SS-Obersturmführer	Chef 4.Bttr. / SS-Flak-Abt.11
Kurt Kühne	9.17.1944	SS-Hauptscharführer	4.Kp. / SS-Pz.Abt.11 "HvS"
Georg Wille	9.17.1944	SS-Standartenoberjunker	Zgf.i.d.4.Kp. / SS-Pz.Abt.11 "HvS"
Herbert Meyer	10.14.1944	SS-Hauptsturmführer	SS-Pz.Gren.Rgt.24 "Danmark"
Per Sörensen	10.14.1944	SS-Hauptsturmführer	Fhr. Kampfgruppe "Danmark"
Richard Braunstein	10.27.1944	SS-Untersturmführer	Stabs-Kp. / SS-Pz.Abt.11 "HvS"
Ernst Stübben	10.27.1944	SS-Obersturmführer	Chef 3.Kp. / SS-Pz.Abt.11 "HvS"
Paul Falke	11.01.1944	SS-Hauptsturmführer	Chef 2.Kp. / SS-Pz.Abt.11 "HvS"
Rudolf Ternedde	11.14.1944	SS-Hauptsturmführer	Kdr.III. / SS-Pz.Gren.Rgt.24 "Danmark"
Karl von Renteln	11.28.1944	SS-Untersturmführer	SS-Pz.Jg.-Abt.11
Karl Theilacker	11.28.1944	SS-Hauptscharführer	Zgf.i.d.7.Kp. / SS-Pz.Gr.Rgt.23 "Norge"
Rudolf Rott	12.18.1944	SS-Obersturmführer	Chef 3.Kp. / SS-Pz.Abt.11 "HvS"
Otto Kroll	12.30.1944	SS-Hauptsturmführer	Fhr. I. / SS-Art.Rgt.11
Siegfried Lorenz	12.30.1944	SS-Obersturmführer	Chef 1.Kp. / SS-Pz.Abt.11 "HvS"
Karl Kutsch	1.7.1945	SS-Oberscharführer Zgf.i.d.9.Kp. / SS-Pz.Gren.Rgt.23 "Norge"	09.06.1942
Walter Plöw	1.13.1945	SS-Obersturmbannführer	Kdr. SS-Flak-Abt.11
August Loderhose	1.20.1945	SS-Hauptsturmführer	Rgt. Artzt. / SS-Art.Rgt.11
Georg Langendorf	3.30.1945	SS-Obersturmführer	Chef 5.Lp. / SS-Pz.Aufkl.-Abt.11
Alfred Wedel	3.30.1945	SS-Oberscharführer	Pz.Kdt.4.Kp. / SS-Pz.Abt.11 "HvS"

H. UNIT COMMANDERS

Div.Kdr.	SS-Brigadeführer und Generalmajor der Waffen-SS Fritz von Scholz
	SS-Oberführer Joachim Ziegler
	SS-Brigadeführer und Generalmajor der Waffen-SS Gustav Krukenberg
Ia	SS-Sturmbannführer Dietrich Ziemssen
	SS-Obersturmbannführer Helmut von Bockelberg
	SS-Obersturmbannführer Erich von Bock und Pollach
	SS-Sturmbannführer Herbert Wienczek
01	SS-Hauptsturmführer Max Kille
	SS-Sturmbannführer Erich Hartmann
	SS-Hauptsturmführer Karl-Otto Schlei
	SS-Hauptsturmführer Alfred Luger
	SS-Obersturmführer Otto Bothe
04	SS-Untersturmführer John Nygaard
Ib	SS-Sturmbannführer Vollmer
	SS-Sturmbannführer Gerhard Noatzke
	SS-Sturmbannführer Joachim Tiburtius
02	SS-Hauptsturmführer Hans-Jürgen Gerosch
Ic	SS-Obersturmführer Walter Faltz
	SS-Hauptsturmführer Günter Greef
	SS-Hauptsturmführer Hans-Gösta Pehrsson
	SS-Obersturmführer Gerhard Riik
03	SS-Untersturmführer Paul Koopman
IIa	SS-Sturmbannführer Harry Willer
	SS-Sturmbannführer Kurt Witten
	SS-Sturmbannführer Albert Bergfeld
	SS-Hauptsturmführer Walter Meyer
III	SS-Sturmbannführer Karl Hackmeister
	SS-Hauptsturmführer Ziak (?)
IV and Kdr. SS-Wi.-Btl.11	SS-Sturmbannführer Siegfried Conrad
	SS-Sturmbannführer Walter Meyer
Ivb and Kdr. SS-San.Abt.11	SS-Standartenführer Hans Schlosser
	SS-Sturmbannführer Wolfgang Trost
V and Kdr. SS-Pz.Inst.-Abt.11	SS-Hauptsturmführer Eugen Popp
	SS-Hauptsturmführer Michael Schindlbeck
	SS-Hauptsturmführer Kurt Buck
VI	SS-Obersturmführer Richard Gram
WaMun	SS-Hauptsturmführer Hans Keil
Kartenstelle	SS-Obersturmführer Siegfried Meissner
Div.Begleit-Kp.	SS-Sturmbannführer Otto Vollmar
SS-Pz.Abt.11 / SSPz.Rgt11 "Hermann von Salza"	SS-Sturmbannführer Otto Paetsch
	SS-Sturmbannführer Paul Albert Kausch
I.Abt.	SS-Hauptsturmführer Artur Grathwold
II.Abt.	SS-Hauptsturmführer Paul Falke
SS-Pz.Gren.Rgt.23 "Norge"	SS-Obersturmbannführer Wolfgang Jörchel
	SS-Sturmbannführer Arnold Stoffers
	SS-Obersturmbannführer Fritz Knöchlein
	SS-Obersturmbannführer Wilhelm Körbel
I.Btl.	SS-Sturmbannführer Finn Finson
	SS-Hauptsturmführer Fritz Vogt
	SS-Hauptsturmführer Robert Haas
	SS-Hauptsturmführer Helmuth Gutowski
II.Btl.	SS-Sturmbannführer Albrecht Krügel
	SS-Hauptsturmführer Michael Thöny
	SS-Sturmbannführer Siegfried Scheibe
	SS-Hauptsturmführer Josef Bachmeier
	SS-Obersturmführer Klaus Kleuker
	SS-Hauptsturmführer Richard Spörle
III.Btl.	SS-Sturmbannführer Hans Lohmann

SS-Pz.Gren.Rgt.24 "Danmark"		SS-Hauptsturmführer Martin Gürz
		SS-Hauptsturmführer Ludwig Hoffmann
		SS-Obersturmbannführer Hermenegild von Westphalen
		SS-Obersturmbannführer Albrecht Krügel
		SS-Obersturmbannführer Rudolf Klotz
		SS-Sturmbannführer Rudolf Ternedde
		SS-Sturmbannführer Per Sörensen
		SS-Obersturmführer Petersen
	I.Btl.	SS-Sturmbannführer Knud Martinsen
		SS-Sturmbannführer Fischer
		SS-Hauptsturmführer Per Sörensen
		SS-Sturmbannführer Helmuth Gutowski
		SS-Sturmbannführer Hermann Im Masche
	II.Btl.	SS-Hauptsturmführer Kurt Walther
		SS-Hauptsturmführer Heinz Hämel
		SS-Hauptsturmführer Albert Bergfeld
		SS-Sturmbannführer Per Sörensen
		SS-Sturmbannführer Albert Bergfeld
		SS-Hauptsturmführer Ellef Rasmussen
	III.Btl.	SS-Sturmbannführer Poul Neergaard-Jacobsen
		SS-Sturmbannführer Hans Kappus
		SS-Hauptsturmführer Rudolf Ternedde
		SS-Obersturmführer Dirksen
SS-Art.-Rgt.11		SS-Obersturmbannführer Friedrich-Wilhelm Karl
	I.Abt.	SS-Hauptsturmführer Wilhelm Müller
		SS-Hauptsturmführer Otto Kroll
		SS-Hauptsturmführer Hans Wischmann
	II.Abt.	SS-Sturmbannführer Alfred Fischer
	III.Abt.	SS-Sturmbannführer Hermann Potschka
SS-Pz.Aufkl.-Abt.11		SS-Hauptsturmführer Rudolf Saalbach
SS-Pi.-Btl.11		SS-Sturmbannführer Fritz Bunse
		SS-Hauptsturmführer Adolf Wolff
		SS-Hauptsturmführer Hermann Voss
		SS-Sturmbannführer Wilhelm Stapper
SS-Nachr.-Abt.11		SS-Sturmbannführer Rüdiger Weitzdörfer
		SS-Obersturmbannführer Eugen Schlotter
		SS-Hauptsturmführer Günther Schnick
SS-Pz.Jg.-Abt.11		SS-Hauptsturmführer Ernst Röntsch
		SS-Sturmbannführer Karl Schulz-Streek
SS-Flak-Abt.11		SS-Sturmbannführer Walter Plöw
		SS-Sturmbannführer Emil Kurz
SS-Div.-Nachs.-Truppen 11		SS-Sturmbannführer Friedrich Gläsker
SS-FEB 11		SS-Sturmbannführer Fritz Lang

I. Cuff Titles

Cuff or sleeve titles, reflecting the name of the unit of affiliation, were worn not only by members of the Waffen-SS, but also by other elite army and Luftwaffe units. These bands of black cloth, with letters embroidered either by hand or by machine, measured 28 mm wide by 490 mm long and were worn on the left sleeve of the uniform almost at wrist level. For some Waffen-SS divisions, more than one title was produced, various versions for the division itself or specific versions for the various regiments within the division. The cuff titles represented a unique element of the SS uniform. They served to identify the unit affiliation and were thus issued to all members of SS formations as an integral part of the uniform. Throughout the war, the cuff titles became increasingly important and were issued during solemn ceremonies to glorify belonging to various military formations.

Cuff title types

On the basis of their manner of production, cuff titles were divided into four categories:

1st Type: Hand-embroidered with aluminum wire thread. This type was produced from 1933 until June 1942. It was used by all NCOs until 1936, but thereafter only by officers.

2nd Type: Machine-embroidered with white cotton thread or silver-gray thread. This type, designated RZM (**R**eich**Z**eug**M**eister, produced by machine), was produced between 1936 and 1943 specifically for NCOs and enlisted troops.

3rd Type: Machine-woven with aluminum wire thread, produced between 1939 and 1943, for use only by officers

4th Type: Machine-woven with thin gray cotton or silk thread. This type, called the BeVo (**Be**teiligung **Vo**rsteher) type, was produced between 1943 and 1945 for all ranks.

"Nordland" cuff titles

Four cuff titles were authorized for members of the "Nordland" division, one with the inscription "Nordland," authorized in 1940 for the regiment of the same name, and three others with the names of the major subunits: "Danmark" (1943), "Norge" (1943), and the "Hermann von Salza" armored regiment (1944).

ENDNOTES

Chapter I

1. The name referred to the Variaghi or Varenghi, the Nordic people (the Nordics were the Germanic populations of south-central Scandinavia and northern Germany) who migrated to the Scandinavian peninsula to the southeast, as pirates and businessmen, and serving as mercenaries, reaching as far as the Caspian Sea and Constantinople. In their chronicles the Byzantines used the term "Variaghi" to refer to both the Scandinavians as well as other Germanic groups associated with them.

2. SS-FHA order number 529/43, dated April 19, 1943.

3. Felix Martin Julius Steiner was born on May 23, 1896, in Stallupönen, East Prussia. After having earned his diploma in March 1914, he volunteered for the army and was assigned to InfanterieRegiment "von Boyen" (5 Ostpreussisches) Nr. 41 (1 Division). On January 27, 1915, he was promoted to Leutnant. He was awarded both classes of the Iron Cross and on October 18, 1918, was promoted to Oberleutnant. After the war he served in several Free Corps in the Memel area, and in May 1920 he joined the Reichswehr. In late 1933, he left the army with the rank of major and transferred to the Landespolizei, where he served as an instructor. It was during that period that he joined the National Socialist Party, joining the SA. On February 1, 1934, he was promoted to SA-Sturmführer. In January 1935, Steiner left the SA and on April 30, 1935, entered the SS (SS-Nr. 253 351), serving on Himmler's staff as an Obersturmbannführer. In early June 1935, he replaced SS-Obersturmbannführer Curt von Gottberg as commander of III./SS-Standarte 1 and led that battalion until July 1936. Meanwhile, on June 17, 1936, he was promoted to Standartenführer. On July 1, 1936, he assumed command of SS-Standarte 1, which became SS-Regiment "Deutschland." Steiner made a name for himself by introducing new training methods for SS troops and for his innovative ideas regarding war of movement and the use of extremely mobile assault units on the battlefield. He is also to be credited for the choice of using camouflage uniforms for SS troops. He led the "Deutschland" regiment during the Polish campaign, as part of Panzer-Division "Kempf." For his actions in Poland, both of his Iron Crosses were reconfirmed. The "Deutschland" became part of the new SS-V.T.-Division in October 1939. Steiner was promoted to Oberführer on January 1, 1940. For valor shown on the battlefield during the campaign on the Western Front, he was awarded the Knight's Cross on August 15, 1940. On November 9, 1940, Steiner was promoted to SS-Brigadeführer und General Major der Waffen-SS, taking command of the new SS "Wiking" division, which he led during the campaign on the Eastern Front in 1941 and on the Caucasus front in 1942. On April 22, 1942, he was awarded the German Cross in Gold and on December 23 with the Oak Leaves for his Knight's Cross. Meanwhile, on January 1, 1942, he was promoted to SS-Gruppenführer, and on July 1, 1943, to SS-Obergruppenführer.

4. This regiment was formed in 1940 following the occupation of Denmark and Norway, when Gottlob Berger, head of the SS-Hauptamt, thought of finding new recruits for the Waffen-SS in those two countries. Thus, on April 20, 1940, the SS-FHA ordered the creation of the SS-Standarte "Nordland" with Danish and Norwegian volunteers. Command of the SS-Standarte "Nordland" was initially assigned to SS-Staf. Gottfried Klingemann, while as of December 1, 1940, the regiment came under the command of SS-Ostubaf. Fritz von Scholz Edler von Rarancze. The regiment was assigned to the "Wiking" division in 1941 and participated in all the campaigns on the Eastern Front. In 1942, a battalion of Finnish volunteers was attached to the regiment.

5. Initially, Gottlob Berger proposed names less linked with national geographic areas for the three regiments, to avoid problems coming from other countries, such as "Thule" or "Germanien"; however, as Heinrich Himmler later explained to Felix Steiner, Hitler had personally intervened in the decision.

6. The number 14 was justified by the fact that at that time, the formation of an 11.Lettische SS-Freiwilligen-Division, a 12.Litauische SS-Freiwilligen-Division, and a 13.Kroatische SS-Freiwilligen-Division had been planned.

7. Fritz von Scholz Edler von Raranancze, born in Pilsen in 1896, served in an artillery regiment of the Austro-Hungarian army during the First World War. Promoted to Oberleutnant in November 1917, for valor in the field he was awarded the Gold Cross for Courage and the Silver Cross for Merit. After the war, he was a volunteer in the "Oberland" Free Corps. In 1932, he joined the Austrian National Socialist Party, and on June 10, 1933, he joined the SS (SS-Nr. 135 638), moving to Germany. He served in the Austrian Legion in Lechfeld until October 1934, when the unit became the II.Bataillon of the future Standarte "Deutschland." On August 21, 1924, he was promoted SS-Untersturmführer and given command first of 5.Kompanie and then as SS-Obersturmführer of 8.Kompanie. On January 30, 1936, he was promoted to SS-Hauptsturmführer. Following the annexation of Austria to the Reich in March 1938, the members of the Austrian Legion formed the 3.SS-Standarte der SS-Verfügungstruppe, which then became the SS-Standarte "Der Führer." Fritz von Scholz assumed command of II.Bataillon and as unit commander was awarded both classes of the Iron Cross during the campaign on the Western Front. On January 30, 1940, he was promoted to SS-Obersturmbannführer, and on January 30, 1941, to Standartenführer, taking command of the "Nordland" regiment of the "Wiking." On November 22, 1941, he was awarded the German Cross in Gold, and on January 19, 1942, with the Knight's Cross. Before assuming command of the "Nordland," for several months Scholz led 1.SS-Infanterie-Brigade (mot.), attached to Army Group Center, and then 2.SS-Infanterie-Brigade (mot.), attached to Army Group North.

8. The Swedish volunteers were mainly concentrated in the 3rd Company of the reconnaissance group, which was baptized the "Swedish Company." The company also included several Estonian volunteers of Swedish "persuasion."

9. The Danish Legion, Freikorps "Danmark," was officially born on June 28, 1941, authorized by the Danish government and by King Christian himself. Recruiting offices were set up throughout Denmark. On July 19, 1941, the first 430 Danish volunteers left Denmark to be transferred to Langenhorn camp in Germany. There the volunteers found another hundred or so

of their compatriots who were veterans of the disbanded regiment SS Nordwest, and on August 10, another three hundred volunteers arrived. The Danes had worn the Waffen-SS uniform with the arm badge with the national colors (the Danish flag) and the armband on the left sleeve of the uniform with the inscription Freikorps "Danmark." The legion was placed under command of Legion-Obersturmbannführer Christian Peder Kryssing, an ex-artillery lieutenant colonel in the Royal Danish Army. The legion was organized with three infantry companies, one machine gun company, and one reserve company. On September 15, 1941, the Danish volunteers were moved to the camp at Treskow, near Poznán in Poland, where they continued their training. In February 1942, command of Freikorps "Danmark" was assumed by Christian Frederik von Schalburg, a veteran of combat in the Ukraine with the "Wiking" division, where he had bee awarded the Iron Cross and had achieved the rank of Sturmbannführer. In early April, the unit was ready for the front: it numbered 109 officers and 781 troops. From the camp at Treskow, the volunteers were sent to Kaliningrad by train. From there, they were transferred to the airport at Heilingebeil, south of Königsberg, then to be moved by air to the area around Demiansk, where they were assigned to "Gruppe Eicke"of the SS "Totenkopf" division, which was surrounded in that area along with other German units. The Danish volunteers were engaged in hard fighting to defend the gap opened by the Germans during the incessant Soviet attacks. On June 2, 1942, SS-Stubaf. Schalburg fell while leading his men during an assault against Soviet positions. On June 9, 1942, a new commander was named, SS-Obersturmbannführer Hans Albert von Lettow-Vorbeck, a German. This new commander also fell in combat two days later, during a Soviet counterattack against the Danish positions at Bolshoi Dubovitsy. SS-Stubaf. Knud Børge Martinsen then assumed command of the legion. The Danish volunteers were engaged in fighting until August 4, when the legion was retired from the front with about three hundred survivors. In early October 1942, thanks to the influx of new volunteers, the unit returned to the Eastern Front. After having been sent first to Mitau in Latvia and then to Bobruisk, in late November the Freikorps was transferred to the area around Nevel in the northern sector of the Russian front. On December 2, 1942, the Danish volunteers were engaged in the Velikje Luki sector northeast of Nevel, in another German pocket surrounded by Soviet forces. Soon after Christmas, Freikorps "Danmark" was shifted farther north to defend the railway line between Nevel and Velikje Luki. In the spring of 1943, the Danish unit came under the command of SS-Hstuf. Per Neeregaard-Jacobsen and was retired from the front and transferred to the camp at Grafenwöhr.

10. Hermenegild von Westphalen, born on March 10, 1909, in Lüdingshausen, SS-Nr. 44 597. He had previously served in 6./Sta. "Deutschland," in command of 14./"Deutschland" and I./"Deutschland," and as adjutant of II.SS-Pz.Korps.

11. The creation of the Norwegian Legion was announced by Reichskommisar Josef Terboven on June 29, 1941. Shortly after the announcement, hundreds of civilian volunteers and about four hundred officers of the Royal Norwegian Army flocked to the recruitment centers to join the Den Norske Legion, or Legion Norwegen (the German designation). Initially it was thought to commit the legion to the Finnish front; in fact, recruitment, which began on July 4, was organized with the help of the Finnish consulate in Oslo. With the roughly 1,500 volunteers available, the unit was organized as an infantry battalion, commanded by a Norwegian, Artur Quist, a former royal army officer, who was given the rank of Legion Sturmbannführer. The unit was organized with three infantry companies, a heavy company, an antitank company, and a platoon of war correspondents. Following the Soviet winter counteroffensive of December 1941, German headquarters decided not to send the legion to Finland, but to the Leningrad front instead. In early February 1942 the Norwegian volunteers were sent by train to Stettin, and from there by air to Gatschina, on the Luga River south of Leningrad. The legion was to be engaged in the Volkhov River sector, subordinate to the SS 2nd Infantry Brigade. After tough fighting and having taken heavy losses, in May 1942 the legion was retired to Konstantinovka to reorganize and to receive fresh reinforcements from the mother country. In June the Norwegian volunteers returned to the Leningrad front and were soon engaged in bitter fighting. In order to make up for the lack of replacements for the legion, in Norway the chief of police, Jonas Lie, organized a company of Norwegian policemen, the 1.Politie.Kompanie. The unit, of about a hundred men, reached the front on September 2, where it was integrated in the legion's 1.Kompanie, which had suffered the most losses. Fighting continued until the month of December, a period during which the strength of the legion fell to only seven hundred men. In early 1943, Jonas Lie replaced Quist in command of the legion. During the second week of February, the Norwegian volunteers participated in the second battle of Lake Ladoga, during which the legion's antitank company distinguished itself. At the end of February, the legion was regrouped behind the front lines at Krasnoje Selo and, from March 1, in groups, began to be repatriated.

12. Finn Finson, born on August 12, 1911. In reality, his real name was Fin Halvorsen, the officer of the torpedo boat that on February 16, 1940, had helped the British board the German merchantman *Altmark* when it was attacked in Norwegian territorial waters. With the German occupation of the country, he decided to change his surname. He then joined the Norwegian Legion, assuming command first of 14.Kompanie and then of 2.Kompanie.

13. Wolfgang Joerchel, born August 19, 1907, in Zaborze, SS-Nr. 272 890. In May 1934, he joined the SA, and in October of the same year he switched to the SS-VT with the rank of Obersturmführer. In October 1935, he served as an instructor at the SS-Junkerschule in Bad Tölz. On February 1, 1937, he was assigned to Standarte "Germania," serving initially in 1.Kompanie, then as a platoon leader in 11.Kompanie (March 1937), and then in command of 6.Kompanie (October 1937). In late October 1937, he passed to SS-Standarte "Deutschland" as a staff officer, participating in military operations during the annexation of Austria and in the occupation of the Sudetenland in 1938. On April 20, 1938, he was promoted to SS-Hauptsturmführer, participating in the Polish campaign in September 1939 with SS-Standarte "Germania" and commanding its 12.Kompanie. In June 1940, he was again with the "Deutschland" regiment, serving in II.Bataillon. On June 29, 1940, he was awarded the Iron Cross First Class. On December 1, 1940, he took command of II./"Germania." The regiment was integrated into the "Wiking" division, and, following it, Joerchel began the campaign on the Eastern Front. On September 1, 1941, he was promoted to SS-Sturmbannführer. On March 1, 1942, he was awarded the German Cross in Gold. As of

January 10, 1943, he took command of SS.Pz.Gren.Rgt. "Nordland." On January 30, 1943, Joerchel was promoted to SS-Obersturmbannführer.

14. Friedrich Wilhelm Karl, born on September 15, 1911, at Frankfurt-am-Oder, SS.-Nr. 101 983. He served initially in 2./LSSAH, then, after having attended an officer's course at the SS-Junkerschule in Braunschweig from 1936 to 1937, he was assigned to 6./Sta. "Deutschland," then in command of 13./Germania, and then of 11./SS-Art.Rgt.5.

15. Fritz Bunse, born on July 4, 1911, in Hagen in Westphalia, SS-Nr 30 303. He had served previously in 1./LSSAH, then after having attended an officer's course at the SS-Junkerschule in Braunschweig between 1936 and 1937, he was assigned to 3./Pi.Btl. SS-VT and then took command of 16.(Pi) Kp./"Germania."

16. Ernst Rönttzsch, born on January 18, 1914, in Bretnig/ Dresden, SS-Nr. 288 514. He had served previously in 2./ LSSAH and in II./Art.Rgt. SS-VT, and in command of 9./SS-Art.Rgt.5 and 5./SS-Art.Rgt.5.

17. Rudolf Saalbach, born on March 18, 1911, at Grossenhain, SS-Nr. 127 697. Initially assigned to an SS-Totenkopfverbände,then attending an officer's course at the SS-Junkerschule in Braunschweig in 1938, he was assigned to command the 1./ SS-Tot.Aufkl.Abt.3 and then to command of SS-Aufkl.Abt.5.

18. Waler Plöw, born on February 3, 1904, in Königsberg, East Prussia, SS-Nr. 29 429. He had previously served in III./"Deutschland" and in command of III./"Nordland."

19. The armored unit bore the name of Hermann von Salza (1165–1239), the fourth great master of the Teutonic Knights, famous for having increased the power and prestige of the order, extending its conquests as far as the coasts of the Baltic Sea.

20. Paul-Albert Kausch, born on March 3, 1911, in Jädersdorf in Pomerania, SS-Nr. 82 578. He had served previously in 4./ LSSAH and after completing an officer's course at the SS-Junkerschule in Braunschweig he was assigned to various SS-Totenkopfverbände before being transferred to the "Totenkopf" artillery regiment and later that of the "Wiking."

21. Franz Riedweg was born in Lucerne (Switzerland) on April 10, 1907. After graduating, he studied medicine at the universities of Bern, Berlin, and Rostock. An anti-Communist firebrand, he became a member of Aktion gegen den Kommunismus (Action against Communism), writing several texts on the topic. He also made a film, titled *The Red Scourge*. This film drew the attention of many German personalities, including Reichsführer-SS Heinrich Himmler, who quickly offered him a position in the SS. In 1938, Riedweg moved to Germany, married a German woman, became a German citizen, and entered the SS-Verfügungstruppe (SS-Nr. 293 744). He was then assigned as a doctor to SS-Standarte "Deutschland" with the rank of SS-Hauptsturmführer and took part in the campaign on the Western Front in 1940 with the SS-VT Division. In 1941, with the help of SS-Gruf. Felix Steiner, commander of the SS-Division "Wiking," Riedweg was able to establish a special office within the SS-Hauptamt for Waffen-SS Germanic volunteers, the Germanische Leistelle. The office registered the volunteers, provided assistance, and helped them overcome all the difficulties of integrating them into the German armed forces and provided aid to their families, In addition, the same office published many periodicals and books for the volunteers to incentivize their enlistment. In 1942, Dr. Riedweg returned to his medical practice with the SS-Division "Wiking" on the Eastern Front and later was involved in the formation of III./ SS-PzKorps. At the same time, he continued to work with Germanische Leitstelle, which had been reorganized as Amstgruppe D. In 1944, SS-Ostubaf. Riedweg assumed command of the III.SS-Pz.Korps military hospital and held that post until the end of the war.

Chapter II

1. The presence of the "Wiking" in Croatia was justified by the fact that the division was initially to be a part of III.SS-Pz.Korps. In addition to the division's panzer regiment, in reality only its new armored battalion led by Mühlenkamp, the III./"Germania," also being reorganized, was present in Croatia.

2. In December 1943, when the "Nordland" was transferred to the Leningrad front, the Italian volunteers were repatriated in order to be attached to the Italian SS legion that was being formed in Italy.

3. Hans Heinrich Lohmann, born on April 24, 1911, at Gutersloh. In January 1935, he joined the SS as part of IV.Bataillon of SS-Standarte "Deutschland." In May 1935, he was promoted to SS-Untersturmführer and was assigned to lead a platoon of the SS-VT. On April 1, 1936, following a long convalescence after an accident, he was promoted to SS-Obersturmführer and was transferred as supervisor at the SS-Junkerschule in Bad Tölz. In February 1937, he was nominated as adjutant to the school commandant. Becoming a company commander in the SS-Regiment "Deutschland," he was promoted to SS-Hauptsturmführer on November 9, 1938. After having served in the army from 1939 to March 1940, he returned again to the SS-Junkerschule in Bad Tölz. On June 5, 1941, Lohmann assumed command of 2.Kompanie of SS-Infanterie-Regiment(mot.) "Westland," with which he campaigned in Russia, subordinate to the SS-Division "Wiking." Hit by an attack of malaria, he was repatriated, not returning to the front until October 1942, when he assumed command of I.Bataillon of the "Nordland" regiment of "Wiking," fighting in the Caucasus until Christmas 1942. With the same regiment, he was engaged in covering the retreat of Heeresgruppe A from the Caucasus. In February 1943, he was awarded the German Cross in Gold and promoted to Sturmbannführer. In May 1943, Nordland was detached from the "Wiking" in order to form its own division, where Lohmann assumed command of III.Bataillon of the new "Norge" regiment.

4. Jens Bernhard Lund, born on May 20, 1918, in Oslo, Norway. He had served previously in 1./SS-Pz.Rgt.1, then following an officer's course at the SS-Junkerschule in Bad Tölz he was assigned to the "Nordland."

5. Per Sörensen, born on September 24, 1913, in Randers, Denmark. He commanded 1./Freikorps "Danmark." On July 19, 1941, he was promoted to Legion-Obersturmführer. He attended the officer course at Bad Tölz between December 1941 and February 1942, returning quickly to again command 1./ Freikorps "Danmark" until May 1943, when he was transferred to command of 1./"Danmark" with the rank of Hauptsturmführer.

6. Helmut Stenger, born on June 9, 1917, in Fechtingen-Saabrücken, SS-Nr. 270 046. He had previously served in 13./ Tot.Inf.Rgt.3 and 2./SS-Tot.Flak.Abt. and in command of 4./ Freikorps "Danmark."

7. Poul Neergaard-Jacobsen, born on February 16, 1901, in Copenhagen, Denmark. He had previously commanded 3./Freikorps "Danmark" and then the Danish Freikorps.

8. Hugo Jessen, born on September 22, 1920, in Niebüll in Schleswig-Holstein. He had previously served in the SS "Der Führer" regiment of "Das Reich."

9. Heinz Hämel was born on October 25, 1914, in Obervellmar/Kassel, SS-Nr. 276 603. He had served previously in 5./Sta. "Germania." Serving on the Eastern Front with this company of the "Wiking," he was promoted as an officer, for merit shown in the field without attending a normal course at an SS-Junkerschule. On April 20, 1942, he was promoted to SS-Untersturmführer der Reserve. On June 11, 1942, for valor shown in combat, he was awarded the German Cross in Gold.

10. SS-FHA, Amt II, Org.Abt. Ia/II, Tgb. Nr. 1574/43 g. kdos, v.22.10.43.

11. SS-FHA, Amt II, Org.Abt. Ia/II, Tgb. Nr. II/9542/43 geh., v.12.11.43, Bezeichnumng der Feldtruppenteile der Waffen-SS.

12. This Tiger-Abteilung had been created on October 16, 1943, to constitute the heavy tank battalion of III.(germanisches) SS-Panzer-Korps.

Chapter III

1. Christian Peder Kryssing, born on July 7, 1891, in Kolding, Denmark. An artillery lieutenant colonel in the Royal Danish Army, he had been designated as the first commander of the Danish Legion, then moving to the "Totenkopf" artillery regiment and later to the "Wiking" division.

2. Kurt Walther was born on July 4, 1912, in Greussen/Thür, SS-Nr. 171 651. He had served previously in the LSSAH, in III./Sta. "Deutschland," and in 11./"Germania," and in command of 7./"Germania."

3. Karl Wichmann was born on March 30,1900, in Spremberg, SS-Nr. 59 774. He had previously commanded III./Waffen-Grenadier-Regiment der SS of the 15.SS.

4. Arnold Stoffers, born on September 1, 1910, in Voorde, SS-Nr. 61 313. He had served previously in II./Sta "Germania" and in command of 2./SS-Flak-Abt.5 and II./SS-Inf.Rgt. "Nordland." On December 5, 1941, he was awarded the German Cross in Gold.

5. Fritz Vogt was born in Munich on March 17, 1918. After two years in the Hitlerjugend, in 1935, he enlisted in the SS-Verfügungstruppe, in the SS-Standarte "Deutschland" (SS-Nr. 270 386). He served initially in 15.Kompanie of that regiment. After having completed his training, he was selected as a potential officer candidate and sent to the SS-Junkerschule at Braunschweig; his course lasted from April 1938 to February 1939. In April of that year, he was promoted to the rank of SS-Untersturmführer. During the Polish campaign in September 1939, he was a motorcycle recon platoon leader, distinguishing himself in several actions and becoming the first member of his unit to receive the Iron Cross Second Class. After having attended a platoon leader course and having been assigned for a brief period to an SS recon unit at Elleangen, he was integrated into the new SS-Verfügungs-Division as a motorcycle platoon leader in 2.Kompanie of the Aufklärungs-Abteilung. He then took command of that same company and on September 4, 1940, was awarded the Knight's Cross. Following a long period of convalescence for typhus, he was assigned to the Totenkopf Division. On February 8, 1942, he was awarded the German Cross in Gold.

6. Albrecht Krügel, born on April 22, 1913. He had previously served in 3./SS-N as adjutant of SS-Inf.Rgt. "Germania," and in command of 6./"Westland" and 6./"Nordland." On February 8, 1943, he was awarded the German Cross in Gold.

7. Siegfried Lorenz, born on June 9, 1920, in Grünwald in the Sudetenland, SS-Nr. 400 106. He had served previously in 15./"Deutschland" and 2./SS-Aufkl.Abt.5.

8. Heinrich Heckmüller, born on July 17, 1906, in Mettmann, SS-Nr. 9 534. He had served previously in 3./"Germania" and then in SS-Geb.Au.E.Btl.7.

9. Hans Schmidt, born on August 22, 1919, in Stadtberger/Augsburg, SS-Nr. 421 133. He had served previously in 13./"Deutschland," in 13./SS-Inf.Rgt.11, and in SS-Aufkl.-Abt.5.

10. Karl-Heinz Schulz-Streek, born on January 21, 1909, in Berlin, SS-Nr. 280 837. He had served previously as Leutnant d.R. and as Zugführer in 1.Batterie of Sturmartillerie Abteilung 192, then as Oberleutnant d.R. and Führer der Stabsbatterie of Sturmgeschütz-Abteilung 184 and as a battery commander in Sturmgeschütz-Abteilung 912. He was seriously wounded in combat in spring 1943 and thus, in autumn of 1943, was assigned as an instructor for "Nordland" assault gun units. When he assumed command of SS-Pz.Jg.Abt.1 (SS-StuG-Abt.11) in January 1944, he was admitted into the SS with the rank of SS-Hauptsturmführer d.R.

11. Helmut Krohmer, born on July 24, 1921, in Stuttgart, SS-Nr. 391 920. He had served previously in 10./"Westland."

12. Kurt Rennert, born on September 26, 1919, in Thalheim/Bitterfeld, SS-Nr. 378 006. He had served previously as adjutant of IV./SS-Art.Rgt.2.

13. Albert Knobelspiess, born on November 2, 1918, in Vienna, SS-Nr. 326 750. He had served previously in SS-Tot. Inf.Rgt.9, in SS-Totenkopf Wachbataillon "Prag," in the SS-StuG-Kompanie of the "Wiking" division, and in SS-Inf.Ers. Btl. "Westland."

14. Kurt Ellersiek, born on April 5, 1901, in Dortmund, SS-Nr. 275 719. He had served previously in 6./LSSAH.

15. Heinz Knepel, born on May 19, 1920, in Celle, SS-Nr. 400 100. He had served previously in 2./SS-Inf.Rgt. "Nordland."

16. Hermann Voss, born on September 16, 1913, in Berlin, SS-Nr. 219 359. Before taking command of 3./SS-Pi.Btl.11, he had served in the army.

17. Wolfgang Rendemann, born on December 11, 1919, in Bremen, SS-Nr. 391 930. He had served previously in SS-Inf. Rgt. "Nordland" in the "Wiking" division.

18. Otto von Bargen, born on October 11, 1915, in Kiel, SS-Nr. 135 189. He had served previously in 4./Sta. "Germania" and in SS-Inf.Rgt. "Nordland."

19. Heinz Twesmann, born on December 17, 1920, in Kamp-Linfort. He had served previously in 6./SS-Inf.Rgt. "Der Führer." He later took command of 3./"Norge."

20. Björn Binnerup, born on January 6, 1910, in Copenhagen. He had served previously as an artilleryman in the "Wiking," first in 2./SS-Art.Rgt.5 and then in command of 6./SS-Art. Rgt.5.

21. Heinz Paul Fechner, born on December 13, 1920, in Trebbin, SS-Nr. 421 026. He had previously served in 7./"Der Führer" and in 7./SS-Inf.Rgt. "Nordland," and then as adjutant of I./"Norge."

22. Heinz Henneke, born on January 14, 1912, in Stassfurt, SS-Nr. 312 936. He had served previously in command of 3./ Frikorps "Danmark" and then was assigned to command 3./"Danmark."

23. Herwarth Arera, born on May 12, 1921, in Düsseldorf, SS-Nr. 466762. He attended the SS-Pionier-Schule before being assigned to command 1./SS-Pi.Btl.11.

24. Georg Langendorf, born on July 28, 1920, in Grafenhausen, SS-Nr. 380 658. He had served previously as a machine gunner and then as a Pak crew member in SS-Pz.Jg.Abt.5 of the "Wiking."

25. Kaspar Antoine Sporck, born on August 10, 1922, in Heerlen in the province of Limburg in Holland. In 1941, he joined the "Nordwest" regiment, later to pass into the Dutch Legion, with which he participated in the first campaign on the Eastern Front. In 1943, he was assigned to the "Nordland's" recon battalion. On May 1, 1944, he was promoted to the rank of SS-Unterscharführer. On October 23, 1944, he was awarded the Knight's Cross as SS-Unterscharführer and Geschutzführer in 5.(schwere) Kompanie / SS-Aufklärungs-Abteilung 11 of 11.SS-Freiwilligen-Panzer-Grenadier-Division "Nordland," based on a recommendation dated September 3, 1944, and signed by Abt.Kdr. Rudolf Saalbach, countersigned on October 5, 1944, by Div.Kdr. Joachim Ziegler and approved on October 8, 1944, by Korps. Kom. Felix Steiner. Toward the end of the war, after having been badly wounded in combat, he died in the Bayreuth military hospital on April 8, 1945.

26. Paul Holtkamp, born on February 15, 1916, in Kaldenkirchen, SS-Nr. 312 814. He had served previously in 3./"Westland" and in command of 6./"Westland."

27. Knud Henrik Ernst Schock, born on May 31, 1899, in Copenhagen, as a former officer in the Danish army. A member of Freikorps "Danmark" as Leg.Hstuf. and commandant of 4.Kompanie. In 1943, after being promoted to Sturmbannführer, he was initially assigned to command SS-StuG.Abt.5, the new "Wiking" assault gun unit. Because the unit was late to be formed, with the only available StuG battery, the nucleus of SS-Panzerjäger Abt. 54 was formed for the "Nederland" brigade.

Chapter IV

1. Bernhard von Matt, born on July 31, in Dornburn/ Vorarlberg, SS-Nr. 400 198. He had served previously in the "Wiking" as adjutant of III./SS-Art.Rgt.5.

2. Walter Seebach, born on November 5, 1920, in Heerlen, Holland, of German parents. Returning to Germany with his family in the 1930s, he joined the Hitlerjugend and then joined the SS (SS-Nr. 405 893), serving as an SS-Scharführer in 6./ Sta. "Germania" during the Polish campaign, distinguishing himself in combat and earning the Iron Cross Second Class. In November 1939, Seebach was selected to become an officer and was first sent to the SS-Junkerschule in Bad Tölz and then, in April 1940, to the SS-Junkerschule in Braunschweig. Promoted to SS-Untersturmführer, on November 9, 1941, he was assigned to SS-Inf.Rgt. "Germania" of SS-Division (mot.) "Wiking." He distinguished himself in defensive fighting on the Mius front and on December 24, 1941, was awarded the Iron Cross First Class. After having been slightly wounded in combat, he was assigned to the battalion staff as a liaison officer. In February 1942, he was designated Adjutant of II./"Germania." After being wounded yet again, he returned to the battalion staff for a period, and it was not until December 1942, that he took

command of 2.Kp./"Germania." During an enemy artillery bombardment against his company's positions, he was again wounded and, on March 25, 1943, was awarded the Wound Badge in Gold (Verwundetenabzeichen in Gold). On April 20, 1943, Seebach was promoted to SS-Obersturmführer, and in May of that same year he was transferred to the Grafenwöhr training area to assume the post as adjutant of SS-Pz.Gr.-Rgt.24 "Danmark."

3. Bent Worsöe-Larsen, born on July 2, 1913, in Jordlose in Denmark. He had served previously in 1.SS-Infanterie-Brigade and then in 2.Kp./Freikorps "Danmark."

4. Josef Schirmer, born on December 9, 1915, in Ornsberg, SS-Nr. 308 337. He had served previously in SS-Standarte "Deutschland" and then in the "Westland" regiment of the SS "Wiking" division.

5. Christen Dall, born on January 5, 1920, in Blans in Denmark. He had served previously in 1./SS-Inf.Rgt. "Nordland" before being assigned to 13./"Norge."

Chapter V

1. In the night between January 26 and 27, 1944, the II. and III.Bataillon of the "Norge" regiment abandoned their positions on the Oranienbaum front. II.Bataillon was tasked with establishing a blocking position between the villages of Martynowo to the north and Ssawoltschina to the south. 7. Kp./"Norge" was deployed on the left flank around the Martynowo area, while 6.Kompanie was on the right flank near Ssawoltschina. When the Soviets attacked this latter locality, the company was engaged in tough fighting at Ssawoltschina, and the battalion commander, SS-Stubaf. Krügel, decided to commit 5.Kompanie and soon after even 8.Kompanie to assist 6.Kompanie, while 7.Kompanie continued to hold the positions at Martynowo to the north. Probably while the rest of the battalion was busy fighting farther south, SS-Ostuf. Kristian Pyritz, commander of 7.Kp./"Norge," lost contact with the battalion headquarters and decided to go there personally to get new orders. He thus left the company under the command of SS-Ustuf. Arne Hanssen. During Pyritz's absence, the company was ordered to pull back. So, when SS-Ostuf. Pyritz returned to Martynowo, his men were not there. He then decided to return to Lamocha, where he joined up with elements of II./SS-Art.Rgt.11 in the withdrawal toward Jamburg. Meanwhile, 7.Kp./"Norge" had begun to pull back to the west. According to surviving witnesses, all the heavy weapons had been abandoned. After several days of marching, the company was attacked by the Soviets. It was then decided to split the men into two groups: the first group, under SS-Uscha. Haase, was completely wiped out by the Soviets, and the few survivors were taken prisoner. The second group, led by SS-Ustuf. Hanssen, in the end made it to Hungerburg.

2. Thomas Peter Sandborg, born on September 1, 1907, in Aalesund, Norway.

3. Knud Henrik Ernst Schock, born on May 31, 1899, in Copenhagen, formerly an officer in the Danish army, a member of Freikorps "Danmark" as Leg-Hstuf. and commander of 4.Kompanie. In 1943, after being promoted to Sturmbannführer, he was initially assigned to command SS-Stug.Abt.5. Because the unit was late to be formed, with the single battery of StuG available, the formation of SS-Panzerjäger Abt. 54 was begun.

4. Walter Landmesser, born on June 29, 1917, in Bachhorst, SS-Nr. 318 0521. He had served previously in 8./"Westland" (1942) and later in III./"Danmark" as battalion adjutant.

5. Michale Thöny, born on November 24, 1915, in Munich, SS-Nr. 353 108. He had served previously in the "Nordland" regiment of the "Wiking," first as adjutant of I./Bataillon and then as commander of 3.Kompanie.

6. Harald Nugiseks was born on October 22, 1921, in the Estonian village of Kayakuela in the province of Saerewere. After having served in the Estonian army, during the Soviet occupation of his country, young Harald was one of the earliest volunteers to join the Estonian security battalions, authorized by the Germans, on October 2, 1941.

7. Provided to Ingvar Bärenklau.

8. Robert Stock, born on June 7, 1918, veteran of 2. Kp./"Nordland" until 1942.

Chapter VI

1. Rudolf Rott, born on January 21, 1918, in St, Pölten in Austria, SS-Nr. 332 114. He had served previously in 10./"Der Führer" (1939), then was in command of 3./"Westland" (1941) and then adjutant of I./"Danmark."

2. Philipp Wild, born on March 28, 1921, in Dornheim. He had been awarded the Iron Cross Second Class on August 25, 1942, and the First Class on March 6, 1944.

3. They were reconstituted in Germany but did not return to the "Nordland," being assigned to the "Wiking" in 1945.

4. Fritz Knöchlein, born on May 27, 1911, in Munich, SS-Nr. 87 881. He had served previously in III./"Deutschland" and in IV./"Deutschland," and in command of 14.Tot.Inf.Rgt.2, of 1./SS-Flak.Abt.3, of äI./SS-Pz.Gr.Rgt.6, and of II./SS-Pz.Gr. Rgt. 36. On November 15, 1942, he was awarded the German Cross in Gold.

5. Siegfried Scheibe, born on May 24, 1916, in Leipzig, SS-Nr. 265 359. He had served previously in 1./LSSAH and in I.Sta. "Germania" and commanded 11./"Germania" and II./SS-Pz.Rgt.5.

6. Martin Gürz, born on January 15, 1918, in Lauda, SS-Nr. 347 280. He had served previously in 3./SS-"N" and in SS-Inf. Rgt. "Nordland."

7. Leo Anton Madsen, born on June 11, 1914, at Copenhagen. He was a veteran of Freikorps "Danmark."

8. Egon Christophersen, born on February 8, 1919, in Strøby in Stevns, Denmark. On April 7, 1941, he joined the Waffen-SS, then was assigned to 11./"Nordland" in August 1941, and soon thereafter to 9./"Nordland." During the campaign in the Caucasus he was wounded and did not return to the front until February 1943. In May of that year, he was promoted to Unterscharführer.

9. Erik Krislian Lärum, born on August 5, 1903, in Oslo, Norway.

Chapter VII

1. After having been employed in Ukraine until April 1944, the Flemish brigade was transferred to Bohemia to be reorganized. Following the deterioration of the situation on the Estonian front, in early July 1944 the Flemings had to quickly organize a combat group to send to the Blue Mountains to reinforce III. SS-Pz.Korps. SS-Ostubaf. Schellong, the brigade commander, decided to commit I.Bataillon, under SS-Hstuf. Rehmann.

2. Paul Otto Trautwein, born on October 4, 1918, in Westerwohld in Schleswig-Holstein, SS-Nr. 357 268. He had served previously in 15./"Germania."

3. Herbert Meyer, born on July 30, 1911, in Kiel, SS-Nr. 9 161. He had served previously in 4./LSSAH, in 8./SS-Inf.Rgt. "Nordland," and in II./SS-Pz.Gren.Rgt.49 and then in command of 9./"Danmark."

4. Ernst-Rihard Stübben, born on June 29, 1918, in Schwerte/Iserlohn, SS-Nr. 342 173. He had previously served in SS-Inf. Rgt. "Germania."

5. Hans Kappus, born on April 7, 1913, in Düsseldorf, SS-Nr. 8 944. He had served previously in 10./Sta. "Deutschland" and in command of 3./SS-Flak.Abt.1.

6. Joachim Ziegler, born on October 18, 1904, in Hanua, SS-Nr. 491 403. After having served in the Legion Condor during the Spanish Civil War, he served as an adjutant in the 3rd Armored Brigade and on September 23, 1939, was awarded the Iron Cross Second Class, followed by the Iron Cross First Class on June 28, 1940. On March 14, 1943, he was promoted to Oberst and served on the staff of XXXXII Armeekorps. On March 15, 1943, he was awarded the German Cross in Gold. In June 1943, he was transferred to the Waffen-SS and, from June 20, 1943, was chief of the general staff of III.(germ.)SS-Panzerkorps.

7. Josef Bachmeier, born on October 27, 1908, in Dingolfing, Bavaria, SS-Nr. 96 239. He had served previously as commander of 4./SS-Inf.Rgt.4 (1941), in SS-Geb.Jäg.Rgt.11 (1943), and as commander of 4./Begl.Btl.RFSS (1944) and then of 5. Kp./"Norge" (1944).

Chapter VIII

1. Jürgen Wagner, born on September 9, 1901, in Strasburg in Alsace. After graduating in 1925 he joined the Reichswehr, which he left in 1929 to attend mechanical-engineering studies. In March 1931, he joined the SS. On April 20, 1933, he was promoted to SS-Sturmführer and in July that year he was assigned to SS-Sonderkommando Jüterborg, a reserve and training unit for "Leibstandarte Adolf Hitler." In October 1933, after being promoted to the rank of SS-Sturmbannführer, he took command of II./LSSAH, which he led until 1939. He then went first to the "Germania" regiment of the SS-Verfügungstruppe and then to SS-Regiment 11 of the "Reich" division. In May 1942, he assumed command of the "Germania" regiment of the "Wiking." On December 11, 1942, he was awarded the German Cross in Gold. On July 24, 1943, he was awarded the Knight's Cross.

2. Degrelle was born in 1906 in Bouillon, to a family of French origin. After having studied at the University of Louvain, he earned a doctorate in law. After joining the Belgian Catholic Action, he soon became its leader. His books and his newspaper soon earned favor in public opinion, and in 1936 his party earned thirty-four seats in the senate. That victory enabled him to meet personalities such as Hitler, Mussolini, and Churchill, while at the same time being exposed to the influence of French nationalist Charles Maurras, Italian Fascism, and the German National Socialist Party. At the beginning of the war in 1939, Degrelle was arrested for his sympathies for Hitler's National Socialism and was imprisoned for some weeks until he was freed by the Germans. In 1941, following the Wallonian volunteer formation for the Eastern Front, Degrelle, thirty-five years old, married and with two children, volunteered, encouraging another thousand Walloons to follow his example. In February 1942, Degrelle participated with his Walloons in a bitter battle against the Soviets at Gromovaya-Balka, during which the Walloon

formation suffered heavy casualties. For valor shown in battle, Degrelle was promoted to lieutenant. During the following summer and autumn, the Walloon volunteers were engaged in the Caucasus campaign, earning the esteem of German headquarters and of Himmler himself, who began to think about transferring the Walloons to his Waffen-SS, which happened in summer 1943. With the 5.SS-Freiwilligen-Sturmbrigade "Wallonien," in January 1944 Degrelle and his men were sent to the Cherkassy sector, subordinate to the SS-Wiking division. During the fighting against Soviet forces and after the death in combat of SS-Sturmbannführer Lucien Lippert, the brigade commander, Degrelle was called upon to take command of the brigade. Coming out of Cherkassy alive, Degrelle was awarded the Knight's Cross by Hitler in person.

3. Rolf Holzboog, born on July 8, 1914, in Stuttgart, SS-Nr. 32 263. He had served previously in 14./Sta. "Deutschland" and in 2./SS-Flak.Abt.5 and then in command of 4./Flak.Abt.11.

4. Albert Bergfeld, born on August 27, 1910, in Altena, SS-Nr. 16 034. He had served in command of 13./"Nordland" and 13./"Danmark."

5. Meino Dirks, born on March 5, 1920, in Neudorf, SS-Nr. 309 889. He had served in 10./SS-Inf.Rgt.7 and in 15./"Nordland" and in command of 10./"Norge."

6. Hans Ahlf, born on August 23, 1914, in Neuhaus, SS-Nr. 202 367. He had served previously in 9./Sta. "Germania" and in 13./"Norge," as an aide in I./"Norge," and in command of 10./"Norge."

7. Max Schäfer, born on January 17, 1907. An SS engineer since its beginning, in June 1935 he was assigned to 2.Kompanie of the SS-VT engineer battalion. In 1941 he was assigned to the "Wiking" division, first as a company commander and then as commander of the division's engineer battalion. On February 12, 1943, he was awarded the Knight's Cross, as SS-Ostubaf. and commander of SS-Pionier Bataillon 5 of the "Wiking." Later he took command of the engineers (Kps.Pi.Fhr) of III. (germ.)SS-Pz.Korps.

Chapter IX

1. Anton Aigner, born on November 30, 1914, in Eggenfelden, SS-Nr. 353 043. He had served previously in command of 8./Pol.Art.Rgt. (1942) and in 14./Waffen-Gren.Div. (1943) and then in command of 2./Art.Rgt.54.

2. Richard Spörle, born on July 20, 1915, in Ludwigsburg, SS-Nr. 244 173. He had served previously in 10./Sta. "Germania" (1935) and in 1./"Westland" (1941) and then in command of 1./"Norge."

3. Hans-Gösta Pehrsson, born on October 10, 1910, in Karlskrona in Sweden. A militant anti-Communist, Pehrsson volunteered for the Waffen-SS in June 1941, when war broke out between Germany and the Soviet Union. On July 25, 1941, he transferred to Freikorps "Danmark." He trained with the Danish Freikorps, first at Hamburg-Langehorn and then from September 1941 at Posen-Treskau. During that same period, Pehrsson attended a course at the SS-Unterführerschule at Posen-Treskau, which lasted until spring of 1942, when he was promoted to SS-Unterscharführer and assigned to 2.Kompanie of the Danish volunteer legion. In May 1942, he was moved with Freikorps "Danmark" to the Damjansk pocket. On June 1, 1942, he was promoted to SS-Oberscharführer and on August 2, 1942, was awarded the Iron Cross Second Class. Soon after, he was assigned to 4.Kompanie, commanding a machine gun

squad. In 1942, he was awarded the infantry assault badge in bronze and the wound badge in black. In December 1942, while Freikorps "Danmark" returned to the Eastern Front, after a brief rest period in Denmark Pehrsson was sent to the SS-Junkerschule in Bad Tölz, attending an officer cadet course from February 1 to July 3, 1943. As an SS-Standartenoberjunker, Hans-Gösta Pehrsson was assigned to the new 11.SS-Panzergrenadier Division "Nordland" that was being formed at Grafenwöhr and on August 20, 1943, was assigned to 3.Kompanie of the division's reconnaissance battalion. On September 1, 1943, he was promoted to SS-Untersturmführer.

4. Kurt Witten, born on December 11, 1913, in Hamburg, SS-Nr. 127 179. He had served previously in Pers.Stab RFSS, before becoming the IIa of the "Nordland."

5. Hermann Potschka was born on November 9, 1911, in Unterannowitz, SS-Nr. 4 016. He had served previously in command of 9./SS-Art.Rgt.5 and then in command of III./SS-Art.Rgt.11.

6. Robert Spahn, born on December 23, 1919, in Mühlheim-Dietersheim, SS-Nr. 466 530. He was killed on January 23, 1945.

Chapter X

1. The heavy armored battalion for III.SS-Pz.Korps was created on October 16, 1943, based on III/SS-Pz.Rgt.11. In that context, SS-Pz.Rgt.11 had been reorganized and reduced to only its I.Abteilung, which was rebaptized as SS-Panzer-Abteilung 11 "Hermann von Salza." The personnel for the new heavy battalion came mainly from the "Nordland" division, but there were also veterans from the "Leibstandarte," "Das Reich," "Totenkopf," and "Hohenstaufen." The battalion was initially commanded by SS-Stubaf. Otto Paetsch. The unit was supposed to consist of a headquarters company and three armored companies equipped with PzKpfw VI Tiger tanks. On November 1, 1943, the battalion was officially christened as schwere SS-Panzer-Abteilung 103. Personnel training was initially conducted at Pasderborn and Sennelager. It was later moved to Holland, at the Wezep-Oldebroeck camp, near Zwolle. There, in February 1944, a railway convoy brought four PzKpfw VI Tiger Ausf.E tanks. Training could thus begin. On March 1, SS-Stubaf. Otto Paetsch was recalled to the "Wiking" division to assume command of II./SS-Pz.Rgt.5 and was then replaced by SS-Stubaf. Kurt Hartrampf. In May 1944 the unit had to cede its six Tigers to 9.Kp./SS-Pz.Rgt.3, along with some of its officers and men to SS-Pz.Abt.101 and 102. On June 30, the unit still had six Tigers, provided on May 26, as training tanks. At the time the battalion numbered thirty-three officers, 154 NCOs, and 850 other ranks. In July, the unit continued its training at the Wezep camp in Holland. At the end of August, SS-Stubaf. Hartrampf was replaced in command of the battalion by SS-Ostubaf. Karl Leiner, Theodor Eicke's son-in-law. In early September 1944 the battalion was transferred to the Paderborn camp in Westphalia. In autumn, to replace the crews that had been ceded to other armored units, the unit was brought to strength with Dutch, Norwegian, and Danish volunteers who had been hastily trained before being transferred to the "Wiking" and "Nordland" divisions. The unit received its first PzKpfw VI B Königstiger tanks on October 19, 1944; only four, and then another six, initially slated for SS-Pz.Abt.502, were delivered in December. Meanwhile, on October 4 the battalion was renamed as SS-Pz.Abt.503. Between January 11 and 25,

1945, thirty-two Tiger IIBs were delivered, while its flak platoon was equipped with eight Flakpanzer IVs. On January 27, 1945, the order to transfer to Heeresgruppe Weichsel was received; the crews had only a few days to train on the new tanks before being sent to the front. On January 19, command of the battalion was assigned to SS-Stubaf. Fritz Herzig. The battalion was sent to the Eastern Front on January 27, 1945. Upon reaching Berlin, the unit was split into two groups: the first, under SS-Stubaf. Herzig, consisting of twelve tanks of the headquarters company and of 1.Kompanie, was sent to Arnswalde in Pomerania, while the second, under. SS-Hstuf. Fritz Natterer, was moved to the Gotenhafen-Küstrin sector.

Chapter XI

1. 11.SS-Panzerarmee was created in Pomerania on January 28, 1945, with personnel from the headquarters of Oberkommando Oberrhein.

2. Leo Madsen, born on June 11, 1914, in Copenhagen. He had previously served in Freikorps "Danmark" before being transferred to "Nordland" in command of 7./"Danmark."

3. Even though it was officially part of 15.Panzergrenadier-Division, in early 1945 this unit was engaged in the Stargard area subordinate to 402.Infanterie-Division.

Chapter XII

1. Erich Seyb, born on August 7, 1909, in Giessen, SS-Nr. 38 859. He had served previously in 8./Sta. "Germania," in 4./"Germania," in 6./"Westland," with the SS-Hauptamt, and in command of 6./"Danmark" and then of 5./"Danmark."

2. Ellef Rasmussen, born on December 26, 1922, in Svendborg in Denmark. He had served previously in the "Wiking" and in 1./"Nordland" and then was assigned as adjutant of II./"Danmark."

3. Willi Hind was born on February 23, 1923, in Wiesbaden, SS-Nr. 391 949. He had served previously in 2./"Deutschland" and then went to "Nordland" in command of 7./"Norge."

4. On March 28, the Wehrmacht reported that "SS-Obersturmbannführer Krügel, decorated with the Knight's Cross with Oak Leaves and commanding SS-Panzer-Grenadier-Regiment 24 'Danmark,' has demonstrated extraordinary courage during a counterattack. He died on the battlefield during this fighting."

Chapter XIII

1. Rudolf Klotz, born on October 2, 1913, in Ichenheim, SS-Nr. 112 350. In 1936, he attended the Führerschule in Braunschweig. During the Polish campaign he was assigned to 2.SS-Totenkopfstandarte and on October 23, 1939, assumed command of 5./II/5.SS-Totenkopfstandarte. In the months that followed, he was transferred first to 12.SS-Totenkopfstandarte, then becoming commander of 4.Kompanie. In 1941, he passed to the "Wiking" division as commander of 8./"Nordland." On November 14, 1944, he was awarded the German Cross in Gold as commander of Kampfgruppe Schill, engaged in repression of a revolt in Slovakia. Klotz replaced Hanns-Heinrich Lohmann in command of SS-Frw.Pz.Gr.Rgt. "de Ruyter" during March and early April, when he was wounded.

2. Wilhelm Körbel was born on July 18, 1912, in Homberg, SS-Nr. 52 817. He had served previously in III./Sta. "Germania" (1936), then was in command of 8./"Westland" (1942) and then of SS-Pz.Gr.Auf.Bt.l5 (1943).

3. The idea of forming a unit of British volunteers to participate in the war on the Eastern Front was an initiative by John Amery, son of an English conservative minister and sympathizer of British movements inspired by Fascism and anti-Communism. In 1940, after the invasion of France, Amery moved to the Vichy area and later to Germany, collaborating with German authorities. With the beginning of the war in the east and the formation of European volunteer legions, Amery began to seriously think about formation of a British anti-Communist legion. Not until October 1942 did Amery have the opportunity to propose to the Germans the formation of a German-British committee to unite all the British anti-Communist forces. Hitler personally authorized Amery's stay in Germany so that a British volunteer unit could be formed to be sent to the Eastern Front: from the military aspect, the Germans thought of the enormous propaganda value of the operation. Amery's original idea was to form a unit of about a hundred men for propaganda purposes as the basis of a larger unit, enlisting some of the many British and Commonwealth prisoners who were disposed toward the idea of an anti-Bolshevik crusade. The Germans approved Amery's project with one reserve: the legion was to be not only a political unit, but above all a combat unit. The German authorities quickly went to work in the stalags and oflags to find ex-members of British Fascist movements, the only prisoners worthy of trust. Initially the new unit was given the provisional name of the Saint George Legion, in honor of the patron saint of England. On April 21, 1943, recruitment for the legion officially began; the first attempts were made at camps in France. After this first round of propaganda, about a hundred Englishmen were recruited, of which only fifty-eight were found to be suitable. When, however, the volunteers came to know that they would have to wear German uniforms, there were many second thoughts; with only eleven volunteers remaining at the end of June 1943, the British volunteer unit was temporarily disbanded. In summer 1943 the project then was passed to the Waffen-SS. Reichsführer-SS Himmler rebaptized the unit as the Britisches Freikorps (in English, British Free Corps). A new recruitment campaign was begun, which netted only about thirty new volunteers. The Britisches Freikorps was initially under the command of SS-Hstuf. Hans Werner Roepke, formerly an officer of the "Wiking" division's artillery regiment. The British volunteers were to wear the SS uniform with a cuff title with the inscription Britisches Freikorps and a patch on the sleeve with the Union Jack colors. Roepke thought to organize the thirty or so volunteers into a single infantry assault platoon to be used exclusively against the Soviets. On February 10, 1944, the BFK was sent to the camp at Lichterfelde near Berlin; there they were joined by six members of the Britisches Freikorps who had been on the Eastern Front with Kurt Eggers's propaganda regiment. In early September 1944 the BFK was transferred to the SS engineer school in Dresden; at that time, the unit consisted of twenty-seven men, of whom two were sergeants, four were corporals, and twenty-one were other ranks. These volunteers were trained to use heavy weapons, clear minefields, remove obstacles, and conduct other engineer tasks. By Himmler's order, once it had finished training the BFK was to be assigned to III.SS-Panzer-Korps. In November 1944, the unit command was assigned to SS-Obersturmführer Dr. Walter Külich. The BFK was split into two sections: one section that included the headquarters staff was sent to Bremen, while the other was sent to a training camp

about 40 kilometers northeast of Berlin, where the volunteers were trained in antitank tactics and the use of the Panzerfaust. On March 15, 1945, the Berlin section finished its training and was officially transferred to the III.SS-Panzer-Korps headquarters; consisting of only eleven men, it was the BFK's only combat unit. SS-Ogruf. Felix Steiner, not keen on employing the British volunteers in combat, transferred the section to the "Nordland" division's recon group on March 22, 1945. SS-Stubaf. Saalbach used the British volunteers in fortification work, digging trenches and antitank ditches. When around mid-April "Nordland" was transferred to Berlin, it was decided not to use the British volunteers in the front line, officially assigning them to III. SS-Pz.Korps headquarters as medical personnel. Some sources report that at least four British SS volunteers fought in Berlin with the "Nordland" recon battalion.

4. Artur Grathwol, born on December 22, 1916, in Freiburg, SS-Nr. 372 382. He had served previously as an officer in I./SS-Inf.Rgt. "Westland" and in 3./SS-Pz.Rgt.5, and in command of 2./SS-Pz.Jg.Abt.11, then of 4./SS-Pz.Abt.11, and finally of I./SS-Pz.Rgt.11.

5. Paul Falke, born on December 26, 1916, in Detmold/Lippe, SS-Nr. 286 645. He had served in 3./Sta. "Deutschland," in 15./"Der Führer," and in 17./SS-Inf.Rgt. "Westland"; then in command of 9./"Westland" and of 1./SS-Aufkl.Abt.5; in 2./SS-Pz.Abt.11; and as Ia of I./SS-Pz.Rgt.11.

6. On April 21, 1945, the Generalkommando III. (germanisches) SS-Panzer-Korps was transformed into Armeegruppe Steiner, with the mission of covering the southern flank of 3.Panzer-Armee, still engaged in the lower Oder sector. Steiner's defensive line followed the course of the Oder-Spree.

Chapter XIV

1. Born on March 8, 1888, in Bonn to a family of university professors, Krukenberg was an officer in active service before the First World War, then left the Reichswehr in 1920 for a post at the Ministry of Foreign Affairs and later in management in German industry. From 1926 to 1931, he was in Paris as the German delegate to the Franco-German Committee of Information and Documentation, a committee that had been formed to draw the political, economic, and scientific personalities of the two countries as a base for a European union. Returning to Germany, he managed a British-owned chemical company in Berlin. On May 30, 1936, he joined the Allgemeine SS, with number 116,685, and was assigned to 6.SS-Standarte in Berlin. On November 9, 1936, he was promoted to SS-Untersturmführer, and on January 30, 1939, to SS-Hauptsturmführer. Mobilized in autumn 1939, he served in various units as a staff officer before being transferred in 1943 to the Waffen-SS. With the rank of Obesturmbannführer d.R., on January 17, 1944, he was nominated as chief of staff of V.SS-Gebirgs-Korps. On May 9, 1944, he was promoted to SS-Oberführer. From May 19 to June 25, 1944, Krukenberg served as chief of staff of VI.Waffen-Armee-Korps der SS (lettisches). On July 25, 1944, he was nominated as commander in chief of the Waffen-SS for Ostland (Befehlshaber der Waffen-SS Ostland), establishing himself in Riga, Latvia. He remained there for two months to supervise the mobilization, training, and reorganization of Latvia units. In early August 1944, he briefly replaced Ziegler as chief of staff of III.(germanisches) SS-Panzerkorps. During that same period, he led Kampfgruppe Krukenberg (within Kampfgruppe Jeckeln) in several antipartisan operations. Fluent in French,

he was well acquainted with the French mentality and customs, which is why on September 23, 1944, he was designated by Himmler to command the "Charlemagne's" inspectorate, contemporaneous with his promotion to Brigadeführer.

2. Henry Joseph Fenet was born on July 11, 1919, in Ceyzerat, in the department of Ain in France. The beginning of the Second World War found Fenet studying literature at the Sorbonne in Paris, and he decided to immediately enlist in the French army. In May 1940, as a lieutenant, he participated in the war against the Germans, during which he was wounded twice and was awarded the Croix de Guerre. After having been released from a prisoner-of-war camp on November 29, 1942, Fenet returned to France and joined the Joseph Damand's Ordre Légionnaire, a police force formed to fight Communist partisans. In October 1943, Fenet volunteered for the Waffen-SS. Sent to the SS Junkerschule in Bad Tölz along with twenty-seven other Frenchmen, he graduated in March 1944 with the rank of Obersturmführer. During the fighting in Galicia, he commanded the 3rd Company of 8.franz.SS-Frei.Sturmbrigade. Wounded in the shoulder on August 22, he was evacuated and sent to a hospital, where he remained until October 1944. On November 10, 1944, at Wildflecken, he was awarded the Iron Cross Second Class. At the age of only twenty-five, he was assigned command of the I Battalion of Franz.Freiw.Gren.Rgt.d.SS.57. After a six-week course for battalion commanders at a German army school, he led his four companies on the Pomeranian front. His battalion was the only cohesive unit of the "Charlemagne" to escape the encirclement, an action that earned him the Iron Cross First Class on March 18, 1945, and promotion to Hauptsturmführer. Placed in command of Sturmbataillon "Charlemagne" during the fighting in Berlin, on April 29, 1945, General Burgdorf awarded him the Knight's Cross.

3. Wilhelm Weber, born on March 19, 1918, in Pivitsheide in Westphalia, was the son of a stonemason. After having completed primary school, Weber worked as a carpenter between 1931 and 1935, then attended commercial school in Detmold for a year. From April 1, 1936, to March 31, 1937, he served in the RAD (the Reich labor service) at Bad Salzuflen, ending his experience as a troop commander. On June 26, 1937, Weber entered the 1st Company of SS-Standarte "Germania" in Hamburg. He later attended an NCO course and was put in command of a reconnaissance armored car. During the Polish campaign he was with the recon troops (he was awarded the Iron Cross First and Second Classes), and he was also in the western campaign, where he was given command of an armored car platoon. At the beginning of the eastern campaign, he served in the 15th Recon Company of the "Germania" regiment. In July 1941, he was promoted to Oberscharführer and was given command of an entire motorcycle recon platoon. From April 1942 to November 1942, he attended the officer's course at the SS Junkerschule in Braunschweig, becoming an Untersturmführer soon after. He remained a platoon leader until 1944. In August 1944, he led an SS training company in the defense of Riga in Latvia. He later was assigned to command the 2nd armored recon training company at Staumuehle. In November 1944, he was promoted to Obersturmführer, and was transferred to Wildflecken to the "Charlemagne" division.

4. Erik Wallin was born on August 2, 1921, in Stockholm. He volunteered twice to fight against the Soviets before joining the Waffen-SS. As an adolescent, Wallin joined the Nordisk Ungdom (Nordic Youth) of the Swedish National Socialist

Party. He participated in the Winter War in Finland with the Swedish volunteer corps and, during the war in 1941, again volunteered and served under captain Harald Bräkenhielm in the Hanko battalion (Svenska frivillingbataljonen). Returning to Sweden in 1942, he returned to service in the Swedish army. In January 1943 he decided to join the Waffen-SS, serving in the SS-Panzergrenadier-Division Wiking, after having attended a training course at the SS-Ausbildungslager in Sennheim. He was later assigned to 11.SS-Freiwilligen-Panzergrenadier-Division "Nordland," acting as a platoon leader, under Hans-Gösta Pehrsson, in 3.Kompanie of SS-Panzer-Aufklärungs-Abteilung 11, the "Nordland" reconnaissance group, also known as Panzergruppe Saalbach. SS-Unterscharführer Erik Wallin stayed with the "Nordland" until the final fighting in Berlin in spring 1945. He ended the war as an SS-Oberscharführer. After the war he wrote a book of his memoirs of his wartime experiences. It was printed by another Swede, an SS-Kriegsberichter of the "Leibstandarte," Thorolf Hillblad. Wallin died in 1997 in Berlin, during a reunion of Waffen-SS veterans. During the war he had been awarded the Iron Cross Second Class, the hand-to-hand badge in silver, the tank killer badge, the wound badge, and other Finnish awards.

5. Thorolf Hillblad, *Twilight of Gods: A Swedish Waffen-SS Volunteer's Experiences with the 11th SS Panzergrenadier Division "Nordland"* (Mechanicsburg, PA: Stackpole Books, 2009), 88–90.

6. Hans-Joachim von Wallenrodt, born on August 27, 1914, in Hannover. He served as adjutant in I./Waffen-Grenadier-Regiment 57.

7. Eugene Vaulot was born in Paris in 1923. An electrician, he volunteered in the LVF, reaching the rank of Obergefreiter. Wounded, he was discharged in 1943, but he then volunteered in the Kriegsmarine, then moving on to the "Charlemagne" SS brigade. During the fighting in Pomerania, he was awarded the Iron Cross First Class.

8. Roger Albert-Brunet, a native of Dauphiné, he joined the Milice in early 1943. He was later transferred to the Ecole des cadres at Uriage. In autumn of that year, he volunteered for the Waffen-SS.

9. Wilhelm Tieke, *Tragedy of the Faithful: A History of the III.(germanische) SS-Panzer-Korps* (Winnipeg, MB: Fedorowicz, 2011), 316–17.

10. Karl-Heinz Gieseler, born on July 30, 1925, in Schweez. He had served previously in the "Totenkopf" before being assigned to the "Nordland."

Chapter XV

1. Herbert Wienczek, born on February 18, 1916, in Kohlfurt/Görlitz, SS-Nr. 400 151. He had served previously in 17./LSSAH (1937) and in 3./SS-Inf.Rgt.6 (1941), then as adjutant of I./SS-Inf.Rgt.6 (1942) and as an ordnance officer (OI) in the SS "Nord" division.

2. After the hospital was moved to Frankfurt-am-Oder and after two failed escape attempts, Kausch's long journey began through many Soviet prison camps; his detention lasted eleven long years. He did not return home until January 16, 1956.

3. Wolfgang Venghaus, *Berlin 1945* (Freudenburg, Germany: Selbst-Verlag, 1998).

4. Ibid.

5. After nine years of prison in East Berlin, including three years of solitary confinement, Krukenberg was able to return home, dedicating the rest of his life to German and French reconciliation. He died on October 23, 1980, in Bonn.

BIBLIOGRAPHY

Primary sources

Public archives
Bundesarchiv Berlin, Lichterfelde, Germany
Bundesarchiv-Militärarchiv, Freiburg, Germany
National Archives, Washington, DC, United States
Vojensky Historicky Archiv, Prague, Czech Republic

Period magazines and publications
Signal magazine, various editions, and numbers
Das Schwarze Korps magazine, various numbers

Secondary sources: published books

On the Waffen-SS in general
Afiero, Massimiliano. *Waffen-SS in guerra*. Vol. 2, *1943–1943*. Afragola, Italy: Associazione Culturale Ritterkreuz, 2010.
Afiero, Massimiliano. *Waffen-SS in guerra*. Vol. 3, *1944–1945*. Afragola, Italy: Associazione Culturale Ritterkreuz, 2011.
Duprat, François. *Le Campagne Militari delle Waffen-SS*. Milan: Ritter, 2010.
Duprat, François. *Storia delle SS*. Milan: Ritter, 2009.
Landemer, Henri. *La Waffen-SS*. Paris: Balland, 1972.
Lumsden, Robin. *La vera storia delle SS*. Rome: Newton & Compton, 2020.
Nordling, S. Erik. *Volontari svedesi nella Waffen-SS europea (1940–1945)*. Pinerolo, Italy: NovAntico, 2010.
Steiner, Felix. *Die Freiwilligen: Idee un Opfergang*. Göttingen, Germany: Plesse Verlag, 1958.
Williamson, G. *La storia illustrata delle SS*. Rome: Newton & Compton, 2001.

On the "Nordland" and foreign units assigned to it
Afiero, Massimiliano. *11.SS-Freiwilligen-Panzergrenadier-Division "Nordland."* Afragola, Italy: Associazione Culturale Ritterkreuz, 2008.
Afiero, Massimiliano. *"Nordland."* Pavia, Italy: Marvia, 2004.
Afiero, Masimiliano. *"Wallonie."* Pavia, Italy: Marvia, 2006.
Afiero, Massimiliano. *"Charlemagne."* Pavia, Italy: Marvia, 2008.
Degrelle, Léon. *SS Wallonien*. Monfalcone, Italy: Sentinella d'Italia, 1981.
Ertel, Heinz, and Richard Schulze-Kossens. *Europäische Freiwillige im Bild*. Osnabrück, (West) Germany: Munin-Verlag, 1986.
Ezquerra, Miguel. *Berlin a Vida o muerte*. Saluzzo, Italy: Edizioni Barbarossa, 1980.
Forbes, Robert. *For Europe: The French Volunteers of the Waffen-SS*. Warwick, UK: Helion, 2006.
Hillblad, Thorolf. *Twilight of the Gods: A Swedish Waffen-SS Volunteer's Experiences with the 11th SS Panzergrenadier Division "Nordland."* Mechanicsburg, PA: Stackpole Books, 2009.

Kurowski, Franz. *SS-Obersturmbannführer Paul-Albert Kausch: Kommandant der Waffen-SS Panzerabteilung "Hermann von Salza."* Würzburg, Germany: Flechsig Verlag, 2007.
Landwehr, Richard, and Holger Thor Nielsen. *Nordic Warriors: SS-Panzergrenadier-Regiment 24 Danmark, Eastern Front, 1943–45*. Halifax, UK: Shelf Book, 1999.
Larsson, Lars. *Hitler's Swedes: A History of the Swedish Volunteers in the Waffen-SS*. Havertown, PA: Helion, 2014.
Lefèvre, Eric. Sturmbataillon *"Charlemagne" a Berlino*. Casteggio, Italy: C.D.L. Edizioni, 1997.
Lucas, J. *L'ultimo anno dell'esercito tedesco*. Bresso, Italy: Hobby & Works, 1988.
Lucioli, Massimo. *Endkampf*. Youcanprint, 2020.
Mabire, Jean. *Division "Nordland."* Paris: Jacques Grancher, 1997.
Michaelis, Rolf. *The 11th SS-Freiwilligen-Panzer-Grenadier-Division "Nordland."* Atglen, PA: Schiffer, 2008.
Norling, S. Erik. *Raza de Vikingos: La Division SS Nordland (1943–1945)*. 2nd ed. Granada, Spain: García Hispán, 1997.
Tieke, Wilhelm. *Tragedy of the Faithful: A History of the III. (germanische) SS-Panzer Korps*. Winnipeg, MB: Fedorowicz, 2001.
Trang, Charles. *Dictionnaire de la Waffen-SS*. Vol. 2. Bayeau, France: Heimdahl, 2012.
Weale, Adrian. *Renegades: Hitler's Englishmen*. London: Weidenfeld & Nicholson, 1994.
Westberg, Lennart, Petter Kjellander, and Geir Brenden. *III. Germanic SS Panzer-Korps*. Vol. 1, *Creation—September 1944*. Warwick, UK: Helion, 2019.
Venghaus, Wolfgang. *Berlin 1945*. Freudenburg, Germany: Selbst-Verlag, 1998.

Second World War
Beevor, Antony. *Berlino 1945: La caduta*. Milan: Rizzoli, 2003.
Bahm, Karl F. *Berlin 1945: The Final Reckoning, April 1945*. London: Amber Books, 2014.
Bernage, Georges. *Berlin 1945: L'agonie du Reich*. Bayeau, France: Edizioni Heimdahl, 2009.
Carell, Paul. *Operazione Barbarossa*. 5th ed. Milan: Biblioteca Universale Rizzoli, 2013.
Liddell Hart, B. H. *Storia militare della Seconda Guerra Mondiale*. 4th ed. Milan: Arnoldo Mondadori, 1971.
Nash, Douglas E. *Hell's Gate: The Battle of the Cherkassy Pocket January–February 1944*. Stamford, CT: RZM Imports, 2009.

Periodicals

Der Freiwillige magazine, various issues

Fronti di Guerra, bimonthly dedicated to Axis formations in World War II, various issues

Ritterkreuz magazine, bimonthly dedicated to Waffen-SS formations, various issues

Siegrunen magazine, periodical published by Richard Landwehr, various issues

Photographic references

Berlin Document Center (BDC)
Bundesarchiv (BA)
Die Deutsche Wochenscahu (DW)
Munin Verlag (MV)
US National Archives (NA)

Private collections

Massimiliano Afiero (MA)
Giorgio Bussano (GB)
Stefano Cecchinato (SC)
Michael Cremin (MC)
Reimo Leol (RL)
Marc Rikmenspoel (MR)
Pierre Tiquet (PT)
Charles Trang (CT)
Olli Wikberg (OW)